From Tolerance to Equality

From Tolerance to Equality

How Elites Brought America to Same-Sex Marriage

Darel E. Paul

BAYLOR UNIVERSITY PRESS

Cover Design by *the*BookDesigners

This book was first issued in paperback in 2019 under ISBN 978-1-4813-0695-9.

The hardcover edition has been cataloged as follows:

Library of Congress Cataloging-in-Publication Data

Names: Paul, Darel E., author.
Title: From tolerance to equality : how elites brought America to same-sex marriage / Darel E. Paul.
Description: Waco, Texas : Baylor University Press, [2018] | Includes bibliographical references and index.
Identifiers: LCCN 2017034302 (print) | LCCN 2017048152 (ebook) | ISBN 9781481308021 (web PDF) | ISBN 9781481308014 (ebook: Mobi/Kindle) | ISBN 9781481306966 (ePub) | ISBN 9781481306942 (cloth : alk. paper)
Subjects: LCSH: Same-sex marriage—United States. | Gay couples—Legal status, laws, etc.—United States
Classification: LCC HQ1034.U5 (ebook) | LCC HQ1034.U5 P38 2018 (print) | DDC 306.84/80973—dc23

For T.M. and J.F.,
who taught me about the sacrifices of marriage

CONTENTS

ACKNOWLEDGMENTS

This book has been long in coming. Its seeds first germinated in late 2008, around the time of the Proposition 8 vote in California, when national same-sex marriage seemed far from a foregone conclusion. Its first public presentation was in February 2009 as part of the Williams College Faculty Lecture Series. It took far longer than I expected for the tree to mature from the seed. That said, I hope the ideas here have seasoned in ways that would not have been possible if the project had been completed before the Supreme Court's 2015 decision in *Obergefell v. Hodges* brought the legal argument for same-sex marriage to its close.

My geographic and social location has proven invaluable in writing this book. I moved to Massachusetts in 2001, just two years before the state's Supreme Judicial Court first brought same-sex marriage to America. I did so in order to take up a position at Williams College, precisely the kind of elite Northeastern liberal arts college that embodies contemporary professional class culture. This context did not simply offer a front row seat on how and why same-sex marriage swept the country; it provided a truly ethnographic experience that influenced the book in many positive ways. This was aided by my own social background. I grew up in Minnesota far from the heartland of the American professional-managerial class, and neither of my parents have four-year college degrees. Being an academic, elite culture has in many ways become my culture. Yet it remains something of which I think I can still take the measure as an outsider.

The ideas and arguments put forth in this book have benefited greatly from many thoughtful comments and insightful critiques received in a number of venues. Four anonymous reviewers of the work in manuscript form forced me to clarify and better defend myself at every step. Panelists and attendees at the 2011 Midwest Political Science Association National Conference, the 2011 American Political Science Association Annual Meeting, and the 2013 American Sociological Association Annual Meeting helped me refine and condense my case. The Williams College students enrolled in my 2014 course "Same-Sex Marriage in America" expressed healthy skepticism and proved worthy readers. Early research assistance was ably supplied by Davi Schoen. Financial support from Williams College enabled the entire process. The maps in chapter 3 were ably produced by Adam Barley, and the patient assistance of Cory Campbell at the Office of Information Technology at Williams aided in their conceptualization and design. Nicolas Robette kindly wrote a new line of code for me that made the scatterplots in chapter 5 more informative. Justin Crowe and Nicole Mellow supplied me with valuable insights on American politics and the judicial process. I have benefited greatly from tremendous moral support provided by Michael MacDonald in particular, as well as by Jim Nolan, James McAllister, Keith McPartland, John and Julie Forbes, Peter Caron, and Fr. William Cyr. I owe considerable thanks to Carey Newman at Baylor University Press for taking on this project with enthusiasm as well as for his great editing. Before meeting him I had not known how valuable a top-notch editor really is. Jenny Hunt at Baylor performed excellent copyediting and made sure all the figures looked sharp. My wife, Kelly, and my children, Hannah, Jacob, Emma, and Michael sacrificed in innumerable small and not-so-small ways over the course of eight years to make this work possible.

This book does not endorse same-sex marriage, and for that reason one anonymous reviewer called it a "conservative" project. This is a label I reject. While this book indeed does not endorse same-sex marriage, neither does it oppose same-sex marriage. My purpose in writing has not been to cheerlead anyone from the sidelines. Nor has it been to present any moral or legal argument. Others more qualified have already provided such a service. The goal of this book is to explain what I take to be the great puzzle of the rapid normalization of homosexuality in American society. Toward that end, the great French sociologist Pierre Bourdieu has provided me with inestimable inspiration. He has also provided a valuable warning. According to Bourdieu, to point out the social conditions underlying ideas and values is to "transgress . . . one of the fundamental taboos of the intellectual world." One is likely to be condemned as "barbarous" in the "attempt to treat culture, that present incarnation of the sacred, as an object of science."[1] If that was true when Bourdieu wrote it nearly forty years ago, how much more so today. I offer this book with full knowledge that some will indeed condemn it as barbarous for precisely this reason.

1

INTRODUCTION

From Outlaw to Married Citizen

The cultural and legal status of homosexuality has experienced one of the most rapid and thorough reversals in American social history. The revolutionary shift played out especially dramatically in 2003. In June of that year the U.S. Supreme Court ruled in the case *Lawrence v. Texas* that the U.S. Constitution guarantees a broad right to sexual privacy, including consensual same-sex sexual conduct. As a result, the country's last fourteen state sodomy laws from Idaho to Florida were immediately overturned.[1] Only five months later, in November, the Massachusetts Supreme Judicial Court mandated in *Goodridge v. Department of Public Health* that "civil marriage" be opened to same-sex couples, thus inaugurating the country's era of same-sex marriage.[2] Only twenty-one months earlier the same high court definitively nullified Massachusetts' own long-standing sodomy law.[3] In the blink of an eye the gay man and lesbian were transformed "from outlaw to married citizen."[4]

The ground for this transformation had been prepared for decades, however. At the beginning of the 1970s forty-nine states had sodomy laws on their books. At the decade's end just twenty-seven did. In 1973 the American Psychiatric Association declassified homosexuality as a mental illness, blazing a trail quickly followed by all the country's major mental health professional organizations. The first same-sex marriage cases wended their way through state and federal judicial systems during the 1970s and reached supreme courts in Minnesota (1971), Kentucky (1973), and Washington (1974), as well as the U.S. Supreme Court (1972).

While cultural change was clearly in the air, just seven years before the *Lawrence* and *Goodridge* decisions it was safe to say that both popular and elite opinion still remained strongly—if not universally—opposed to treating homosexuality as normal. In December 1996 a Hawaii state circuit court judge ruled that a strictly opposite-sex definition of marriage was in violation of the state constitution's commitment to equal protection.[5] Public reaction was swift and decisive. Marshaling a peremptory strike in anticipation of just such a ruling, in September of that year the U.S. Congress passed and President Bill Clinton signed into law the Defense of Marriage Act (DOMA). The law both defined marriage for federal purposes as a strictly opposite-sex institution and allowed states to refuse recognition of same-sex marriages conducted in other jurisdictions. While it may be hard to fathom today, DOMA received overwhelming support from both political parties. Among Republicans, not a single senator and but one member of the House of Representatives voted against it. Democrats strongly supported the legislation, too, with House members voting in favor by a nearly two-to-one margin (118–65) and Senate Democrats surpassing even that mark (32–14).[6] Strong Democratic support granted the bill a veto-proof majority and Democratic President Bill Clinton signed the measure. While doing so somewhat reluctantly—the professed degree of reluctance growing notably over the decades—Clinton nonetheless stated clearly at the time, "I have long opposed governmental recognition of same-gender marriages and this legislation is consistent with that position."[7] His signature completed a fast-track process for the legislation, which took a mere four months to travel from congressional subcommittee to law of the land.

As it turned out, DOMA was premature by nearly a decade. The Hawaii threat was repelled nearly as soon as it arose. In 1997 the Hawaii state legislature passed a proposed constitutional amendment that if passed by referendum would allow it to define marriage as a strictly opposite-sex institution. In 1998 residents voted in one of the country's first two state marriage referenda. One of the bluest of blue states rebuked its own court and backed the measure by a lopsided 71%–29% margin.[8] Even down to the late 1990s, a clear societal consensus existed on marriage.

By the time the country's first legally recognized same-sex marriage ceremony took place in 2004, this broad national agreement had disintegrated. The national Democratic Party's reversal on DOMA was the most dramatic. In 2004 House Democrats strongly opposed the Marriage Protection Act—a bill designed to insulate DOMA from federal court interpretation or challenge—by a 176–27 margin. This reflected a tremendous collapse of support within the party's House caucus for a traditionalist definition of marriage, from 64% in 1996 to a mere 13% in 2004. It also represented an implicit repudiation of DOMA itself. In the 1990s even the most liberal Democrats avoided clear public endorsements of same-sex marriage, carefully couching their opposition to DOMA as opposition to discrimination. By 2004 all three minor Democratic candidates for president were calling openly for national same-sex marriage.

Corporate America also came to embrace the normalization of homosexuality in this period. When DOMA was passed in 1996, slightly over 500 U.S. firms offered domestic partner health benefits to their same-sex partnered employees. By 2004 the figure had skyrocketed to over 8,200. The country's largest corporations in particular were becoming increasingly gay-friendly. At the time DOMA was passed only 28 of the Fortune 500 were offering domestic partner health benefits. By 2004 the number had risen to 216.[9] Moreover, the largest firms in the country were the private sector's pioneers in granting spousal equivalency to unmarried same-sex couples across a broad range of employee benefits, including life insurance, pensions, and family leave. According to former Human Rights Campaign President Joe Solmonese, "Corporate America is far ahead of America generally when it comes to the question of equality for GLBT people."[10]

The courts also began trending decisively toward same-sex marriage. Judges from Hawaii to Massachusetts and Iowa to Texas began discovering constitutional rights their predecessors a generation earlier had either decisively rejected or never imagined existed. The weight of such a "significant change in the definition of marriage as it has been inherited from the common law, and understood by many societies for centuries" was embraced by more and more members of the judiciary who now found the older views fundamentally irrational.[11] Beginning in 2003 state court judges inaugurated same-sex marriage in Massachusetts, California, Connecticut, Iowa, New Jersey, and New Mexico. Federal judges in more than half a dozen states and ultimately in Washington, D.C. found both federal and state DOMAs unconstitutional.

American elites have largely embraced same-sex marriage, but the wider public remains divided on the issue. When the polling organization

Gallup first asked a same-sex marriage question in 1996, just 27% of Americans were in favor while 68% opposed it. Support rose markedly in the mid- and late 2000s to a 37%–46% range, and in 2011 Gallup reported that a majority of Americans favored same-sex marriage for the first time. Notable opposition was raised throughout the early 2010s, however. Until 2012, all thirty-one states that held a marriage referendum rejected same-sex marriage. Even in that year North Carolina became the country's thirty-second state to constitutionally define marriage as strictly opposite-sex. In 2010 Iowans turned three state supreme court justices out of office who had mandated same-sex marriage. In 2012 three of the four Republican state senators instrumental in passing same-sex marriage in New York the previous year failed to survive the next election. In 2013 and 2014, after federal judges found that state DOMAs in Utah and Oklahoma violated the U.S. Constitution, the governors of those states fought the rulings rather than capitulating. In two polls over 2016 and 2017, Gallup found over one-third of the country still continued to oppose same-sex marriage.[12]

Marriage has become the social and legal touchstone for the normalization of homosexuality in the United States. At the same time, it has everything to do with the family, the country's most volatile social, cultural, and political fault line. This clash reaches into every facet of public and private life. In the United States at least, the family is the foundation upon which both the state and the market are organized. Economically speaking the family is the primary site of consumption, of social reproduction, and even today of some aspects of production (for example, domestic services). Socially the family remains the primary provider of housing, an important secondary provider of welfare and education (and primary provider for young children and adults outside employment), and the primary site of social interaction. Politically the family continues to be the primary generator of tax revenues, and its ability to carry out economic and social tasks requires constant political support through legislation and government spending.

Regardless of class, race, ethnicity, or region, as recently as the 1970s Americans largely lived and promoted a single dominant family model of husband, wife, and their natural-born children. This is usually called the "nuclear family" or the "natural family" model. Today there are many new models—the blended family, the single-parent family, the cohabitating family, the same-sex couple family—both lived and promoted. These increasingly define the country's politics. Proof lies in the fault lines that now characterize the American electorate. Marital status has become one of the most important determinants of voting behavior. Larger than the much more publicized gender gap, the marriage gap produces an increasingly married Republican partisan and an increasingly divorced, separated, or never-married Democratic partisan.[13]

At the same time, marriage has increasingly become an institution for elites. In 1950 a negative relationship existed among women between marriage rate and level of education. At the time, those with a bachelor's degree or more were the least likely to be married while those without a high school degree were the most likely. By 2011 some 60% of women with a bachelor's degree or more were married, while among women without a high school diploma the figure was under 30%.[14] In 1960 the marriage gap between all adults with at least a bachelor's degree and those with a high school diploma or less was just 4%. In 2010 the gap was 17%. No wonder 45% of persons with a high school education or less agreed that marriage is "becoming obsolete" while only 27% of adults with college degrees said the same.[15] The gap isn't due to the least educated eschewing marriage. By age 46, 89% of Americans over the years 2003–2010 with a bachelor's degree or higher had been married while the same was true for 87% of those with a high school diploma and 81% of those with less than a high school education. The gap is more due to high divorce rates on the lower rungs of the class ladder, where 58% of first marriages of the lowest educated group end in divorce as do 48% of those among high school graduates. Among college graduates the figure is less than 30%. The marriage gap by education has become especially large among men. Between those with a bachelor's degree and those without a high school diploma, the difference is 11% for ever being married, 24% for ever being divorced, and 34% for still being in a first marriage.[16] While cohabitation has become much more common throughout the United States in recent decades, there is a large and growing difference by education level. In 1995 among women ages 22–44, those without a high school degree had a 12% higher rate of first union as cohabitation compared to those with a four-year degree or more. By 2006–2010 the gap had nearly doubled to 23%. While dissolution rates of first unions were roughly the same across all educational groups, the highly educated tended to turn cohabitation into marriage much more often than did others. At three years from the formation of first union, 53% of college educated women in the late 2000s had turned cohabitation into marriage while only 39% of high school graduates had done so and just 30% of women lacking a high school diploma. A pregnancy during cohabitation is especially likely to transition the most educated women in America to marriage but is not likely to transition the least educated. While the probability of marriage after cohabitation within one year of pregnancy is 53% for the college educated, it is only 30% for those with only high school diplomas and a mere 19% among those without.[17]

A once-small racial marriage gap in America has also swelled. From 1880 to 1950 the difference in marriage rates between white and black women was never more than 5%.[18] As of 2010 the gap stood at a yawning 24%.[19] While much of the marriage gap by education is due to high divorce rates among the least educated, the marriage gap by race is driven much more by very low marriage rates among blacks. In the years 2003–2010, by 46 years old 90% of whites had been married but only 68% of blacks had been.[20] Combined with the fact that at the end of the period a mere 31% of all black adults were married, prominent observers were moved to ask, "is marriage for white people?"[21]

This dramatic and widening divide in family formation along both ideological and sociological lines prompted some to transfer the "red state-blue state" story of American presidential politics onto the American family. According to law professors Naomi Cahn and June Carbone, "red families" characteristic of conservative parts of the country—although not necessarily typical among conservative families—"insist on the unity of sex, marriage, and procreation; the complementary nature of the relationship between men and women; and the importance of commitment (and, indeed, acceptance of the 'authority of marriage') to marital stability." On the other hand, the "blue family" typical of liberal regions of the country—although, again, not necessarily typical among liberal families—"emphasizes autonomy and [individual] responsibility"; rejects gender roles in favor of "egalitarian values"; and accepts and even celebrates nonmarital sex as long as it is also nonprocreative. These models of the family are based in differences in family law across the country and the cultural debates and practices that animate them. By focusing only on law to the exclusion of actual social behavior, however, these models oversimplify. Rival ideals of marriage cannot be reduced simply to "external authority" (red) versus "individual freedom" (blue). The blue model is, after all, a socially imposed cultural script as much as is the red model. Both are held out as norms of belief and behavior for all.[22]

The real differences turn on two key factors. The first is the social meaning of gender. The second is the desirability of unifying sex, marriage, and procreation. Notably these are the very divisions that lie at the foundation of the country's radical disagreements over same-sex marriage. Wrapped up in that clash of worldviews and ways of life is a struggle between rival groups for influence, authority, and power. This shouldn't be surprising. Ideas, after all, do not float freely about the world but are carried by persons and institutions that create, promote, and defend them. The dominance of one set of ideas and behaviors over another is tied up with the dominance of one social group, its institutions, and its way of life. This is the very nature of what we typically call a "revolution" whether or not it involves violent change of government. After all, the Industrial Revolution and the Sexual Revolution were no less transformational for having avoided guillotines and grapeshot.

From Tolerance to Equality

In his second inaugural address Barack Obama became the first president of the United States to interpret same-sex marriage as a dogmatic element of the American Creed. After pointing to "Seneca Falls and Selma and Stonewall" as the peaks of the country's symbolic geography, Obama stated, "Our journey is not complete until our gay brothers and sisters are treated like anyone else under the law—for if we are truly created equal, then surely the love we commit to one another must be equal as well." The phrase "marriage equality" has become so commonplace that it is easy to forget how recently supporters of same-sex marriage publicly anchored their project to a different value. In 2000 the *New York Times* Editorial Board referred to that year's California ballot issue on marriage as "a referendum on tolerance." Likewise it urged a negative vote on Oregon's 2004 marriage referendum as a "message of tolerance." U.S. Senator Jim Jeffords characterized his vote against the Federal Marriage Amendment in 2004 as consistent with "the great American tradition of inclusiveness and tolerance and acceptance." The *Boston Globe* Editorial Board praised the 2007 passage of civil union legislation in New Hampshire as a widening of the "circle of tolerance," while the editors of the *Washington Post* lamented passage of three state marriage referenda in 2008 as ultimately futile interruptions of the societal "flow in the direction of tolerance." The *Los Angeles Times* Editorial Board praised Mexico City's 2009 legalization of same-sex marriage as "a triumph of tolerance" and in 2011 New York State Senator Stephen Saland, one of the four decisive Republican votes that brought same-sex marriage to the Empire State, interpreted his support as a function of being "respectful, tolerant and accepting of others."

Similar examples are countless.[23] Back in the 2000s a "discourse of liberal morality" prevailed among supporters of same-sex marriage.[24] They struck agnostic public poses on the moral value of same-sex sexual relations—although quite obviously presuming the moral value of marriage—and expected others to do the same. This repudiation of judgment was presented as the moral virtue of toleration, the "central liberal value."[25]

In the 2010s this language of toleration fell into a near total eclipse behind the language of equality. Consider the *New York Times* Editorial Board, one of the country's most prominent champions of same-sex marriage. Prior to 2007 it never used the phrase "marriage equality." Even down to 2009 it still preferred discussing same-sex marriage as a matter of "tolerance" or "fair(ness)."[26] By 2011, however, the phrase "marriage equality" was everywhere. The board used it eleven times in seven editorials advocating for same-sex marriage in New York that year and did not use the word "tolerance" once.[27] In its 2013 editorial hailing the Supreme Court decisions on same-sex marriage in *United States v. Windsor* and *Hollingsworth v. Perry*, in under eight hundred words the board used the phrase "marriage equality" three times and the word "equal(ity)" without modifier seven times. The word "fairness" made but a single appearance and "toleration" not at all.[28] In its 2015 column praising the Court's opinion in *Obergefell v. Hodges* that brought same-sex marriage to every state and territory in the country, "(in)equality" appeared seven times and "equal" four times. "Fair(ness)" and "toleration" fell into total disuse.[29]

The shift from toleration to equality involves a transformation in moral judgment. Toleration asks for public neutrality while allowing ample room for private disapproval. Without negative judgment there is no virtue of toleration at all but instead indifference or even affirmation posing as virtue. Equality is something altogether different. It demands public affirmation backed by state power and restricts the private scope for negative judgment to the narrowest range possible. In fact the most ambitious renderings of marriage equality go beyond even that and hope for the eradication of judgment itself. Massachusetts Justice John Greaney showed as much in his concurring opinion to the *Goodridge* decision back in 2003:

> I am hopeful that our decision will be accepted by those thoughtful citizens who believe that same-sex unions should not be approved by the State. I am not referring here to acceptance in the sense of grudging acknowledgment of the court's authority to adjudicate the matter. My hope is more liberating. The plaintiffs are members of our community, our neighbors, our coworkers, our friends. . . . The plaintiffs volunteer

in our schools, worship beside us in our religious houses, and have children who play with our children, to mention just a few ordinary daily contacts. We share a common humanity and participate together in the social contract that is the foundation of our Commonwealth. Simple principles of decency dictate that we extend to the plaintiffs, and to their new status, full acceptance, tolerance, and respect. We should do so because it is the right thing to do.[30]

Although he used the word "tolerance," Greaney doesn't really call for toleration from opponents of same-sex marriage at all. He seeks their personal transformation. He wants equality not merely in law but deep within the private sphere where, from a liberal perspective, moral disagreement is supposed to exist and even thrive.

This step beyond tolerance is widely depicted by supporters as just such a personal transformation. Consider a characteristic example in the 2010 book *From Disgust to Humanity* by University of Chicago law professor Martha C. Nussbaum.[31] The argument there is distinguished from general liberal opinion only by the prominence of its author, a past president of the American Philosophical Foundation and one of *Foreign Policy* and *Prospect* magazines' "Top 100 Public Intellectuals" in the world three times over. Nussbaum understands all political and legal struggle around the status of homosexuality as a Manichean clash of opposing psychologies. On one side stand the "forces of imagination and humanity" practicing a "politics of humanity, a political attitude that combines respect with curiosity and imaginative engagement."[32] Arrayed against them are a rogue's gallery of high-caste Indians, Southern white supremacists, German Nazis, and their fellow travelers practicing a "politics of disgust" animated by an irrational and "primitive idea of stigma and taint" and reflecting "some deeper sort of anxiety or aversion (animus, to use the language of [the Supreme Court majority in] *Romer*)."[33] In the contemporary United States the darkness is "under siege" from the light—not from the latter's greater political and economic power but instead from "the friendships of young people and, perhaps above all, from the arts."[34] For Nussbaum the story of the normalization of homosexuality is a power-free tale of imaginative engagement, empathy, and personal conversion "at the level of the human heart."[35] Because "democratic majorities can't yet be trusted to put aside bigotry," she is open to the exercise of state power by judges aligned with the forces of humanity.[36] Yet in Nussbaum's account this is not a material and moral struggle between equals so much as an act of policing against outlaws.

At first impression, Harvard Law School Professor Michael Klarman presents a more intellectually satisfying account of the movement of gays and lesbians "from the closet to the altar" in his 2013 book by the same name.[37] Activists, politicians, and judges rather than ideas and emotions play the central roles in his account, with special emphasis on what he calls "'coming out' as a political act."[38] While Klarman's causal argument is hazy, he seems to believe that the LGBT movement is the author of normalization and ultimately of same-sex marriage. The sympathetic yet "elite bias of judges" which Nussbaum celebrates has actually stoked political backlash and retarded broader social progress though their countermajoritarian actions.[39] Yet despite the copious descriptions of political struggle throughout the book, on closer inspection Klarman is actually making a less Manichean version of Nussbaum's argument. In the clearest presentation of a causal claim, Klarman describes coming out as the "perhaps most important" aspect of normalization because over time it forces the majority to understand how gays and lesbians are *already* completely normal. On many occasions he appeals to the "power of the coming-out phenomenon" to engage heterosexuals imaginatively and emotionally, to elicit their sympathy, and to transform them personally.[40] While power does play an important descriptive role in the journey from closet to altar, all the foundational action—the dramatic and rapid changes in public opinion that validate LGBT activists and their allies—takes place in the power-free zone of the human heart.

One might expect that political scientists would generate more compelling accounts based on the exercise of power. Yet even in that field one finds the very same story advanced by Nussbaum and Klarman. Temple University Professor Gary Mucciaroni, among the country's leading scholars of LGBT politics, sums up "the story of sexual politics" in the contemporary United States as "a narrative about a heterosexist majority that has used religion and ideology to maintain its cultural and legal privileges and a story of social learning in which disproportionately younger, more educated citizens have come to know openly gay people and have responded with greater tolerance and support for LGBT equality."[41] He stresses the importance of "'coming out' [as] a form of political resistance" because it necessarily and unproblematically elicits "tolerance" and "support for [LGBT] political demands." As with Nussbaum and Klarman, Mucciaroni mentions power but analyzes it in a transparently ideological manner. On one side is positive or good power: educational, noncoercive, individually transformative, liberating. On the other side is negative or bad power:

irrational, coercive, traditionalist, repressive. Such an approach undermines Mucciaroni's otherwise insightful points that ably describe—but ultimately fail to explain—the move from tolerance to equality. *Why* is it that college towns, the highly educated, judges, and the entertainment industry have become signal supporters of normalization? *Why* has a conservative view of LGBT persons as "normal" rather than a liberationist "queer" image triumphed? *Why* has framing normalization as a matter of civil rights and equality been so successful? *Why* does "coming out" lead not only to toleration (rather than renewed repression) but ultimately to affirmation, normalization, and same-sex marriage?

Existing accounts emphasize the role of activists and the process of moral growth so much that the contributions of Corporate America, normalization's most powerful ally, are invisible. Perhaps this is because the movement for normalization and same-sex marriage understands itself and is understood by others as a force of the political Left. Some have even been so bold as to call it "the civil rights movement of our time."[42] It begs explanation then how a supposedly left-wing movement became the cause célèbre of the country's rich and powerful. Support for normalization, after all, has always been positively correlated with income and level of education. Big business' endorsement should be especially puzzling. Corporations marketing directly to the public are usually highly sensitive to public opinion. They tend to follow, not lead, the herd when it comes to controversial social issues. Yet in this case corporate support came well before public support.[43] This is a puzzle that cries out for a solution, an answer to the question of how and why elites brought America to same-sex marriage.

2

THE ELITE EMBRACE OF NORMALIZATION
AND SAME-SEX MARRIAGE

The New Normal

On March 23, 2014, Brendan Eich was known to the world—to the extent he was known at all—as the inventor of the JavaScript programming language and cofounder of Mozilla, the organization and foundation that produces and supports the globally popular Firefox web browser. On March 24 and for ten intense days afterward, he was primarily known as the nation's premier homophobic bigot. Tech industry colleagues publicly condemned his "hateful views" and pledged to boycott his company. His own employees called for his resignation. A petition signed by over 75,000 labeled Eich "Mozilla's new anti-gay CEO" and demanded he issue "an unequivocal statement of support for marriage equality" or else be fired immediately.

As Silicon Valley is not generally known as a hotbed of cultural conservatism, this public firestorm was all the more dramatic. What had Eich done or said to provoke it? Six years earlier while serving as Mozilla's Chief Technology Officer, Eich donated $1,000 to the campaign for California's Proposition 8, the state's 2008 marriage referendum that proposed to overturn a state supreme court ruling and return marriage in California to a strictly opposite-sex institution. Both Eich's contribution and his views on same-sex marriage were publicly unknown until 2012 when the *Los Angeles Times* published a searchable database of all contributors to the then-four-years-past campaign. Eich had buried his opinions so deeply that even Mozilla cofounder and Executive Chairwoman of the Board of Directors Mitchell Baker, someone with whom Eich had worked side by side for nearly twenty years, hadn't a clue "that Brendan and I aren't in close alignment here."[1] While the initial storm around Eich's donation subsided in 2012, it broke out with renewed intensity the day Eich was named Mozilla's new CEO. Within hours of the March 24 announcement, both social and internet media exploded in angry opposition. Outrage became so intense that both Eich and Baker were forced within two days to publicly defend the company and its commitment to "equality and welcome for LGBT individuals at Mozilla." Eich in particular expressed "sorrow at having caused pain" and begged for an opportunity to "show, not tell" his dedication to full inclusion and support for "LGBT individuals at Mozilla."[2] That opportunity never came. Pressure increased dramatically on March 31 when the dating website OkCupid changed its home page specifically for Firefox users, replacing its slogan "Start meeting people now!" with a nearly two-hundred-word political statement. It read in part:

> Mozilla's new CEO, Brendan Eich, is an opponent of equal rights for gay couples. We would therefore prefer that our users not use Mozilla software to access OkCupid. . . . If individuals like Mr. Eich had their way, then roughly 8% of the relationships we've worked so hard to bring about would be illegal. . . . OkCupid is for creating love. Those who seek to deny love and instead enforce misery, shame, and frustration are our enemies, and we wish them nothing but failure.

At the end of the message, active links appeared for downloading and installing all of Firefox's rivals' web browsers.[3] OkCupid's intervention proved decisive. Three days later the enemy resigned not only as CEO but from Mozilla altogether.

Chairwoman Mitchell Baker proceeded to issue a letter of apology for the entire controversy. "We know why people are hurt and angry, and they are right," she wrote. "We haven't stayed true to ourselves." While professing Mozilla's commitment to "stand for both" equality and freedom of speech, class values stood above all. In Baker's words, "we failed to listen, to engage, and to be guided by our community."[4] That community of technology specialists, venture capitalists, and libertarian internet users spoke with a united and powerful voice. Regardless of any official corporate policy of welcome toward persons of "very diverse personal beliefs," the Mozilla community showed that personal beliefs against the normalization of homosexuality are clearly not welcome at all.[5]

Silicon Valley is hardly the only place in America where opposition to normalization is anathema. Consider another corporate entanglement and walk-back over same-sex marriage. In June 2012 Dan Cathy, the president and chief operating officer of the national fast food chain Chick-fil-A, gave two public interviews to evangelical media outlets. The purpose of each was to discuss how Chick-fil-A's corporate practices are an expression of its owners' evangelical Christian values. Alongside closing on Sundays and supporting college football, Cathy mentioned the firm's support for "the Biblical definition of the family unit."[6] While Cathy implicitly criticized divorce and fatherlessness, the mainstream media was interested only in his insinuations regarding same-sex marriage:

> I think we are inviting God's judgment on our nation when we shake our fist at Him and say, "We know better than you as to what constitutes a marriage." I pray God's mercy on our generation that has such a prideful, arrogant attitude to think that we would have the audacity to try to redefine what marriage is all about.[7]

Cathy donated far more than $1,000 to this cause. Through the Cathy family-financed WinShape Foundation, he, his parents, and his siblings donated millions of dollars to culturally conservative organizations dedicated to promoting traditional marriage and families, including the Marriage and Family Foundation and the Family Research Council. They also donated small amounts to some of the country's most controversial conservative family groups, including Focus on the Family and Exodus International. While Brendan Eich's views were wholly invisible and even undetectable before 2012, Dan Cathy was a well-known quantity. His remarks nonetheless ignited an online firestorm that quickly spread to the mainstream media and even to elected politicians, who eagerly joined the fray. Three big-city mayors publicly rebuked Cathy in the name of their constituents' values. Thomas Menino insisted, "Chick-fil-A doesn't belong in Boston."[8] Rahm Emanuel asserted, "Chick-fil-A values are not Chicago values."[9] Edwin Lee expressed disappointment that the restaurant chain "doesn't share San Francisco's values."[10] These mayors didn't stop at words, either. Each explicitly or implicitly threatened to use city permitting and zoning powers to block the creation of any new Chick-fil-A restaurants. Menino was clearest on this point: "If they need licenses in the city, it will be very difficult—unless they open up their policies."[11] All three mayors eventually backtracked on early promises of government action against the fast food chain, if only because the U.S. Constitution clearly denies city governments the power to punish speech. That is beside the point, however. The 2012 Chick-fil-A imbroglio showed clearly how vigorous public support for normalization and same-sex marriage in professional- and managerial-class cities is not only well within the bounds of acceptable opinion, it is a pure symbol of moral—if not legal—virtue. Among elites in their political and cultural bastions, support for same-sex marriage has become as natural and obvious as praising motherhood or cheering the hometown team.

Who Are the Elites?

Americans are not generally used to thinking about their society or their politics in terms of social class. Common European or Latin American labels such as "bourgeois interests" or "labor party" have a distinctly foreign ring. Over half of all Americans refer to themselves as members of a broad "middle class." Less than a third understand themselves as "working class," a term much more common in Europe, while nary a "peasant" nor an "aristocrat" is to be found. The most the tiny strata at the pinnacle of the American social pyramid can manage to say about themselves is that they are "upper class."[12] Politicians are even more fond of a broad, sweeping "middle class America." They fight for the middle class and uphold middle class values. They repeatedly campaign on tax cuts for a homogenous middle class. If the tax rhetoric of the 2012 presidential campaign can be believed, American politicians think 97%–99% of the population is "middle class."

Yet the country has at the same time a long and vibrant history of populism. The Left version identifies a tiny and corrupt yet powerful business elite at odds with the country's mass of hardworking commoners. In 1896 the Democratic presidential candidate William Jennings Bryan delivered his famous "Cross of Gold" speech in which he summed up American politics as a contest between the "office-holding class" and "idle holders of idle capital" on one hand, and the "producing masses of the nation" on the other. Over a century later Vermont Senator Bernie Sanders nearly captured the Democratic Party nomination for president on a platform of "political revolution" against the power of the "billionaire class" and the "top one percent."[13] From the Right, populism targets an elite of educated persons with cosmopolitan tastes and habits lording over the mass of regular Americans. In the 1970s Alabama Governor and erstwhile presidential candidate George Wallace juxtaposed the "average citizen" against "pointy headed pseudo-intellectuals."[14] More recently, former senator and presidential contender Rick Santorum echoed the sentiment by contrasting "good decent men and women who go out and work hard every day" against the "snobs" produced by the contemporary university.[15] In 2016 Donald Trump ran tirelessly against "the establishment" of party leaders, campaign donors, special interests, and the legacy media. The eternal popularity of such language suggests that Americans have a much more acute sense of class politics than they are generally given credit for.

Social class is both an objective and a subjective category. As an objective social entity defined by scientific analysis, a social class is a group of persons who share a similar position in a social order. Society can be thought of as a structure into which different classes fit, engaging in different yet interdependent behaviors and enjoying different yet mutually produced social outcomes that together define the whole. For example, it is often said of medieval Europe that three "orders" or "estates" existed: the nobility, who fought; the clergy, who prayed; and the peasants, who worked. Any particular person's life experience—his or her wealth, health, lifestyle, values—was strongly defined by their class. Among sociologists the most important (although rarely the only) factor in defining a class today is the relationship to the economy in general and to wealth-producing property in particular. It wasn't only Karl Marx who believed that the most basic division in any capitalist society is between those who own such property and those who don't. Adam Smith, too, saw a basic class divide in every capitalist society between the "masters" who control productive private property in land and capital and the "workmen" who labor with and upon it.[16] To speak of class isn't to be a crypto-Marxist. It is simply to speak sociologically.

At the same time, class is not only about material matters but about cultural practices as well. Whether someone plays tennis or basketball, enrolls in an Ivy League school or a state university, joins a labor union or fights against one, marries or cohabitates, identifies as a Democrat or a Republican, is healthy or ill, aspires to become a professor or a police officer, can be explained as a function of class. Social class distinguishes groups of people who share common thought patterns, common social practices, and common subjective social identities. They are social actors with a subjective sense of self and a self-interest created through political, social, economic, and cultural struggle.

Because a social class can only be defined through its interactions with other classes, social class is a fundamentally relational concept. It is also a hierarchical concept. Classes are not simply different. They are unequal. They engage in an eternal quest for distinction and status. Those at the top of society own property, garner high incomes, wield political and cultural influence, and enjoy social prestige. Those at the bottom are subject to the power of those at the top, own little if any wealth, garner low incomes, and are socially marginalized.

The foundation of class power today is capital. Dominant classes hold sway over the rest of society because they enjoy the highest concentrations of both economic and cultural capital. Consider as a rough cut recent measures of economic capital and cultural capital by occupation. Following the internationally recognized Standard Occupational Classification (SOC) system, the U.S. Bureau of Labor Statistics identifies twenty-two "major occupational groups" in the American economy, corresponding to two-digit codes. Two are managerial, eight are professional, and the other twelve are middle- and low-skilled service and goods production jobs, everything from police officers to sales clerks to factory workers to secretaries (a full list and description can be found in table A.4 in appendix D). Figure 2.1 plots each of the twenty-two occupational groups along two axes. Annual median wage is used as the measure of economic capital. Percent of the group having at least a four-year bachelor's degree is used as the measure of cultural capital. Managerial groups are colored dark grey, professional groups are colored light grey, and all others are transparent. The size of each bubble represents the total number of employees in each group. The figure is tilted forty-five degrees counterclockwise to aid in interpretation. The result is a new vertical axis representing the total volume of capital and a new horizontal axis representing the relative balance between cultural and economic capital.

The gap in figure 2.1 between professionals and managers on one hand and everyone else on the other is stark. The ten managerial and professional groups have high levels of both economic and cultural capital. The remaining twelve have low levels of both. No group has moderate levels of total capital, a function of the great gulf in educational attainment between elite occupations and the rest of society. The least educated elite group is the very broad category of managers. Yet even here 52% have at least a four-year degree. The best-educated nonelite group is sales and related occupations where just 29% have a bachelor's degree or higher.

Heterogeneous capital endowments distinguish groups within the large category of managerial and professional occupations. Managers have the most economic capital-heavy endowment thanks to their combination of a relatively low (for elites) education level and the highest median annual wage of any group at $99,000. On the other end are community and social services occupations, the most cultural capital-heavy group among the elite. Over 70% of people in such occupations have a bachelor's

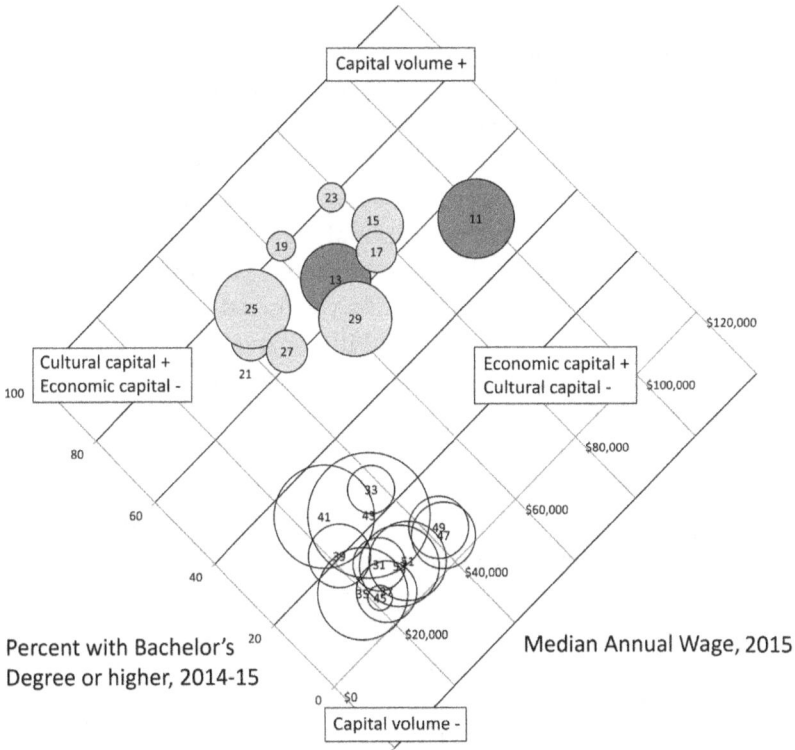

FIGURE 2.1. Occupational Groups in Social Space

SOURCE: *Department of Labor, U.S. Bureau of Labor Statistics, "Employment Projections: Occupational Data," tables 1.1 and 1.11, last modified November 9, 2016, https://www.bls.gov/ emp/ep_data_occupational_data.htm.*

degree or higher while the group's mean annual wage is just $42,000. Legal occupations enjoy a relative balance between economic and cultural capital. By these two simple measures they also enjoy the largest overall capital endowment of any group.

The historic rise of the country's professionals and managers has been a long process intertwined with dramatic changes in the economy and the growth of the state. In the nineteenth century most firms were small. Even new behemoths were controlled by entrepreneurial founders or their descendants. Neither state governments nor the federal government did much to manage the economy, and their powers to tax and spend were unimpressive. The main social classes were capitalists who owned the means of production, industrial and agricultural workers who owned only their own labor, and the traditional middle class of small property owners such as shopkeepers and yeoman farmers. This was a fairly typical arrangement throughout the Western world. As early as the late nineteenth century, however, German academics began to identify and analyze what they called a "new middle class" of salaried employees and state functionaries in new corporate and governmental bureaucracies.[17] Unlike both capitalists and the traditional middle class, members of this new class owned no physical means of production and thus appeared to be workers. At the same time, unlike the industrial and agricultural working classes, they had significant skills, enjoyed special employment benefits, and exercised real if limited control over their own labor. A new social class was born.

The growth of this class over time is impressive. As early as the 1900 census the federal government reported data on a category of occupations it labeled "professional service," which included actors, architects, clergy, dentists, engineers, journalists, lawyers, musicians, government officials, physicians, teachers—the same rough definition of "professional" in use today.[18] At the time, over 1.2 million persons worked in such occupations, totaling 4.3% of the workforce. Teachers alone made up over one-third of the class while physicians, lawyers, clergy, and journalists together comprised another 40%.[19] Over the next fifty years the absolute number of "professional, technical and kindred workers" more than quadrupled to almost five million and their relative weight in the labor force nearly doubled to 8.7% of all occupations. Teachers continued to be the largest group but diminished to barely one-fifth of the class. Now engineers, nurses, and accountants followed numerically in their wake.[20] Thirty years after that, the number of people working in "professional specialty occupations" had more than doubled to over twelve million and composed 12.3% of the labor force, with the same four subsets of teachers, engineers, nurses, and accountants the most numerous.[21] By 2010 nearly thirty million adults and 21% of the workforce were in a "professional and related" occupation.[22]

The U.S. Census Bureau didn't create a distinct "managerial" occupational category until 1940. That year the census recorded 3.8 million persons in the category "proprietors, managers and officials," making up 8.4% of the country's workforce.[23] By 1980 the figures for "executive, administrative, and managerial occupations" stood at just over ten million or 10.4% of the labor force.[24] As of 2010, over twenty million workers or 14.3% of the workforce are in "management, business, and financial occupations."[25] By these rough Census Bureau definitions, the relative size of professionals and managers has grown from not quite 16% of active workers on the cusp of World War II to over one-third of the workforce a decade into the twenty-first century.

This top 20%–25% of households is a broad working definition of the American "elite."[26] It captures that broad group of persons whose income has actually grown over the past thirty-five years, and that social class that has most separated itself from the rest of the country in terms of educational attainment, family structure, residence, lifestyle, and cultural values.[27] It is the mass base for the cultural projects and political activism of the gay rights movement. Whether known as the "upper middle class," "knowledge workers," "symbolic analysts," "creatives," or "bobos," this is the class that turned the dreams of a very small percentage of the American population into reality.[28]

Normalizing the Gay Individual

The evolution of the normalization of homosexuality in the United States has traveled along two parallel tracks. The first emphasizes equality between individuals. Professionals worked to destigmatize homosexuality as a sexual orientation and to promote legal toleration. They urged policies of nondiscrimination in employment and housing, and argued for the repeal of sodomy laws. While this track began in the early 1970s, in many ways it continues today. The second emphasizes an equality of family forms. While mental health professionals performed crucial early work on child custody and foster care, the corporate sector is the more important mover. The country's largest firms began to normalize LGBT families by extending employment benefits to same-sex partners. Professionals pressed on to issues of adoption, artificial reproduction, domestic partnerships, and ultimately to same-sex marriage. While LGBT activists attempted to open this track in the early 1970s, it carried little traffic until the 1990s. With the Supreme Court's 2015 *Obergefell* decision, the family track was complete after twenty years, while the individual track still carries on into its fifth decade. This unusual difference says a great deal about elite values and the importance of elite support in shaping the overall normalization project.

Professional Elites

In Western countries a common way of depicting the human condition is to place us a little lower than the angels while a step above the animals. Unlike them, we human beings are simultaneously spirit (or "selves" or "wills" or "souls") and matter with the latter routinely confounding the former. The eternal tension between the two gives rise to the eternal problem of the "flesh," regulated and controlled by means of three central social institutions: medicine, law, and religion.[29] Excepting perhaps food, sex is the most obvious consequence of human embodiment calling out for social regulation. Every society establishes and polices boundaries for sexual behavior—who may have sexual relations with whom, when, where, and how. Even half a century into the Sexual Revolution, American society is rife with formal legal and informal cultural rules of sexual desire and behavior. Stark lines continue to be drawn between adults and children.[30] Lines nearly as stark are drawn between private and public spaces and between the most closely related persons. Mutual consent occupies the cornerstone of moral as well as legal reasoning. On the nation's college campuses, consent ever more intimately regulates each discrete sexual act. Americans continue on the whole to expect monogamy and demand sexual fidelity from their partners. Sex that is "safe" is a cultural totem.

Prior to the 1970s same-sex sexual desire and behavior were generally unproblematic objects of the country's cultural and legal regulatory apparatus. Homosexuality was nearly universally understood as a psychological disorder (medicine) generating social (law) and moral (religion) problems. In 1968 the American Psychiatric Association published the second edition of its *Diagnostic and Statistical Manual*. This "bible" of psychiatry defined homosexuality as a "sexual deviation" in the same category with fetishism, pedophilia, voyeurism, and sadism.[31] Forty-nine of fifty U.S. states maintained laws against sodomy at the time. The American legal apparatus was only just coming off an "antihomosexual kulturkampf."[32] Not one mainstream Christian or Jewish religious body ordained openly gay men or lesbians. In the first nationally representative survey, taken in 1973, asking Americans their views of same-sex sexual behavior, 80% of respondents who expressed an opinion believed it to be always or almost always wrong.

The mental health professions proved the true pioneers of normalization. This is profoundly ironic in light of their historic role in suppressing homosexuality. From their origins in the nineteenth century, psychiatrists successfully medicalized a wide array of social deviancy. Behaviors that had been long understood as the products of sinful desire or self-deception became diseases. Doctors began to displace clergy and monastics, churches lost control over hospitals, and asylums became commonplace. The concepts "sexuality" and "sexual orientation" expanded out of psychiatry into general cultural use. By the early twentieth century in the United States, psychiatrists had established dominance over the social meaning of same-sex sexual relations. They defined it as an abnormal sexual orientation, labeled it a mental illness, and assigned themselves the task of curing it.[33]

The American Psychiatric Association's definition of homosexuality as a departure from "normal sexual behavior" and "normal sexual objects" made it an obvious early target for gay rights activists.[34] Such activists began picketing and disrupting panels of annual APA conferences in 1970, hoping to force the profession to declassify homosexuality as a mental illness. Together with LGBT and allied members of the APA itself, in 1973 they successfully convinced the organization's Board of Trustees to remove homosexuality from the *Diagnostic and Statistical Manual* (replacing it with "sexual orientation disturbance"). The APA's membership ratified the board decision the following year.[35]

Other mental health professions followed closely behind. In 1975 the American Psychological Association not only endorsed the APA's change but moved well beyond it, advocating for a broad normalization of homosexuality throughout society. The country's psychologists lent the prestige of their profession to political efforts to include sexual orientation in government lists of suspect classifications under civil rights law. They likewise urged "all mental health professionals to take the lead in removing the stigma of mental illness that has long been associated with homosexual orientations."[36] Professional social workers moved in close synchronization. In 1976 the National Association of Social Workers (NASW) formed a "Task Force on Gay Issues" as an internal committee dedicated to advancing the full inclusion and normalization of gay men and lesbians. The following year the organization issued its first policy statement on homosexuality, a forceful document that directed the profession to work toward the "eradication of prejudice and discrimination against Lesbians and Gay men" in all areas of public life.[37] By 1979 the NASW's code of ethics included sexual orientation in its list of protected classes. All three mental health professional organizations expanded their efforts in the 1980s and 1990s. In 1988 the APA passed a resolution against "irrational employment discrimination on the basis of gender and sexual orientation" and in 1993 the American Psychological Association formally opposed any legal effort in U.S. states that "prohibits anti-discrimination legislation for lesbian, gay, and bisexual persons." All three leading mental health organizations supported the normalization of homosexuality in the military in the early 1990s and, led by the NASW, condemned in the late 1990s so-called "reparative therapies" that seek to reduce or eliminate same-sex sexual desire.

Mental health professionals have been the elite's vanguard of normalization. A 1982 study of San Diego area physicians showed that psychiatrists were far and away the most positive in their views of homosexuality, with 62% having what researchers termed "homophilic" attitudes and a mere 2% having "homophobic" ones. Those in surgery, general and family practice, and obstetrics and gynecology were much less positive, with homophilia rates in the 20%–33% range and homophobia levels above 30%.[38] Another study of New Mexico physicians in the late 1990s showed considerable consistency over time in the discrepancies between specialties. Psychiatrists once again exhibited the most positive support for normalization, with 86% reporting homophilic attitudes and just 1% homophobic sentiments. Surgeons and general practitioners again fell into the least supportive camp, although their levels of support had dramatically increased over the preceding fifteen years. Their homophilic range rose to 42%–58% while homophobic attitudes fell to a mere 3%–8%.[39] This pattern is reflected in the history of the American Medical Association (AMA), the profession's largest and oldest U.S. organization. In 1981 the AMA adopted a policy report on "the health care needs of homosexuals" that offered endorsement of sexual orientation change therapies. It also refused recognition to a proposed gay and lesbian caucus around the same time, persisting in such refusal until 1998. Not until 1993, after seven failed attempts, did the AMA include sexual orientation in its own nondiscrimination policy. It removed homosexuality from its own list of treatable disorders only in 1994.[40] By the end of the 1990s, however, all major medical professional organizations had come to embrace normalization. In 1999 ten professional health, education, and religious organizations, including the American Psychological Association, the National Association of Social Workers, the American Counseling Association, and the American Academy of Pediatrics, formed the

"Just the Facts Coalition" to counteract what each saw as the continued social legitimacy of sexual orientation conversion therapy for minors. In a pamphlet mailed to every school superintendent in the country, the group endorsed the strong position that "homosexuality is not a mental disorder and thus there is no need for a 'cure.'"[41]

Legal professionals traveled a similar if slower path from chief regulators and suppressors of homosexuality to ardent social champions of normalization. As early as 1955 the American Law Institute (ALI), an organization of the profession's intellectual elite with a self-stated mission to "clarify, modernize, and otherwise improve the law,"[42] recommended through its *Model Penal Code* that states decriminalize all consensual noncommercial same-sex sexual behavior. At the time of publication, every U.S. state maintained a sodomy law on its books. The American Bar Association (ABA) expressed formal approval of the ALI's *Model Penal Code* in 1974 amid a wave of legal change sweeping the country. Between 1969 and 1983 over thirty states either decriminalized consensual same-sex sexual relations completely or reduced their criminal status from a felony to a misdemeanor.[43] In comparison Gallup found that a plurality of Americans rejected the legality of "homosexual relations between consenting adults" down into the early 1990s.

The legal profession remained content largely to follow the mental health professions rather than stake out a leadership position within the elite. Fifteen years after the American Psychological Association expressed support for inclusion of sexual orientation in nondiscrimination law, the Association of American Law Schools (AALS) amended its bylaws to include sexual orientation in its own nondiscrimination policy. As some 90% of accredited U.S. law schools are members of the AALS, the practical impact of this rule change was to ban employers lacking the same policy from recruiting at the country's law schools. In 1995 the ABA filed an amicus brief with the Supreme Court against Colorado's ban on local governments recognizing LGBT persons as a protected class. In 1999 the ABA included sexual orientation in its Model Code of Judicial Conduct list of "bias or prejudice" from which every judge must refrain. The growth in the legal profession's support for normalization over the course of the 1990s was so thorough that in 2003 Supreme Court Justice Antonin Scalia called out "the law profession's anti-anti-homosexual culture." By this he meant "a law-profession culture, that has largely signed on to the so-called homosexual agenda, by which I mean the agenda promoted by some homosexual activists directed at eliminating the moral opprobrium that has traditionally attached to homosexual conduct."[44] While many criticized Scalia's language and argument concerning the role of this "culture," none disputed the observation itself.[45]

With the demise of the U.S. military's "Don't Ask, Don't Tell" policy in 2011, the country's religious bodies became the last site of organized opposition to normalization in the United States. Yet even here there have been dramatic changes. Many mainstream religious bodies spoke out in favor of public nondiscrimination in the 1970s, including the Unitarian Universalist Association (1970), the United Church of Christ (1975), the Episcopal Church (1976), Reform Judaism's Union of American Hebrew Congregations and Central Conference of American Rabbis (1977), the Christian Church (Disciples of Christ) (1977), and the Presbyterian Church (USA) (1978). Change of beliefs and doctrines regarding homosexuality within the denominations themselves came later. Among Christians the United Church of Christ (UCC) has been the clear leader. Descended from the Puritans and one of the "seven sisters of mainline Protestantism," the UCC has been the mainstream religious pioneer of every step in the history of normalization. Its Council for Christian Social Action condemned all sodomy laws five years before the ABA did so. In 1972 the UCC became the country's first Christian denomination to ordain on openly gay person. In 1975 the UCC's highest legislative body made its first of many calls for inclusion of LGBT persons in nondiscrimination law and by 1983 was condemning itself for "institutionalized homophobia." The UCC embraced full normalization in 1985 when 98% of voters at its General Synod meeting supported a resolution urging every UCC congregation to adopt a "Covenant of Openness and Affirmation of persons of lesbian, gay and bisexual orientation within the community of faith." Reform Judaism has been pioneering outside the country's dominant Christian tradition. It reached a position of full normalization by 1990 with statements by the Union of American Hebrew Congregations for "full inclusion" of LGBT Jews "as singles, couples and families" as well as the formal acceptance by the Central Conference of American Rabbis of openly gay rabbinical candidates.

Liberal if less strongly progressive denominations embraced normalization in the 2000s and 2010s. In 1996 The Episcopal Church formally refused to discipline a bishop for knowingly ordaining a sexually active gay man, functionally establishing a new interpretation of church canons on the morality of same-sex sexual behavior. Full normalization came in 2003 when, in open defiance of the worldwide Anglican Communion,

Episcopalians famously ordained V. Gene Robinson as bishop. In 2006 Conservative Judaism opened the door for its congregations to appoint openly gay rabbis in same-sex relationships under a sort of "don't ask, don't tell" policy regarding their sexual conduct. The Evangelical Lutheran Church in America voted in 2009 to permit the ordination of noncelibate gays and lesbians, and elected its first partnered gay bishop in 2013. The Presbyterian Church (USA) voted to overturn its own ban on ministerial same-sex sexual behavior as early as 1997, but due to its internal political structure did not institute the policy change until 2011.[46] The Disciples of Christ likewise endorsed sexually active LGBT clergy in 2013.

This pattern of normalization within the country's religious bodies has a class basis shown in table 2.1. The seven large denominations that had normalized homosexuality by the end of 2016 are among the eight most highly educated in America. The pioneering Christian denomination, the United Church of Christ, has more than twice the national average of members with an advanced degree. The pioneering body outside Christianity, Reform Judaism, has over three times the national average and alongside Conservative Judaism is the most highly educated religious denomination in the country. The only three denominations with more than half of their members holding four-year college degrees are three of the first four to normalize. On the other side of the class divide, no denomination having one-third or fewer members with four-year degrees has normalized or is even seriously discussing doing so. The one outlier in the list is the United Methodist Church (UMC), the last highly educated large denomination yet to normalize homosexuality. The church's unusual polity explains the exception. Unlike most other Protestant denominations in the United States, the UMC's highest legislative body is a global one in which non-Americans have notable representation. At the 2016 meeting of the Methodist General Conference, for example, only 58% of the delegates were from the United States.[47] It is precisely the UMC's large and growing minority of mostly African and Filipino members that keeps it officially committed to a traditional position on homosexuality. If the UMC was a strictly American church, there is no doubt it, too, would have endorsed normalization long ago.

Managerial Elites

Compared to the mental health and legal professions, the corporate sector's journey to normalization has been complex. From a business perspective sexual orientation is not simply a question of professional values.

TABLE 2.1. Level of Education and Median Family Income, 2014,

Denomination	% of adult members with bachelor's degree or higher	% of adult members with postgraduate degree
Conservative Judaism	62 (2013)	30 (2013)
Reform Judaism	61 (2013)	30 (2013)
The Episcopal Church	56	27
Presbyterian Church (USA)	47	23
United Church of Christ	46	24
United Methodist Church	37	14
Evangelical Lutheran Church in America	36	15
Christian Church (Disciples of Christ)	35 (2007)	17 (2007)
Presbyterian Church in America	33	12
Church of Jesus Christ of Latter-Day Saints	33	10
Lutheran Church—Missouri Synod	32	12
All U.S. adults	28	11
Seventh-Day Adventist Church	28	10
Catholic Church	26	10
National Baptist Convention	19	7
Southern Baptist Convention	19	6
Churches of Christ	18	7
Assemblies of God	15	4
American Baptist Churches USA	13	5
Church of God in Christ	12	5
Jehovah's Witnesses	12	3
Church of God (Cleveland, Tenn.)	11	3

TABLE SOURCES: Pew Research Center, *America's Changing Religious Landscape,* 2015; Pew Research Center, *A Portrait of Jewish Americans,* October 1, 2013; Pew Research Center, *A Portrait of American Orthodox Jews,* August 26, 2015; Pew Research Center, *U.S. Religious Landscape Survey: Religious Affiliation, Diverse and Dynamic,* February 1, 2008.

and Date of Normalization by Religious Denomination

% of adult members with family income above $100,000	Full normalization of individuals by	Full normalization of families by
41 (2013)	2006	2012
47 (2013)	1990	2000
35	2003	2012
25	2011	2015
29	1985	1997
26		
26	2009	2009
20 (2007)	2013	
25		
20		
22		
19		
15		
19		
9		
16		
16		
10		
9		
9		
4		
8 (2007)		

Table includes all denominations with at least 0.4% of the 2014 adult U.S. population as members. The Christian Church (Disciples of Christ) was added despite being under the size cutoff so as to include all "seven sisters" of mainline Protestantism.

It is also a matter of human resource management, legal compliance, and profit and loss. Hiring openly LGBT individuals may clash with the desire to maintain a harmonious workplace. Promoting traditional values may conflict with the demands of the law. An interest in marketing to gays and lesbians may contend with a fear of alienating culturally conservative consumers. During the 1990s and early 2000s, Corporate America worked through these competing pressures, and by the first half-decade of the twenty-first century its highest echelons had become one of the country's most significant forces for normalization.

Prior to the 1990s business barely recognized sexual orientation. In 1989 just ten LGBT employee organizations existed in the entire country.[48] That same year Massachusetts became only the third state (including D.C.) to ban discrimination in private sector employment on the grounds of sexual orientation. The 1990 Gay Games, a sort of Olympics plus international cultural festival, attracted but one corporate sponsor who donated just $5,000.[49] The largest U.S. firms did begin engaging HIV/AIDS in the late 1980s, although this should not necessarily be read as a growing acceptance of homosexuality. The prominence of Ryan White, the Indiana teenager who contracted HIV/AIDS through a blood transfusion and became nationally famous in 1985 for being denied admittance to his middle school, likely did much more to destigmatize the disease. By the mid-1990s, however, a great deal had changed. Fifty new LGBT employee organizations had been created.[50] One hundred thirty-two of the largest American corporations maintained nondiscrimination policies including sexual orientation in 1993, two-thirds of them initiated in the 1990s.[51] The 1994 Gay Games raised nearly $1 million in corporate sponsorships.[52] Corporate efforts to fight HIV/AIDS even became a fashionable element of corporate social responsibility.[53]

The Human Rights Campaign, the country's most powerful LGBT rights organization, has tracked the practices of the country's largest firms in the area of sexual orientation and gender identity since the early 2000s. Its "Corporate Equality Index" reports show that sexual orientation nondiscrimination policies had become ubiquitous in Corporate America by the early twenty-first century. Over 90% of firms answering the organization's survey had them. By the late 2000s, diversity training covering sexual orientation had reached a similar status. In 2010 the Human Rights Campaign for the first time reported scores for every Fortune 500 firm whether or not each firm had completed a formal survey. The group found that 89% included sexual orientation in their nondiscrimination policies. Among the largest one hundred firms, fully 95% did so, and among the top fifty the tally was 98%.[54] For greater comparison, only 75% of Fortune 1000 firms had such policies.[55] Not only is there a clear association between financial size and support for normalization. Corporate America outpaced the fifty-one state governments (including the District of Columbia) as gay-friendly employers, only thirty-two of which listed sexual orientation in their nondiscrimination employment policies.

Marketing to LGBT consumers is another indicator of support for normalization, important enough for the Human Rights Campaign to include in its Corporate Equality Index reports. Such efforts began largely in the early 1990s. In 1994 the inaugural Gay Press Report found that only nineteen Fortune 500 corporations were targeting LGBT consumers. By 2005 over 175 of these firms—even socially conservative ones like Walmart—were intentionally positioning their products and services in the LGBT market.[56] Corporate sponsorship of LGBT organizations and events has proven an important part of this marketing strategy. Before the early 1990s few major national brands provided such support, and those that did tended to be concentrated in early gay-friendly industries such as alcoholic beverages.[57] By the 2000s, however, major corporate sponsorship had become normal and the range of industries had expanded dramatically. Today LGBT advocacy organizations proudly tout their corporate sponsors. San Francisco Pride, the country's largest LGBT pride festival, boasts recent sponsorship from Fortune 500 giants Nike, Verizon, Bank of America, Wells Fargo, Coca-Cola, Macy's, Google, and Apple. New York City Pride sponsors include State Farm, New York Life, Delta Airlines, and Citibank. The "national corporate partners" of the Human Rights Campaign's 2016 National Dinner included fifteen Fortune 100 firms as well as several members of the Fortune Global 100 list.[58] Nearly half of all Fortune 500 firms now make what the HRC calls a "public commitment to the LGBT community" through marketing and philanthropy.[59]

Perhaps the most far-reaching corporate contribution to normalization is an increasing use of LGBT-themed advertising to mainstream audiences. The first wave of "lesbian chic" hit U.S. magazines in 1993. As early as 1994 Ikea featured a same-sex couple in its advertising to a general American audience.[60] Alcoholic beverage manufacturers integrated gay themes and characters into their mainstream advertising early on, pulled by the desire to tap a lucrative market without the constraints imposed by a fear of criticism or boycott from conservative religious consumers. The travel, fashion, and financial industries have also pressed gay men and lesbians into advertising service as carriers of brand values such as stylishness, sexiness, distinction, nonconformity, and cosmopolitanism.[61] In 2014 events as mainstream as the Super Bowl and the Winter Olympics first ran LGBT-inclusive television ads from Coca-Cola and General Motors. Same-sex couples became so common in advertising in 2015 that CNBC declared it "the year of LGBT ads" and a *Washington Post* columnist described it as the year "advertisers embraced 'the gays' with open arms."[62] Homosexuality has become so normal among Fortune 500 firms that they even market products generally associated with children with gay-inclusive ads. During Pride Month 2012, for example, Kraft Foods posted to its corporate Facebook page a photograph of its well-known Oreo cookie stuffed with six layers of frosting, each a different color of the rainbow. It simultaneously took to Twitter with the image and suggested that subscribers "celebrate your pride for love." The following year General Mills launched its "#LuckyToBe" advertising campaign during Pride month across all social media platforms, enlisting its Lucky Charms cereal (and particularly its rainbow marshmallows) as a celebration of those "lucky enough to be different." General Mills intentionally played up the shared symbolism between the cereal and the gay rights movement as the cereal's marketing director referred to the rainbow as "one of the universal symbols of acceptance."[63] In 2014 Nabisco (a former subsidiary of Kraft Foods) featured a male same-sex couple in its mainstream advertising of Teddy Grahams snacks under the theme "this is wholesome." The symbolic power of advancing normalization is so great that even Mormon-owned Marriott International uses gay-themed ads for general audiences. In the words of one of the firm's marketing vice presidents, "multiculturalism today is mainstream. . . . This is what best-in-class brands do."[64]

The general success of normalization across Corporate America is proved by the trends recorded in the Human Rights Campaign's Corporate Equality Index. The reports measure (and thus advocate) the overall commitment of the largest American companies to "an ethos of LGBT inclusion."[65] Since the scorecard's inauguration in 2002, both the number of firms voluntarily participating in the rather involved evaluation process, as well as the number of corporations receiving perfect scores, has increased dramatically. The first index received completed surveys from 319 employers. By 2017 the total had nearly tripled to 887. The first index featured just thirteen firms with perfect scores. The most recent iteration presents 515 corporations at 100%, a nearly forty-fold increase on a measuring stick that, according to the Human Rights Campaign, has only become more demanding over time. It's hard to argue with the view that these trends are proof that "a new normal has arrived" in Corporate America.[66]

Normalizing the Gay Family

The normalization of LGBT families involves both same-sex coupling and gay parenting. Despite the two issues being raised together in the early 1970s, gay parents became normalized—at least among elites—well before same-sex unions. This is likely because the issue of gay parents first emerged as an individual matter of sexual orientation in child custody cases between biological parents and later in foster care and adoption by individuals. Normalizing gay parents played an important role in the later normalization of same-sex coupling and ultimately marriage.

Professional Elites

Here again mental health professionals were society's vanguard. Their earliest policy statements on gay parenting involved matters of child custody after divorce. In 1976 the American Psychological Association became the first to oppose sexual orientation as either the "sole or primary" consideration in child custody decisions. At the time not a single U.S. state adhered to such a policy. Judges in professional class centers such as the San Francisco Bay Area, New York City, Boston, Washington, and Chicago advanced the cause of normalization slowly through the 1980s and early 1990s. The expert testimony of mental health professionals played a critical role in the earliest same-sex couple adoption cases.[67] The fact that these couples were almost always highly educated and wealthy professionals themselves surely didn't hurt matters. The first such case in New York, *In the Matter of Evan* (1992), involved two female Ph.D.s living in Manhattan. The first in Massachusetts, *Adoption of Tammy* (1993), involved two female surgeons living in Cambridge. In New Jersey's *In the Matter of the Adoption of Two Children by H.N.R.* (1995), the adoptive couple was composed of two female radiation therapists living in "a prosperous suburban community," one of which was the administrative director of a department of radiation oncology. The District of Columbia's first such adoption was *In the Matter of M.M.D. and B.H.M.* (1995) involving two men with master's degrees, one in computer engineering and the other in public administration.

Mental health professional organizations said little officially on gay parenting, however, until the late 1990s. In 1997 the American Psychiatric Association became the first to endorse the developing practice of "second parent adoption" pioneered by the National Center for Lesbian Rights. The American Psychological Association followed in 1998. Consider that when these statements were issued, fewer than half a dozen states explicitly allowed a same-sex couple to adopt, while many legally banned joint adoption by same-sex partners. In the 2000s the trickle of elite support for LGBT parenting became a torrent as every major medical professional organization formally endorsed second-parent adoption, including the American Academy of Pediatrics (2002), the National Association of Social Workers (2002), and even the traditionally recalcitrant American Medical Association (2004). The American Psychological Association issued a particularly well-publicized brief in 2005, supported by an annotated bibliography of sixty-seven published and unpublished research manuscripts, that concluded, "There is no evidence to suggest that lesbian women or gay men are unfit to be parents. . . . Not a single study has found children of lesbian or gay parents to be disadvantaged in any significant respect relative to children of heterosexual parents."[68] As with LGBT individuals, the legal profession followed medicine on questions of gay families. The American Bar Association (ABA) endorsed a policy of sexual orientation nondiscrimination regarding child custody and visitation rights in 1995, nearly twenty years after the American Psychological Association did the same. The ABA endorsed individual LGBT adoption in 1999 and rapidly assimilated to elite opinion by supporting second-parent adoption in 2003. The American Law Institute (ALI) has been particularly revolutionary in matters of family law and homosexuality. In 2000 it issued the model legal code *Principles of the Law of Family Dissolution*, largely building upon the work of lesbian legal scholars Nancy Polikoff, Martha Fineman, and Martha Ertman. The ALI took the primary goal of family law to be the promotion of family diversity, and its proposal on parental rights and obligations was particularly dramatic. The organization openly rejected the biological basis of parenthood for what they called "functional parenthood" based on shared household status. For the ALI same-sex parenting became itself the norm against which all other families were to be measured.[69]

The evolving social and legal status of same-sex couple parents strongly contributed to the final step in normalizing the gay family. As early as 1998 the American Psychological Association began calling for same-sex marriage in all but name, appealing particularly to the welfare of children already being raised in same-sex couple households. The American Psychiatric Association approved a position statement in 2000 supporting same-sex civil unions after the Vermont model that had just been enacted, strongly emphasizing the children of gay couples in its statement. The National Association of Social Workers became the first major mental health professional organization explicitly to endorse marriage for same-sex couples when it joined an amicus brief to the Massachusetts Supreme Judicial Court in the *Goodridge* case.[70] The American Psychological Association formally endorsed same-sex marriage in 2004, just two months after it had become a legal reality in Massachusetts, and the country's psychiatrists followed quickly behind in 2005.[71] Consider that at this time only one state had recognized same-sex marriage—and that by judicial fiat in a one-vote margin with threatened reversal through a popular referendum.

Although legal elites may have embraced an "anti-anti-homosexual culture" by the mid-2000s, this did not necessarily translate into support for same-sex marriage. As the country's mental health professional organizations were stepping out boldly in support of same-sex marriage, the ABA could only pass a resolution in 2004 opposing the Federal Marriage Amendment. The ABA's language on this point is revealing, carefully noting that its position was based strictly on respect for federalism and the rights of states to regulate marriage. It was certainly not "to place the ABA on record as either favoring or opposing laws that would allow same-sex couples to enter into civil marriage."[72] As elites came to embrace same-sex marriage in the 2000s, however, such fence-straddling proved an embarrassment. By 2009 the ABA officially called for repeal of section 3 of the federal Defense of Marriage Act, something carried out by the Supreme Court four years later. In 2010 the ABA abandoned its former deference to federalism and completed the final step, calling for nationwide recognition of same-sex marriage by every "state, territorial and tribal government."[73]

The country's most elite judges united behind same-sex marriage at this time. Throughout the 1990s and 2000s numerous state courts had found strictly opposite-sex marriage fully consistent with their constitutions, even in the most liberal of states such as New York and Maryland. Once federal judges began reviewing same-sex marriage lawsuits beginning in 2010, however, state-level DOMAs fell like dominoes. The legal elite's consolidation around same-sex marriage at this point proved remarkably rapid and thorough. In 2011 former U.S. Solicitor General Paul Clement had to resign as partner from the powerhouse Washington law firm King & Spalding in order to continue providing legal support for the House of Representatives' defense of the federal Defense of Marriage Act. In mid-2014 the news organization Reuters found that over one hundred suits had been filed in federal court regarding same-sex marriage since the *Windsor* decision a year earlier. While at least thirty of the legal profession's largest two hundred firms filed briefs in support of plaintiffs seeking to overturn state DOMAs, not one defended democratically passed state constitutional marriage amendments. In the estimation of Reuters, "the legal industry has reached its Mozilla moment" when dissent on the question of the normalization of homosexuality would no longer be tolerated.[74] Law had indeed established itself as the country's most gay-friendly industry by this time. The Human Rights Campaign's Corporate Equality Index for 2014 reported that 89% of law firms it surveyed earned perfect scores. In the second most supportive industry, banking and financial services, just 49% received the group's top rating.[75]

The cultural power of normalization among American elites shows most dramatically in their religious denominations. Historically, sexual behavior in both Christianity and Judaism—even in their most liberal manifestations—had only ever been endorsed within marriage. This is not to say that every denomination maintained the very same doctrinal teachings or disciplinary policies regarding either sexual relations or marriage. It is to say, however, that all agreed on the broad normative standard. Yet despite this ancient and shared foundation, the denominations that normalized LGBT individuals did so by abandoning their belief that sexual relationships are fully legitimate only within marriage. While the explicit intent of normalizing homosexuality has been to bring same-sex couples into marriage, the implicit effect has been to denormalize marriage for everyone.

There are a host of examples. A recent one is the Presbyterian Church (USA). In 2011 the denomination officially removed the "requirement to live either in fidelity within the covenant of marriage between a man and a woman, or chastity in singleness" as a standard for ordination. The clear purpose was to facilitate partnered LGBT clergy. The abandoned language was not replaced with new text incorporating same-sex couples into a covenantal bond, however. Instead, all mention of sexual standards for clergy candidates simply disappeared. In 2014 the church's General Assembly voted to change its definition of marriage to a union of "two persons" rather than "a man and a woman." The next year that new defini-tion became church law. Yet no simultaneous effort was made to reinstate the old sexual standards of fidelity and chastity.

The Episcopal Church (TEC) has traveled the same path much longer. In 1996 a panel of the church's bishops dismissed charges against a priest who had six years earlier knowingly ordained a partnered gay man. At that moment TEC's requirement that sexual relations occur only within marriage came to an effective end. The well-known ordination of Gene Robinson as bishop in 2003 merely confirmed the fact. Strangely enough, Episcopal priests were not allowed to officiate at same-sex marriages, civil unions, or domestic partnerships until 2009, a year *after* Robinson had entered into his own state-recognized civil union. Only in 2012, sixteen years after partnered gay clergy were effectively permitted, did Episco-palians approve a formal liturgy for same-sex marriage. This does not mean that TEC insists its partnered clergy be married, however. Even a bishop can quite respectably cohabit with her "life partner" long after state recognition of same-sex marriage.[76]

Among Christians the diminution of marriage is furthest along in the United Church of Christ (UCC). As early as 1977 the UCC was urging governments to grant legal status to intimate associations beyond "tra-ditional marriage."[77] In both 1981 and 1983 its General Synod passed resolutions of support for "all families . . . and that persons regardless of their family patterns, be affirmed and supported in the life of the church." The latter resolution was explicitly couched in the context of homosexu-ality, preparing the ground for full normalization in the UCC in 1985. By 1997 the church freely declared marriage to be simply one among many forms of "covenanted relationships" in which sexual behavior could be approved, ratifying a de facto policy that had been evolving since the ordination of the UCC's first openly gay minister in 1972.[78] Although the UCC endorsed civil same-sex marriage in 2005, it was careful to reaffirm its belief in "the right to lead lives that express love, justice, mutuality, commitment, consent and pleasure" beyond "a single marriage model."[79]

Managerial Elites

The United States is unusual among wealthy postindustrial countries in that employers deliver many of society's most basic social welfare benefits, including health insurance and retirement pensions. This is especially true for elites whose private benefits strongly supplement public sys-tems like Medicare and Social Security. The U.S. system is also distinct for its continued use of marriage as an important means of accessing social welfare. While most European countries—particularly those in Scandinavia—have individualized social welfare, in the United States tens of millions gain access to basic benefits through their spouses. Because of this feature of the American political economy, normalization of LGBT families has always been closely bound to the material benefits that come through marriage. As soon as gay and lesbian employees began demanding their same-sex partners be treated as spouses, employers were forced to make very concrete material decisions concerning the social meaning and status of the gay family.

In 1982 the *Village Voice* became the first U.S. employer to extend spousal benefits to same-sex partners. The issue did not become widely debated until the 1990s, however. In 1990, the Human Rights Campaign counted fewer than two dozen firms offering health insurance benefits to same-sex partners of their employees. Yet by the time of the federal Defense of Marriage Act six years later, the figure had risen to slightly over 500. In 2004, the year of the country's first same-sex marriage, the number had skyrocketed to over 8,200. By 2008 the tally was over 9,300 and so high that the Human Rights Campaign simply stopped counting.[80] With a greater number of employers came a greater number of covered employees. Early data on strictly same-sex couples is not available. In 1999, however, 11% of all workers (including government employees) who were offered health insurance benefits by their employer could extend those benefits to same-sex partners. By 2004 that figure had risen slightly to 14%. In 2015, the last calendar year before the federal courts began overturning all state DOMAs, the tally hit 42%.[81]

While these figures demonstrate the significant change in the behavior of corporate managers over the past twenty-five years, they mask the leadership role played by the largest firms. At the time the federal DOMA was passed in 1996, only 28 of the Fortune 500 firms were offering domestic partner health benefits. By 2004 the number had swelled to 216, a more than seven-fold increase in a mere eight years. By 2015, 318 companies—almost two-thirds of the list—did so.[82] At firms with 5,000 or more workers, 15% of employees were offered access to medical benefits for same-sex partners in 1999. By 2004 the number had more than doubled to 32%, and in 2015 it had essentially doubled again to 61%.[83]

Support for same-sex marriage has come naturally for large globe-spanning corporations. In 2013 forty Fortune 500 firms—including eighteen of the top one hundred—signed an amicus brief with the U.S.

Supreme Court urging it to overturn the federal Defense of Marriage Act.[84] Their argument amounted to pleading the "burden of a dual regime" in which employees are simultaneously married (in state law) and unmarried (in federal law). This included in part the legal "compliance burdens" involved. The more substantial injury, however, was DOMA's burden on "corporate missions" and "core principles," namely diversity and nondiscrimination on the basis of sexual orientation. These firms contended both that "DOMA does violence to the morale of the institution itself" and, echoing contemporary arguments from businesses for religious freedom, forces corporations to "renounce these principles or, worse yet, betray them." One could hardly invent a clearer expression of Corporate America's dedication to the full normalization of homosexuality.

Print and electronic media firms have played especially important supporting roles in this process. A rather mundane yet important step toward normalization was treating same-sex partners as spouses in newspaper announcements. In the early 1990s major newspapers began mentioning the names of same-sex "companions" in obituaries, and by the late 1990s major dailies in liberal cities such as Austin (TX), Minneapolis, and Seattle were running announcements of same-sex commitment ceremonies and civil registrations of same-sex partnerships in their wedding sections.[85] Widespread change swept the industry after the *New York Times* adopted the practice in 2002. Within a month the number of newspapers making such announcements doubled.[86] According to the Gay and Lesbian Alliance Against Defamation (GLAAD), by 2004 approximately half of all newspaper readers in the country could access same-sex marriage or commitment ceremony announcements.[87]

The transformation at the *Times* was so rapid and thorough that in just two years the paper went from refusing same-sex union announcements to, in the words of its own public editor, "present[ing] the social and cultural aspects of same-sex marriage in a tone that approaches cheerleading." The public editor even characterized a series of the paper's articles that year on same-sex couples as "a very effective ad campaign for the gay marriage cause."[88] The same can be said for the *Washington Post*. In 2013 its ombudsman freely admitted that journalists at the *Post* "have a hard time giving much voice to those opposed to gay marriage." The reason lies, so he claimed, in the social libertarianism at the heart of journalism. "[M]ost journalists have a problem with religionists telling people what they can and cannot do," the ombudsman observed. "We want to write words, read books, watch movies, listen to music, and have sex and babies pretty much when, where, and how we choose." Since "legitimate media outlets routinely cover gays . . . because it is the civil rights issue of our time," they reflexively recoil from social conservatives who are essentially "cousins, perhaps distant cousins" of segregationists Orval Faubus, George Wallace, and Bull Connor.[89]

It is hardly surprising, then, that a Pew Research Center study conducted during and shortly after the U.S. Supreme Court hearings on the *Windsor* and *Hollingsworth* cases in early 2013 found significant bias in media reporting on same-sex marriage. Stories that emphasized supporters outnumbered stories that highlighted opponents by a 5-to-1 margin. On news radio, including National Public Radio, supportive stories outnumbered opposing stories 2-to-1. In online news sources such as *Huffington Post* and *Politico* the ratio was 5.3-to-1, while in the country's newspapers it was 5.4-to-1. Even Fox News, which ran the largest percentage of neutral segments on the topic, had 3.5 times more supportive than opposing stories. Amazingly, on broadcast television news, including PBS and the morning and evening news programs of the country's three major networks, the ratio was infinite—none ran a single story focusing on opponents of same-sex marriage.[90]

The profound success of normalization in elite circles has freed Corporate America to take up direct political action as well. Spurred by developments in neighboring New Mexico, in early 2014 the Arizona legislature passed a bill modifying the state's Religious Freedom Restoration Act explicitly to mention the right of businesses in the state to refuse service to customers on religious grounds. Arizona's corporations marched into battle against the bill virtually in unison. Eighty businesses based in the state penned a letter to the governor urging a veto, warning her that failing to do so would "haunt our business community for generations to come."[91] Numerous Fortune 500 firms made public statements supporting a veto, including American Airlines, Delta Air Lines, AT&T, Marriott, Apple, eBay, Intel, JPMorgan Chase, Southwest Airlines, United Continental Holdings, Verizon, and Wyndham Worldwide. So, too, did the country's top three major sports leagues. The National Football League even threatened to pull the scheduled 2015 Super Bowl out of Phoenix in response. The statement of Delta Air Lines captures corporate sentiment perfectly:

> As a global values-based company, Delta Air Lines is proud of the diversity of its customers and employees, and is deeply concerned about proposed measures in several states, including Georgia and Arizona, that

would allow businesses to refuse service to lesbian, gay, bisexual and transgender individuals. If passed into law, these proposals would . . . violate Delta's core values of mutual respect and dignity shared by our 80,000 employees worldwide and the 165 million customers we serve every year.[92]

Under intense local and national pressure, including opposition from the state's leading Republicans, the governor vetoed the bill. The contributions of the business lobby confirm that Corporate America has, according to the Human Rights Campaign, "transformed itself into a beacon of progress when it comes to LGBT equality" and "become legislative and social change agents."[93] Today the Chick-fil-As of the corporate scene retreat into isolated backwaters. The vocal majority of major firms get on the "right side of history."[94]

3

NORMALIZATION AS A CLASS VALUE

Class Values

Former Vice President Joe Biden has a well-deserved reputation for verbal indiscipline. From "close talking" to cursing into open microphones to causing a diplomatic row with the country's closest allies in the Middle East, Biden is famous for putting his foot in his mouth. During a routine taping of the television news program *Meet the Press* on Friday, May 4, 2012, the vice president committed one of his most consequential gaffes. Responding to a question on whether or not his views on same-sex marriage had "evolved," Biden replied that he was "absolutely comfortable" with the idea and admitted he didn't "see much of a distinction" between same-sex and opposite-sex couples.

The problem with Biden's confession was less a reversal of his clearly stated 2008 opposition to same-sex marriage. It was more his open dissent from the stated policy of his president. Since the 2008 presidential campaign Barack Obama had carefully crafted a position of both political and religious opposition to the legal recognition of same-sex marriage. While Biden emphasized that he was not speaking for the president nor announcing a new administration policy, no one missed the import of the vice president's remarks. That Biden made the comment the weekend before the country's thirty-fifth state marriage referendum in North Carolina only reinforced the media's surprise. While few observers really believed President Obama personally opposed same-sex marriage, most assumed he was making a strategic political gambit with his public opposition and that he would openly endorse same-sex marriage at a safe political moment, perhaps after the Democratic National Convention in September or more likely after the presidential election in November. Flushing Obama's true views out into the open prior to that was thought to be as wise as taking a stick to a hornet's nest.

Both the vice president's and the president's handlers quickly jumped into action to begin damage control. David Axelrod, chief strategist for the president's reelection campaign, took to Twitter early Sunday morning even before the Biden interview aired to claim the vice president hadn't said anything new or notable. Sunday evening the Office of the Vice President issued a "clarifying" email making the same claim. White House Press Secretary Jay Carney faced reporters Monday morning and deflected over fifty questions for twenty straight minutes on whether Biden's comments indicated a change of administration policy. Axelrod was called to duty for a conference call with reporters Monday afternoon during which he claimed the president and vice president enjoyed total agreement on same-sex marriage.

The administration fire brigade convinced no one. So on Tuesday Obama decided to settle the controversy himself. The White House set up a one-on-one interview between the president and ABC talk-show host Robin Roberts for Wednesday afternoon. Rumors began flying that morning. ABC even interrupted its regular programming to show key excerpts from the interview only an hour after taping. Four years previously in another one-on-one interview, then-Senator Obama told evangelical megachurch pastor and author Rick Warren, "I believe that marriage is the union between a man and a woman." Roberts' first question—"So Mr. President, are you still opposed to same-sex marriage?"—elicited the reversal everyone was waiting for: "I think same-sex couples should be able to get married."[1]

In the interview Obama did not describe his reversal as a change of mind. Likewise Roberts never accused the president of a "flip-flop." Instead Obama called it "going through an evolution." Three times during the interview he used "evolution" or "evolving" to characterize his and the country's views on same-sex marriage. This was a familiar turn of phrase for the president, one he had been using for a year and a half. He did so publicly for the first time in October 2010, observing that on same-sex marriage "attitudes evolve, including mine." Two months later he revealed that his "feelings about this are constantly evolving."[2] By mid-2011 the president's political allies were capitalizing on the metaphor and urging him to evolve faster. Once the president had completed his evolution, everyone from sitting U.S. senators to retired directors of homeland security to future Democratic party presidential nominees began "evolving" as well into support for same-sex marriage.

The timing could not have been more fortuitous. Polls in 2010 and 2011 showed for the first time a majority of Americans supporting legal recognition of same-sex marriage. In November 2012 three states recognized same-sex marriage by referendum. Apparently the country was evolving, too. By 2014 federal judges were overturning state DOMAs with direct appeals to "society's evolution."[3] In Justice Anthony Kennedy's 2015 *Obergefell* opinion mandating national same-sex marriage, he described repeatedly how the institution of marriage had "evolved" over time. These "changed understandings of marriage" have always been rooted in "new insights and societal understandings" as "new dimensions of freedom become apparent to new generations" and "we learn [the] meaning" of liberty.[4] One could hardly hope for a more elevated account of policy change.

All the attention paid to mass opinion and politicians hides the fact that the views of social elites had evolved long before those of Biden and Obama. As early as 2005 polls showed a plurality of persons with advanced degrees supported same-sex marriage.[5] College graduates overall tilted to supporting marriage for same-sex couples around 2008.[6] Analyses of state-level gay-rights and marriage referenda over the period 1996–2008 show the strong positive correlation between higher levels of education and support for same-sex marriage.[7] "Creative class" cities pioneered broad societal LGBT normalization.[8] In the 1970s and 1980s they were the first to include gays and lesbians in municipal nondiscrimination ordinances and to elect openly gay politicians, and their states were the first to repeal same-sex sodomy laws and ban discrimination in civil service hiring. By the 1990s such cities were enacting domestic partnerships and their states were legalizing adoption by gay and lesbian individuals and then by same-sex couples. In the 2000s, of course, American same-sex marriage originated in Massachusetts, a state with one of the highest concentrations of professionals. In the 2010s fourteen of the first sixteen states (including the District of Columbia) to recognize same-sex marriage were located in the Northeast or Pacific Coast regions. While we usually explain this geography of normalization by noting these cities and states are the most liberal in the country, beneath their ideology is their sociology. America's sites of normalization and same-sex marriage are at the same time its sites of greatest elite concentration.

The previous chapter showed that elite peak organizations representing those with the highest endowments of cultural capital led the way to normalization in the 1970s and 1980s. They were joined in the 1990s and 2000s by elite peak organizations of persons with the highest endowments of economic capital. This chapter shows that this activism has not been an anomaly. While elite peak organizations certainly led elite opinion, they also represented it as the bulk of elites followed. The nation's most powerful psychiatrists and CEOs set the cultural agenda for the country's engineers, purchasing managers, high school teachers, and office supervisors.

The embrace of normalization is not simply a class story, however. It is also a story of geography. Elites are unevenly distributed across the country. They are highly concentrated in "creative class" cities, university towns, the Boston-Washington corridor, and the Pacific coast, while diluted in fading Rust-Belt cities, natural resource regions, and the Deep South. If geography matters we shouldn't expect software engineers in Silicon Valley to have exactly the same cultural views as software engineers in Nashville, or hospital managers in Boston to see eye-to-eye with hospital managers in Las Vegas. Just as living organisms evolve not simply by expressing tendencies in their genes but in and through their environment, social classes (not to mention politicians) evolve in a social environment. The most important characteristic of that environment is class concentration.

Defining Social Class

Up to this point in the book, social class has been a somewhat amorphous concept. A rigorous measurement of class values, however, requires a rigorous definition of class. Social classes are not things so much as relationships—to forms of capital, to dispositions, to other classes, and to the overall social order. A rough depiction of those relationships appeared in chapter 2. Using the U.S. Bureau of Labor Statistics' 2010 Standard Occupational Classification (SOC) system, figure 2.1 showed how the country's twenty-two major occupational groups map onto a simple representation of social space. Professionals and managers enjoy relatively high accumulations of capital while the rest of society has low accumulations. Within the elite, managers tend toward higher concentrations of economic capital. The endowment of social service professionals tends toward cultural capital. Legal professionals show a balance between the two.

A much more sophisticated approach leverages fine-grained distinctions between occupations. For example, the 2010 SOC identifies 840 "detailed" occupations in the contemporary American economy, grouped into 461 "broad groups," 97 "minor groups," and ultimately the 22 "major groups" of figure 2.1.[9] This process of grouping and differentiating is based on a theory of society, how hierarchies of skill, education, prestige, autonomy, and income organize society, distribute social goods, and shape social outcomes. The family is also a key institution producing and transmitting status and needs to be included in any theory of social class. The analysis of this chapter is based upon a combination of both occupational and familial characteristics defining nine "class fractions," grouped into three social classes. Every person (excluding career military) can theoretically

TABLE 3.1. Social Class Fractions

	Abbr.	Class fraction	Common occupations
Elites	HM	Higher managerial	Chief executives, public administration officials, managers, financial managers
	HP	Higher professional	Engineers, computer systems analysts and scientists, accountants and auditors, college and university professors, lawyers, physicians
	LP	Lower professional and higher technical	Elementary and secondary school teachers, nurses, social workers, health technicians, therapists, wholesale sales representatives
	LM	Lower managerial and higher supervisory	Sales supervisors, office supervisors, unclassified managers, supervisors of intermediate occupations
Middle Class	I	Intermediate	Secretaries and administrative assistants, bookkeepers, office clerks, nursing and health aides, police officers
	SB	Small business owners	Small business owners, self-employed, independent farmers
	LST	Lower supervisory and lower technical	Supervisors of semiroutine and routine occupations, mechanics and repairers, plumbers, electricians, inspectors
Working Class	SR	Semiroutine	Retail salespersons, cashiers, receptionists, cooks, janitors, machinists, assemblers, machine operators
	R	Routine	Waiters, carpenters, textile workers, truck drivers, heavy equipment operators, construction workers, childcare workers

be assigned to one of these class fractions. Table 3.1 lists them alongside examples of the most common occupations in each. Appendix A describes their construction and theoretical justification in depth. To give us confidence that these nine class fractions are indeed combining and differentiating people on the basis of their (or their families') relative capital

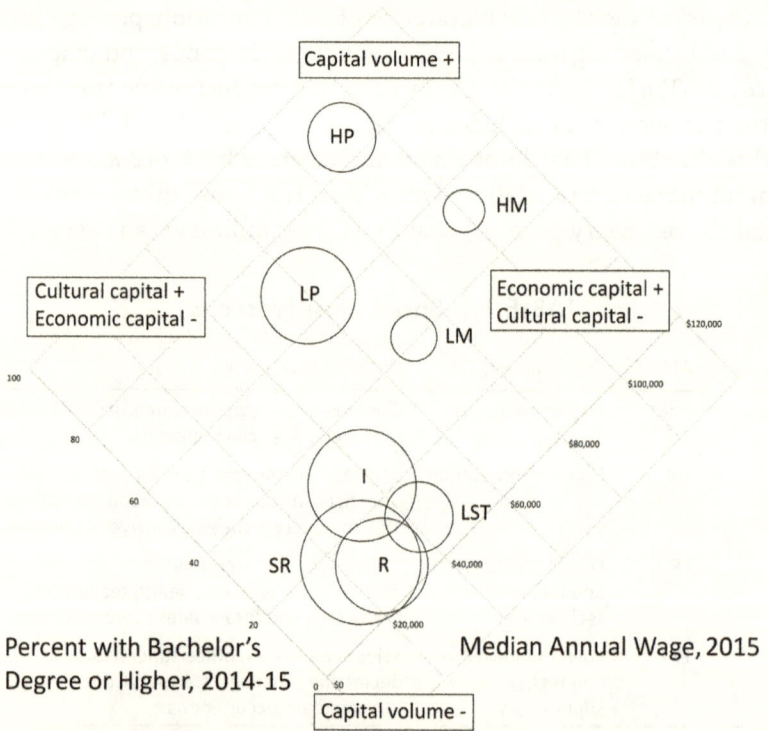

Capital volume +

HP

HM

Cultural capital +
Economic capital -

LP

Economic capital +
Cultural capital -

$120,000

LM

100

$100,000

80

$80,000

I

60

LST

$60,000

SR

R

40

$40,000

20

$20,000

Percent with Bachelor's
Degree or Higher, 2014-15

Median Annual Wage, 2015

0    $0

Capital volume -

FIGURE 3.1. Class Fractions in Social Space

SOURCE: Bureau of Labor Statistics (BLS), U.S. Department of Labor, May 2015 OEC Estimates, Occupational Employment Statistics (OES) Survey; Employment Projections program, Employment Projections: 2014–24, table 1.11, "Educational Attainment for Workers 25 Years and Older by Detailed Occupation, 2014–15." Class fractions are defined roughly in accord with appendix A. The two significant exceptions are as follows: (1) the unit of analysis here is the employed individual, not the household; and (2) no self-employment data are available and thus no small business class can be identified. Thus the positions of the eight class fractions here should be taken as rough approximations of what an analysis completely in accord with appendix A would produce. Class fraction means are weighted by the size of each component occupation group. The area of each bubble reflects the number of employed persons in the fraction. Eight occupations in SOC 29-1000 had annual median wages greater than the BLS measured maximum of $187,200 and were thus coded with an annual wage at $187,200. Four occupations in SOC 27-2000 had no annual wage data and were thus coded with an annual wage calculated as the occupational median hourly wage times 2087 (the U.S. Office of Personnel Management definition of "full-time") rounded to the nearest $10.

endowments, we can plot them in the same social space as figure 2.1. They lie just where we expect, which is reassuring because neither level of income nor level of education are direct inputs into this classification system. We see that higher managers and higher professionals have by far the highest volumes of capital. While the overall volume is very similar, managers tend more toward economic capital while professionals accumulate more cultural capital. We see the same pattern in the lower elite at a lower overall volume of capital where again (lower) professionals tend more toward cultural capital while (lower) managers tend more toward economic capital. The capital volume gap between elites and the middle and working classes is large, and considerable overlap exists among the four remaining fractions depicted (small business owners are not included due to lack of data from the Bureau of Labor Statistics on income and education levels among the self-employed). The middle class fractions do have a slightly higher volume of capital than the working class fractions as expected, and there is some minor differentiation between intermediate occupations and lower supervisory and technical occupations on composition of capital. The lowest level of capital volume is found among the working class fractions with virtually no differences in capital composition at all.

Social Class and the Progress of Normalization

Social classes are not simply defined by their capital or their relationship to the labor market. They are just as much defined by cultural practices and attitudes around language, art, leisure, and food—as well as sexuality, marriage, and the family. That is, positions in objectively defined social space are congruent with positions in the subjective "space of lifestyles." The General Social Survey (GSS)—a nationally representative survey of American attitudes designed and conducted by the National Opinion Research Center at the University of Chicago—allows us to access that subjective social space.[10] From its beginning the GSS has asked its respondents a battery of questions on sexual behavior and the family. Prefaced by the phrase, "There's been a lot of discussion about the way morals and attitudes about sex are changing in this country," it has included intermittently since 1973 the following question as part of that battery: "What about sexual relations between two adults of the same sex—do you think it is always wrong, almost always wrong, wrong only sometimes, or not wrong at all?" Looking at the responses over time, we can see a dramatic evolution of American opinion on homosexuality.[11]

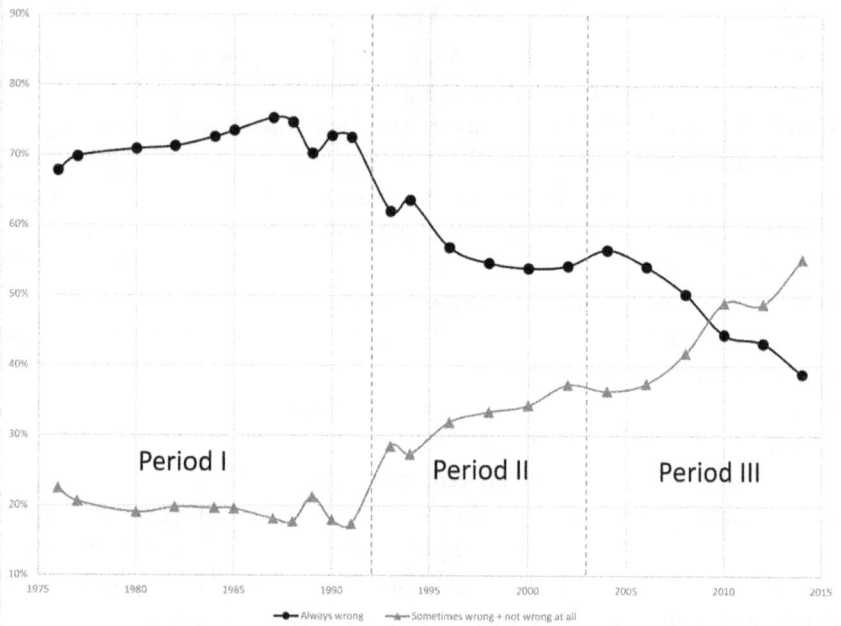

FIGURE 3.2. Americans' Views on Homosexuality, 1976–2014

SOURCE: *General Social Survey. The question was, "What about sexual relations between two adults of the same sex—do you think it is always wrong, almost always wrong, wrong only sometimes, or not wrong at all?" Responses of "don't know" are included in the calculation of percentages. Responses are weighted with the GSS weight variables WTSALL and OVERSAMP.*

In the 1970s and 1980s—and presumably long before that—the public's view of same-sex sexual relations was both very negative and very stable. Between two-thirds and three-quarters of all Americans believed them to be "always wrong." Pronormalization responses of "sometimes wrong" and "not wrong at all" are given by only around one-fifth of the population.[12] If any trend can be said to exist in this period, it was a strengthening of opinion *against* normalization in the 1980s.

This long era of stability ended abruptly in the early 1990s. The GSS data show "always wrong" responses fell from 73% to 62% of the total in only two years. Over the same 1991–1993 period the number reporting "sometimes wrong" and "not wrong at all" views jumped an equal eleven points from 17% to 28%. This was neither a measurement error nor a temporary fluctuation. It was a dam break. From 1995 onward "always wrong" responses never again exceeded 60% while "sometimes wrong" and "not wrong at all" combined never again fell below 30%.

The early 1990s period of rapid change eventually slowed and even stopped in the early 2000s. However, a second period of more steady change followed, ushered in by the first same-sex marriages in Massachusetts in 2004. Between 2004 and 2014 the pro- and anti-normalization positions essentially swapped places in terms of popularity, with pronormalization views surpassing antinormalization around 2009.

This is the general and well-known story for the country as a whole. To investigate the class dimensions of opinion over time, however, we need a different approach. GSS sample sizes almost never exceed three thousand respondents per survey, and prior to 1994 they are only about half that size. In the 1970s and 1980s especially there are often under one hundred respondents per year in some class fractions. These numbers are far too small to allow one to draw reliable and meaningful conclusions. Aggregation of the annual data is necessary. Three periods described above suggest themselves: one of stability covering the years 1976 to 1991; one of normative change beginning in 1993 and lasting through the end of the trend in 2002; and one of normative change since the first same-sex marriages from 2004 to 2014.

The mean response of each class fraction is plotted by period in figure 3.3. Error bars show the range within which we can be 95% confident the true class fraction means lie. When the opinion data is aggregated and plotted this way, two patterns immediately jump out. The first is that every class fraction becomes more positive in its views of homosexuality over time. This is so much so that the least positive fraction in Period III, lower technical and supervisory occupations (LST), is more positive (although not outside the 95% confidence interval) than the most positive fraction in Period I, higher professionals (HP). The second pattern is that the relationship between class fraction status and views on same-sex sexual relations is more or less positive. The dots within each period roughly align in a southwest-to-northeast pattern. The higher the class status, the more positive an opinion one tends to hold on normalization.

Higher professionals are far and away the most positive in any period. They have the highest mean scores and their confidence intervals overlap only with higher managers in Periods II and III. In the first period 34% of higher professionals held pronormalization opinions. This is an extraordinarily high figure for the time. In Period I among the seven nonprofessional fractions combined, only 16% held normalizing views—just half the level of higher professionals. The views of elite professional

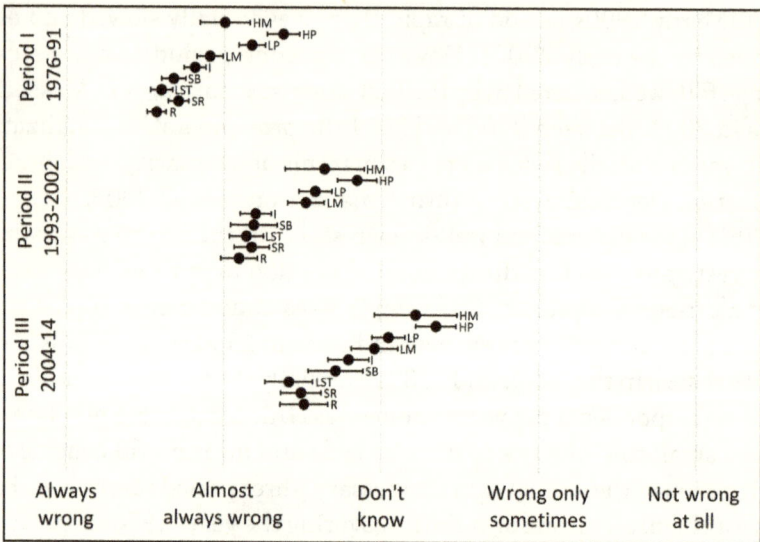

FIGURE 3.3. Americans' Views on Homosexuality
by Class Fraction and Period

SOURCE: *General Social Survey. The x-axis indicates class fraction means on the GSS homosexuality question (see the figure 3.2 information). Weighting is performed by year within the period as well as by using the GSS weights WTSSALL and OVERSAMP. Confidence internals are at 95%.*

organizations shown in chapter 2 seem to have reflected the views of a large number of higher professionals more broadly.

The transformation in the views of managers can also be seen clearly in figure 3.3. During the 1970s and 1980s both higher and lower managers were more similar to middle class fractions than to professionals. From the 1990s and onward, however, managers begin to agree with professionals and distance themselves from the middle and working classes. Compare the means of higher and lower managers in Period I to their means in Period II. Higher managers made a tremendous positive leap, although their large error bars make it difficult to say exactly how far they jumped. It may be that by the 1990s they were as positive in their views on homosexuality as higher professionals. Lower managers make a similarly large positive jump in the 1990s and become indistinguishable from lower professionals in Periods II and III. The opinion data here match the trajectory depicted in chapter 2. While Corporate America was largely unfriendly to homosexuality in the 1970s and 1980s, its views and policies began to evolve rapidly in the early 1990s and ultimately made the group one of the most LGBT-friendly of American society.

In the current period, stretching back to 2004, all four professional and managerial class fractions have possible means above the "don't know" line of neutrality. The lower confidence interval of higher professionals does not even dip to the left of neutrality. The GSS finds a remarkable 58% of psychiatrists, engineers, lawyers, and other higher professionals holding normalizing opinions across this decade. By the early twenty-first century American elites—those with the greatest concentrations of economic and cultural capital—had indeed embraced normalization.

The middle and working classes always hold more negative views on homosexuality than do elites. Their means lie to the left of the "don't know" line of neutrality in every period and usually by a wide margin. Four of these five class fractions (excepting Intermediate occupations) have overlapping confidence intervals in every period. This indicates that their mean values are statistically indistinguishable from each other, and thus it makes analytic sense to discuss them as a group. In Period I only 15% of persons in these four class fractions collectively held pronormalization views, while a full 78% believed same-sex sexual relations were "always wrong." While their views certainly became more positive over time, by Period III still 56% of the vast bulk of the middle and working classes maintained "always wrong" opinions. Compare this to higher managers and higher professionals as a group, in which just 36% said the same. The gap between elites and the rest of the country is particularly stark in Period II. As managers joined professionals in the 1990s in favoring normalization, three of the four elite fractions became statistically indistinguishable. On the other side of the class divide, the five middle and working class fractions were likewise statistically indistinguishable. This dramatic gulf eroded in Period III. As the rate of growth in pronormalization views slowed among managers, it sped up among some of the middle class fractions. The Intermediate fraction saying same-sex sexual relations were "wrong only sometimes" or "not wrong at all" leaped from 27% to 44%, while the Small Business fraction made a similarly impressive jump from 26% to 42% over the same interval. By Period III both of these middle class fractions even became statistically indistinguishable from lower managers. Just as elites made their decisive shift toward normalization in the 1990s, much of the middle class made theirs in the 2000s and early 2010s.

As capital is distributed and concentrated in geographic as well as social space, we can gain more insight into the class dimensions of normalization by adding a geographic component. The GSS makes this possible by providing residence information for every survey respondent at the level of the country's nine "divisions" as defined by the U.S. Census Bureau. Nine class fractions times nine geographic regions makes eighty-one regional class fractions for analysis. Comparing the eighty-one mean scores on the GSS homosexuality question over time demonstrates the influence of elite concentration or dilution in geographic space on their support for normalization.

American elites are most concentrated in three U.S. census divisions. New England has both the highest volume of capital and the highest concentrations of workers in managerial and professional occupations. In 2015 the median household income in these six states was nearly $67,000, 38% of adults age 25 and older had at least a bachelor's degree, and some 36% of all employed persons were either managers or professionals per the 2010 SOC definition. Following New England are the Middle Atlantic and Pacific regions. In 2015 both had similar median household incomes and educational attainment levels, with the Middle Atlantic having a somewhat higher concentration of cultural capital and the Pacific area—driven by Silicon Valley in northern California and by aerospace and Hollywood in southern California—having a somewhat higher concentration of economic capital. Both ranked second in the concentration of managerial and professional occupations in 2015 at 33%. If the Baltimore and Washington, D.C. metropolitan areas were more sensibly included in the Middle Atlantic region, its capital volume and concentration of elites would be even higher.

Elite class fractions from these three "elite heartland" regions are consistently the ones that express exceptional pronormalization views. We can measure just how much via the degree to which they diverge from the GSS homosexuality question mean score of all eighty-one regional class fractions in each period. Any score that lies more than two standard deviations above the group mean and having a lower confidence interval at least one standard deviation above the group mean gets counted here as "exceptionally high." One could justifiably say "extreme."

In Period I there are three extreme pronormalization class fractions: the higher professionals of New England, the Pacific, and the Middle Atlantic regions. The mean for higher professionals in New England in particular was remarkably high, already over the "don't know" line of neutrality (although the lower confidence interval bar lay to the left of that line). Even the lower confidence interval bar for New England higher professionals lay more than two standard deviations above the group mean.

Capital Volume +

New England

Middle Atlantic   Pacific

Mountain   West North Central

Cultural capital +
Economic capital -   South Atlantic   East North Central

Economic capital +
Cultural capital - $70,000

West South Central

$65,000

$60,000

East South Central $55,000

$50,000

Capital Volume - $45,000

Percent with Bachelor's
Degree or higher, 2015   Median Household
Income, 2015

$40,000

Capital Volume +

Pacific

New England

Cultural capital +
Economic capital -   Middle Atlantic

Economic capital +
Cultural capital - $450,000

South Atlantic   Mountain $400,000

West North Central $350,000

East North Central   West South Central $300,000

$250,000

East South Central

$200,000

Capital Volume -

Percent with Bachelor's
Degree or higher, 2015 $150,000

Median House
Value, 2015

$100,000

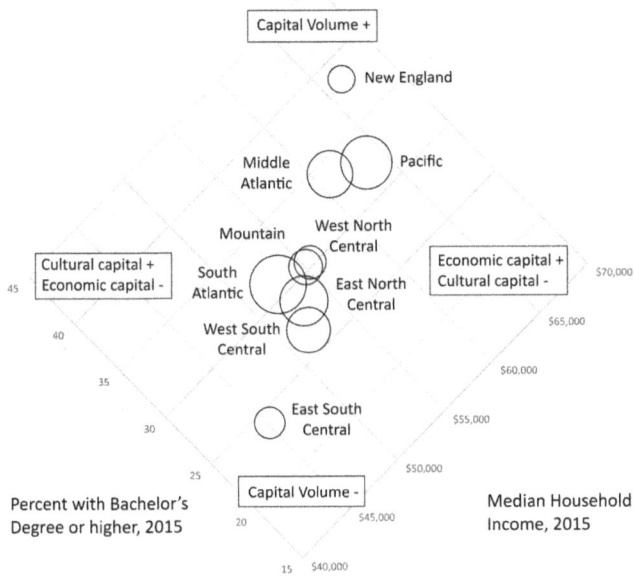

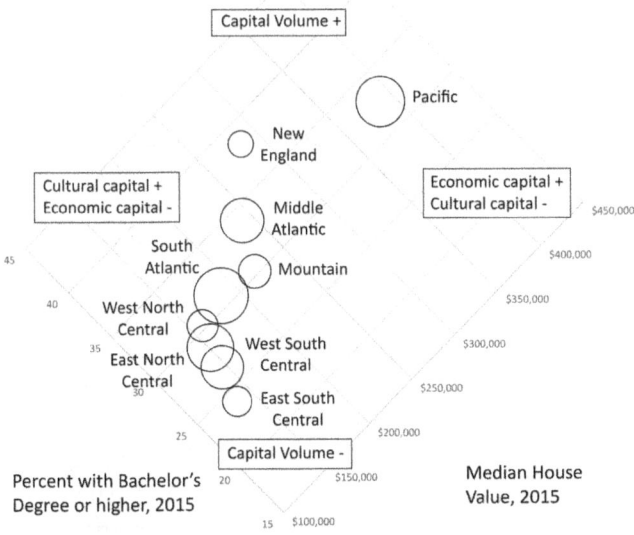

FIGURE 3.4. Census Bureau Divisions in Social Space

*SOURCE: U.S. Census Bureau, 2015 American Community Survey one-year estimates, table S0201
(for median household income); tables S0201 and B25077 (for median house value).*

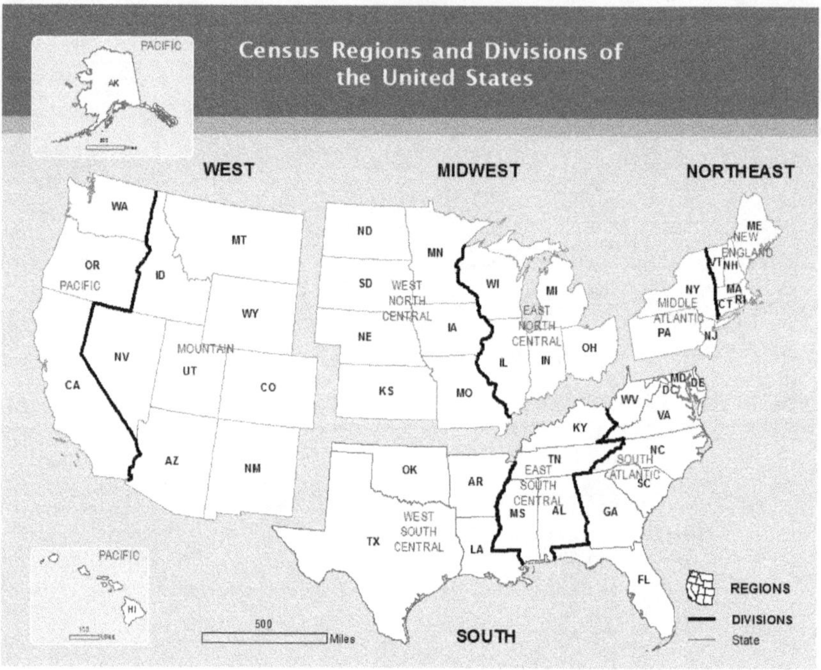

FIGURE 3.5. U.S. Census Bureau Divisions

SOURCE: U.S. Census Bureau.

This is an astounding degree of support in a period in which over 70% of all Americans believed same-sex sexual behavior to be "always wrong." The higher confidence interval bars for higher professionals in the Pacific and Middle Atlantic states were also over the line of neutrality, suggesting that their true means might also have been already pronormalization as well. These elites are the clear avant-garde of America's cultural change.

Period II was the era of greatest differentiation between elites and the middle and working classes. There are three exceptionally high pronormalization fractions in this period: New England higher professionals, New England lower professionals, and New England lower managers. Due to their very wide confidence intervals (due in turn to a particularly small sample size in the GSS), New England higher managers just missed making the list. Six other regional class fractions had mean scores more than one standard deviation above the group mean labeled here as "high" support. Four are unsurprising: Middle Atlantic higher managers, Middle Atlantic higher professionals, Pacific higher professionals, and Pacific

TABLE 3.2. Most Pronormalization Regional Class Fractions, by Period

Period I	Extremely high	New England	Higher professionals
		Middle Atlantic	Higher professionals
		Pacific	Higher professionals
	High	New England	Lower professionals Lower managers Small business
		Middle Atlantic	Lower professionals
		Pacific	Higher managers Lower professionals
		West North Central	Higher managers Higher professionals
		Mountain	Lower professionals
		South Atlantic	Higher managers
Period II	Extremely high	New England	Higher professionals Lower professionals Lower managers
	High	New England	Higher managers Small business
		Middle Atlantic	Higher managers Higher professionals
		Pacific	Higher professionals Lower professionals
		Mountain	Higher professionals
Period III	Extremely high	New England	Higher managers Higher professionals
	High	New England	Lower professionals Lower managers Intermediate Small business
		Middle Atlantic	Higher managers Higher professionals Lower managers
		Pacific	Higher managers Higher professionals Lower professionals
		West North Central	Higher professionals

TABLE SOURCE: *Author's calculations from the General Social Survey.*

lower professionals. The final two are unexpected, however, and give some insight into the spread of pronormalization views. Higher professionals in the Mountain states are the first elite fraction outside the class heartland to hold especially positive views on homosexuality. The sixth regional class fraction was New England small business. In this area of greatest elite concentration in the country, pronormalization views had not only come to dominate professionals and managers but had even begun to define the cultural values of all New England classes.

New England distinguished itself yet again in Period III. Between 2004 and 2014 there are three exceptionally high fractions: the upper managers, upper professionals, and lower professionals of New England. The first two even have mean scores to the right of the "wrong only sometimes" line. This signifies the complete triumph of normalization among the region's elites. Notably three other class fractions in New England—lower managers, small business, and intermediate—have high pronormalization scores with the upper confidence interval to the right of "wrong only sometimes." Pacific and Middle Atlantic managers and professionals also distinguished themselves in Period III. Outside the elite heartland, however, only upper professionals in the West North Central states had high support.

The case of New England suggests that perhaps location is the real story of normalization. While New England elites are clearly the most strongly pronormalization regional class in the country across every time period, it may be that New England's middle and working classes also differentiate themselves just as strongly from their kindred classes in other parts of the country. The GSS data does not bear this out. Classes share similar values on homosexuality where elites are few. Where elites are plentiful, classes differentiate.

Figure 3.6 plots the mean scores on the GSS homosexuality question for the three major social classes in each of the nine U.S. census divisions for each period. Consider the three elite heartland areas. In every period New England elites are more supportive of normalization than the working class of their own region. In two periods the same is true of New England elites relative to the local middle class. There is a similar pattern in the Pacific region. In every period Pacific elites are significantly more positive in their views of homosexuality relative to the middle class and in two periods relative to the working class. In the Middle Atlantic states in every period elites are more supportive of normalization than both their middle and working classes. Not only are these differences statistically significant, the differences are also large. The top 10% largest class gaps

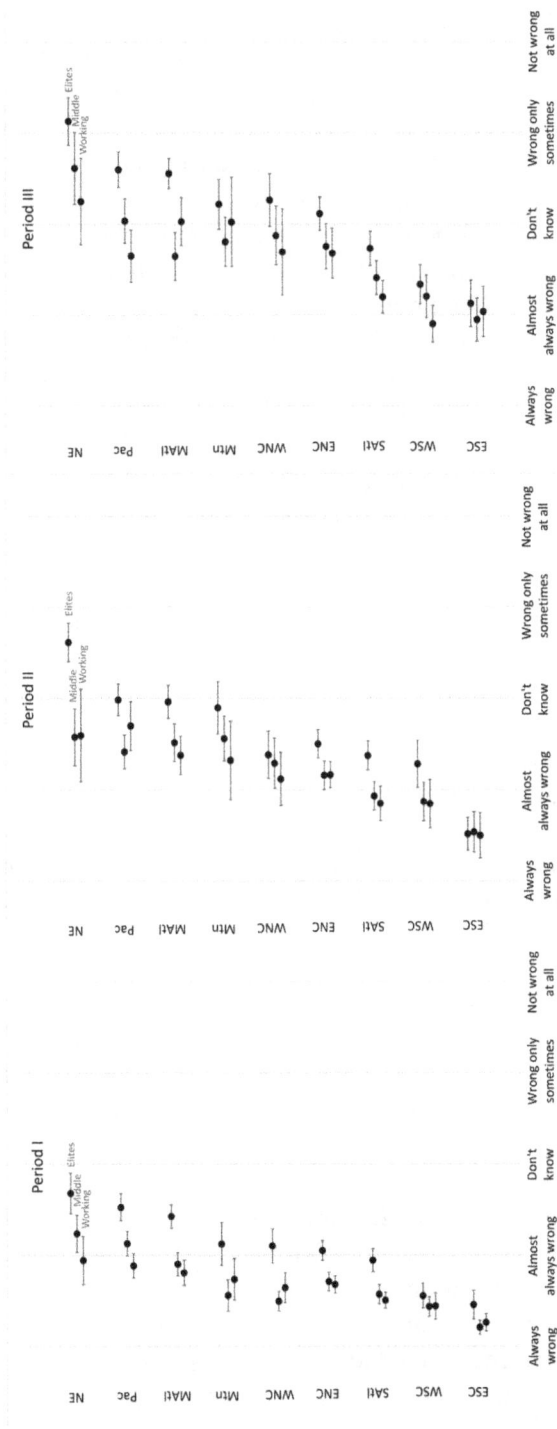

FIGURE 3.6. Views on Homosexuality by Class and Division, Periods I–III

SOURCE: Author's calculations from the General Social Survey. The x-axis indicates class fraction means on the GSS homosexuality question (see figure 3.2 above). Weighting is performed by year within the period as well as by using the GSS weights WTSSALL and OVERSAMP. Confidence internals are at 95%.

across all three periods are all recorded in either New England, the Middle Atlantic, or the Pacific regions. This is because an exceptionally pronormalization elite lives alongside a working class that is no more in favor of normalization than the working class in the Midwest or the Mountain West. This is no regional culture misrecognized as a class culture. Elites in their heartland broke away from the other classes of their own region.

We can emphasize the point by looking more closely at the six U.S. census divisions outside the elite heartland. In the East South Central, West South Central, and Mountain divisions, elites have significantly more positive views than other classes in only one period, relative to only one class. West North Central elites are more positive than both their middle and working classes but only in one period. Even though elites in the East North Central division are significantly more positive than their middle and working classes in four of six comparisons, these differences are all among the smallest 6% of statistically significant cases, less than half the size of the gap recorded in the elite heartland.

From Normalization to Same-Sex Marriage

The General Social Survey began regularly asking a same-sex marriage question in 2004. Not surprisingly the patterns of class and geographic opinion on same-sex marriage largely mirror those on same-sex sexual relations. Particularly wide confidence intervals on all the data prevent us from saying much about the patterns with certainty, however.

State-level marriage law and marriage referenda provide a rich alternative source of information on class and regional opinion regarding same-sex marriage. With a single exception, prior to December 20, 2013 the legal status of same-sex couples in the United States was determined solely by state governments.[13] Thirty-three states defined marriage by means of popular referendum, another eight (including the District of Columbia) did so by legislative act uncoerced by a court, and one (Hawaii) did both. Even the five states forced by state court order to adopt same-sex marriage offer some worthwhile information on local political sentiment.

The pattern of recognition suggests a central political role played by pronormalization elites. Figure 3.7 plots the fifty states in social space with 2012 data, the year of the country's final state marriage referenda.[14] Of the nineteen states (including the District of Columbia) with the highest concentrations of both economic and cultural capital, fifteen recognized same-sex marriage without federal compulsion. This includes five of six New England states, two of three Middle Atlantic states, and three of five Pacific states. It also includes the two northernmost states from the South Atlantic as well as the District of Columbia. Of the remaining thirty-two states, only three recognized same-sex marriage of their own accord.

Six states are anomalies to this strong association between capital concentration and support for normalization. Yet even these outliers ultimately reinforce the pattern with interesting qualifications. Maine, New Mexico, and Iowa are the three states with relatively low levels of capital volume and elite concentration that nonetheless recognized same-sex marriage. Maine is a borderline case and appropriately one of only three states to take both positions on same-sex marriage. Voters approved a constitutional amendment recognizing only opposite-sex marriage in 2009, while three years later they overturned it in a second marriage

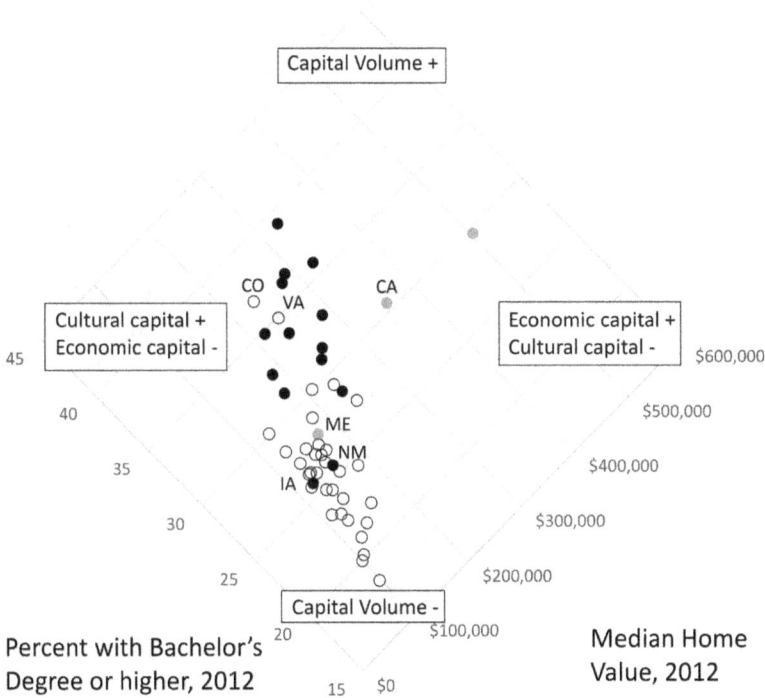

FIGURE 3.7. Concentration of Capital by State and Same-Sex Marriage Status

SOURCE: U.S. Census Bureau, 2010–2012 American Community Survey, tables S0201 and B25077. "Median home value" is the median value of owner-occupied housing by state. Black circles indicate recognition of same-sex marriage. White circles indicate nonrecognition. Gray circles indicate both recognition and nonrecognition. The District of Columbia is an extreme outlier and is not depicted.

referendum at the very end of the period of state self-determination. Maine's 2012 vote also made New England the only Census Bureau division to have unanimous recognition of same-sex marriage. Both Iowa and New Mexico have much lower levels of capital and elite concentration. In that respect it is unsurprising that both required court orders to bring about same-sex marriage. New Mexico's came just one day before the wave of federal district court decisions culminating in the *Obergefell* decision. The political reaction to the Iowa Supreme Court demonstrates the dearth of popular support for same-sex marriage in this elite-deficient state. In April 2009 all seven members of the court ruled unanimously that the Iowa constitution demanded state recognition of same-sex marriage. At the next election nineteen months later, voters removed all three justices facing a retention vote. They also elected a new Republican majority in the state House of Representatives as well as the state's first Republican governor in twelve years. House Republicans quickly used their new power to pass legislation approving a 2012 constitutional referendum on the state's court-directed marriage law. The Democratic-controlled state Senate blocked the legislation, however. Iowa never did hold its referendum.

Another three states are outliers in the opposite direction. Colorado, Virginia, and California each have relatively high levels of capital volume and elite concentration but nonetheless did not recognize same-sex marriage. Colorado voters approved a referendum measure against same-sex marriage in 2006 despite having one of the highest mean education levels in the country. Support for that position waned considerably over time, however. In 2013 the state legislature instituted marriage-like civil unions for same-sex couples and in 2014 a state district court struck down the 2006 constitutional amendment. One might say, therefore, that Colorado is an anomaly more on technical than substantive grounds. Virginia stands as a more robust and surprising outlier. The expansion of the Washington, D.C. metropolis has made northern Virginia one of America's greatest sites of elite concentration and propelled the entire state up the ranks of economic and cultural capital concentration. Despite this, Virginia voters passed a highly restrictive constitutional amendment on marriage in 2006 that not only refused recognition to same-sex marriage but went further to ban recognition of any relationship "of unmarried individuals that intends to approximate the design, qualities, significance, or effects of marriage." In that referendum a mere thirteen of Virginia's 134 counties and independent cities voted against the proposal that "only a union between one man and one woman may be a marriage valid in or recognized by this Commonwealth and its political subdivisions." Those thirteen, however, included precisely the places we would expect: the two counties (Arlington and Fairfax) and three independent cities (Alexandria, Falls Church, and Fairfax) of core northern Virginia. The only other county in the state to reject the amendment was Albemarle County surrounding Charlottesville, the home of the University of Virginia. Charlottesville itself turned out the smallest percentage of "yes" voters in the entire state, while other college towns dominated the list of cities rejecting the amendment. Inside core northern Virginia and Albemarle County/Charlottesville, only 41% of voters supported the marriage amendment. The referendum ultimately succeeded through strong support beyond the bastions of elites. In the rest of Virginia, 62% of voters supported constitutionalizing opposite-sex-only marriage, making for a massive twenty-one-point gulf between the regions.

Finally California provides an especially interesting and illuminating case. Like Maine, prior to December 2013 California both recognized and did not recognize same-sex marriage. In May 2008 the state supreme court ruled in a 4–3 decision that same-sex marriage was a "fundamental right" according to the California Constitution. County clerks began issuing marriage licenses to same-sex couples the following month. A popular opposition movement rose up immediately and secured enough signatures to place a constitutional amendment recognizing only opposite-sex marriage, dubbed "Proposition 8," on the November ballot. California voters surprised many observers by approving it by a narrow 52%–48% margin. While the state continued to recognize the same-sex marriages contracted between June and November, it stopped issuing any further licenses to same-sex couples.

Analysis at the level of California's roughly 7,000 census tracts allows a unique fine-grained look at a marriage referendum's results. The Proposition 8 vote was strongly correlated with social class. Areas of high capital concentration mostly opposed the question and supported same-sex marriage, while areas of low capital concentration mostly supported Prop 8. The correlation between the "yes" vote and the percent of residents with at least a bachelor's degree is negative, as expected, and quite high (-0.65). Using median home values as an indicator of economic capital, the correlation with the "yes" vote was nearly the same (-0.60).[15]

The elite heart of California is the Greater San Francisco Bay Area. The seven most educated counties in the state and the five counties with the highest median house values are all located there.[16] Its core is the more narrowly drawn San Francisco metropolitan area.[17] In those five counties the correlation between the Prop 8 vote and the concentration of cultural capital was measurably tighter than in the rest of the state (-0.69 vs. -0.60). San Francisco County, coterminous with the city of San Francisco, had one of the highest correlations in the entire state (-0.80). No surprise then that the San Francisco area was the core of opposition to Prop 8. Only 20% of census tracts in the San Francisco metro supported Prop 8, compared to 74% in the rest of the state. The intensity of opposition was also most extreme here. Of the 5% of California census tracts with the lowest "yes" vote, more than half were located in the San Francisco metropolitan area despite the region having a mere 12% of all census tracts statewide.[18]

Figure 3.8 shows a map of the Prop 8 vote and the percent of residents with at least a bachelor's degree for the core Greater San Francisco Bay Area. Nearly all of San Francisco, northwest Alameda County covering the cities of Berkeley and parts of Oakland, and Marin County show black dots in the top panel, indicating census tracts in the lowest quarter of votes in favor of Prop 8. A similar concentration of black dots in the bottom panel indicates tracts in the highest quarter of educational attainment. A similar pattern of black dots in both panels also covers the northwest corner of Santa Clara County into much of San Mateo County. This is Silicon Valley. It is difficult to find many census tracts with the highest levels of cultural capital that supported Prop 8.

The opposite pattern is also prevalent. Tracts in the lowest quarter of educational attainment tend to exhibit the highest levels of support for Prop 8. In San Francisco almost all of these are located in the low-income southeast corner of the city. Another is the tiny low-education section in the northeast part of the city, which is at the same time the only census tract in the city to fall in the highest quarter of Prop 8 supporters. This is Chinatown. The northeast section of Santa Clara County is composed of the working class parts of San Jose that supported the amendment. In northwest Alameda County, one can see Oakland is a city deeply divided both by class and by same-sex marriage. The elite sections along the border with Berkeley and in the hill neighborhoods on the city's the east side strongly opposed Prop 8. This is shown by the black dots in the upper panel and the black and dark grey dots in the lower panel. Working class (and largely black) East Oakland, on the other hand, supported the referendum.

Like the San Francisco metro, Los Angeles County census tracts showed a very strong negative correlation between education and the

FIGURE 3.8. California Proposition 8 Vote and Level of Education, by Census Tract and Metropolitan Region

SOURCE: Statewide Database, University of California, Berkeley School of Law, http://statewidedatabase.org/index.html; U.S. Census Bureau, 2005–09 American Community Survey, table S1501. One dot = one census tract. "Yes" on California Proposition 8 (2008) is the total "yes" vote divided by the total number of "yes" and "no" votes. Blank or spoiled ballots were not included in the denominator. Statewide Database created "consolidated precincts" for statistical merging purposes, and vote tallies for such precincts were used here. The votes were converted to census tract-level votes using the data conversion file "SRPREC to 2000 BLK" for each county provided by Statewide Database. 22,755 (0.2%) valid votes could not be assigned to a census tract and thus were not included in the final dataset. Twenty-six (0.4%) census tracts were missing either vote results or educational attainment data and thus were not included in the final dataset.

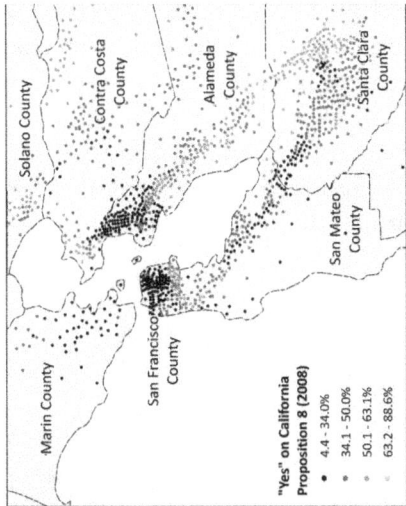

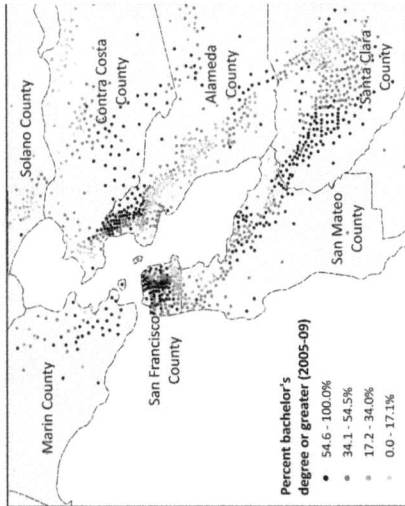

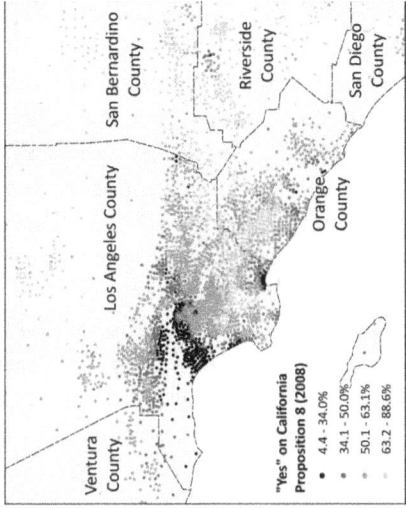

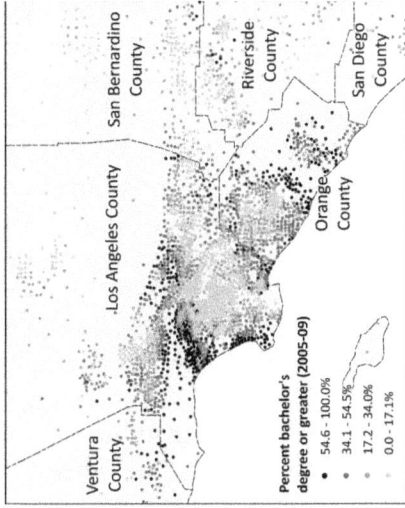

same-sex marriage vote (-0.66). Although the county overall supported Prop 8, its southwest end was the heart of opposition. Black dots for this area in the top panel representing the lowest vote totals for the referendum are reproduced in the bottom panel showing levels of education. The most densely populated parts are the Los Angeles neighborhoods of Brentwood, Bel-Air, and Hollywood as well as the independent cities of Santa Monica, Beverly Hills, and West Hollywood—among the wealthiest areas in the country and home to the elites of the American entertainment industry. Just over the Hollywood Hills to the north, however, lies the San Fernando Valley and its tracts of moderate and low educational attainment combined with mostly moderate support for Prop 8. South and southeast of the Hollywood Hills lies a large region of lighter-colored dots in both panels covering much of both Los Angeles and Orange Counties. This is the heart of working class (largely Hispanic and black) metropolitan Los Angeles, which helped carry the vote statewide.

One unusual feature is a number of census tracts in southern California that combined high levels of education with an overall "yes" vote.[19] One can see many of these on the map in central and southern Orange County, represented by black and dark grey dots in the bottom panel but mostly medium gray dots in the top panel. Statewide there were 319 such tracts, with 214 (67%) in the Greater Los Angeles area and another 50 (16%) in metropolitan San Diego.[20] In these two regions combined, 38% of elite census tracts voted for Prop 8. The number in the Greater Bay Area was just 6%. Since this is geographic and not individual vote data, we cannot say with certainty that southern California elites are less supportive of same-sex marriage than those in northern California. We can be sure, however, that elite regions in the south of the state differ notably from their counterparts in the north. The contour lines of class geography run not only along but across state lines.

It is often said that elites support normalization and same-sex marriage because they are liberal. The data presented here suggest it is more accurate to say that liberals support normalization and same-sex marriage because they are elites.

4

BEYOND TOLERANCE

From Toleration to Equality

The largest glass building in the world stands just to the west of the Santa Ana Freeway in Orange County, California. Known until 2013 as the "Crystal Cathedral," this one million cubic foot, auditorium-like structure once housed the megachurch Crystal Cathedral Ministries, led by the televangelist Robert H. Schuller. From this building Schuller broadcast the "Hour of Power" television program and his "positive thinking" pop psychology approach to Christianity. At its peak in the 1990s the program reached over twenty million viewers per week in more than 180 countries.

The winds of religious change began to turn against Schuller in the early 2000s, however. When he retired in 2010, Schuller turned a financially floundering organization on the edge of bankruptcy over to his daughter Sheila Schuller Coleman. In an attempt to save the ministry and the building, Schuller Coleman took the congregation in a new, more evangelical direction. She replaced the choir and orchestra with praise and worship bands. She cancelled the church's lavish and long-running Christmas and Easter pageants. But what caught the media's attention was Schuller Coleman's introduction of a controversial covenant statement demanding all ministry volunteers profess that "sexual intimacy is intended by God to only be within the bonds of marriage, between one man and one woman." This stance drew outrage not only from church members interviewed by the press, but also from Schuller Coleman's father. From retirement the old patriarch, too, objected; the covenant was a betrayal of his "principles of being positive." Contacting the media himself, Schuller explained his position this way: "I have a reputation worldwide of being tolerant of all people and their views. I'm too well-educated to criticize a certain religion or group of people for what they believe in. It's called freedom."[1]

Schuller's self-understanding is a common one among elites. Since the 1940s social science has shown that elites in Western countries are tolerant while those at the bottom of the social hierarchy are not. The classic work in the field is the book *The Authoritarian Personality*, published in 1950 by the German social theorist Theodor Adorno and colleagues at the University of California, Berkeley.[2] Basing their work on Freudian psychoanalytic theory, Adorno and his coauthors created a personality scale ranging from "libertarian" to "authoritarian." While the contemporary version of the scale is generally known as the "right-wing authoritarianism scale," it was originally called the "F scale," where "F" stood for "fascism." Adorno and his team used this scale to measure the susceptibility of subjects to far-right political causes, an important question in the immediate aftermath of World War II. They found that a significant minority of their subjects, particularly working class men, exhibited symptoms of an "antidemocratic personality." Should a significant fascist movement form in the country, these people were those who could be politically activated through it and pose a mortal threat to democracy.

Why would social class be associated with personality type? The contemporary explanation is that highly educated people develop cognitive skills and accumulate factual knowledge that allow them to navigate a world wracked by ambiguity, uncertainty, and difference. The undereducated, on the other hand, are buffeted by events and retreat to false certainties, external authorities, and all types of xenophobia.[3] No wonder *The Authoritarian Personality* contributed mightily to the now well-worn tradition of defining right-wing political opinions as a mental disorder.[4] From the 1950s to the present day it has been commonplace to hear elites warn against "working-class authoritarianism," lament a working class that "cling[s] to guns or religion or antipathy toward people who aren't like them or anti-immigrant sentiment," and castigate a "basket of deplorables. . . . The racist, sexist, homophobic, xenophobic, Islamophobic—you name it."[5]

Opinions on homosexuality have long served as popular measures of toleration. In Adorno's work three questions about sexual behavior were included in the battery measuring "fascist receptivity," with one explicitly testing views on homosexuality. Many contemporary scholars see opposition to same-sex marriage as especially indicative of right-wing authoritarianism and support as a hallmark of liberal tolerance.[6] Because of the association between liberal views on homosexuality and elite social status, some researchers are even bold enough to suggest higher education as an "antidote to intolerance."[7]

Toleration was once American elites' preferred frame for thinking about homosexuality. As they came to support normalization, however, mere toleration fell out of fashion. Equality is now the dominant frame of discourse. The New York Times editorial board is as good an authority as any on the ideological shift. In 2011 the New York state legislature vigorously debated and ultimately passed a same-sex marriage bill. In 2012 five states held the country's final marriage referenda, including three that explicitly asked voters to approve same-sex marriage. During those two years the Times published twenty-six separate editorials related to same-sex marriage. It used the phrase "marriage equality" forty-nine times and the word "tolerance" only once. In the board's 2013 editorial hailing the Windsor and Hollingsworth Supreme Court rulings, it used the phrase "marriage equality" three times and "equal(ity)" without modifier seven more. The words "tolerance" or "toleration" were not used once.[8] After the Supreme Court's Obergefell ruling in 2015 the editors at the Times penned an editorial with "(in)equality" appearing seven times and "equal" four. Neither a "tolerance" nor a "toleration" could be found.[9]

With the power of the state now fully behind normalization, toleration has itself become morally compromised. After the Boy Scouts of America modified their internal rules in 2013 to allow for openly gay scouts but not scoutmasters, the editors at the Times charged the organization with "bigotry" for "tolerating a loathsome belief, pressed by religious activists, that equates homosexuality with deviance."[10] To those editors the cost of such toleration can be counted in dead bodies. Although the Islamic State sympathizer Omar Mateen fired the bullets that killed forty-nine people at a gay night club in Orlando in 2016, the Times editorial board ultimately blamed American social conservatives. "Hate crimes don't happen in a vacuum," the Times insisted. "They occur where bigotry is allowed to fester, where minorities are vilified and where people are scapegoated for political gain." This then-deadliest mass shooting in American history was interpreted as an attack on LGBT equality. Its victims were "casualties of a society where hate has deep roots."[11] If these are the wages of tolerating anti-LGBT bigotry, what virtue can exist in toleration?

Luckily elites have come to support normalization and same-sex marriage not because they are tolerant of homosexuality in any meaningful sense of the word. They have done so because they affirm it. Mere toleration has long since become passé. Elites have moved beyond it.

An Affirming Elite

The literary theorist Stanley Fish has described toleration as "the central liberal value" and liberals' "favorite virtue."[12] No wonder so many have been so reluctant to surrender the word even as their beliefs and practices have moved beyond tolerance. Some philosophers now define toleration as equal social respect, while others go further to define it as "esteem" or even "appreciation."[13] Finding mere state forbearance or even neutrality insufficient, they call upon the state to engage in positive acts of attention, compensation, and cultivation so that all moral frameworks—as long as they are essentially liberal—may be not only legally equal but also socially equal.

It should seem strange to grant the label "toleration" to a project that seeks to eliminate meaningful kinds of moral judgment, because objection is an essential element of toleration. For a person to "tolerate" something, she actually has to believe the object in question is deficient, false, or wrong in some way. This is the "objection component" of toleration. Without it, we are left at the very least with indifference and at the most with outright affirmation. Objection has to be counterbalanced, of course, by an "acceptance component," a positive act of association (or at the very least a positive act of noninterference) with that which one finds objectionable. Otherwise toleration lapses into rejection or repression.[14] Such association can simply reflect self-interest. It can also be the result of acceptance operating on a "higher ground." Some argue it can even be the product of philosophical skepticism and moral relativism.[15]

As already noted, the General Social Survey (GSS) asks several questions regarding homosexuality that allow us to test the relationship between toleration and social class. Suppose that supporting same-sex marriage is an act of toleration that does not inherently affirm same-sex sexual relations. In this case a combination of moral objection to same-sex sexual relations with acceptance of same-sex marriage is the act of toleration. Any other combination—affirmation and acceptance, affirmation and rejection, or objection and rejection—expresses something else altogether (see table 4.1, panel A).

Since 2006 the GSS has asked its respondents both a question on the morality of same-sex sexual relations and a question on same-sex marriage. Combined data from the five surveys between 2006 and 2014 show that the overwhelming majority of Americans (86%) fall into one of two camps: affirmation-acceptance or objection-rejection. A fair interpretation is that almost all Americans want state marriage policy to reflect their personal attitudes toward same-sex sexual relations. Less than 10% of respondents can be classified as "tolerant" in any meaningful sense with no significant change in that figure over time (see table 4.1, panel B).

TABLE 4.1A. Cross Tabulation of Opinions on Same-Sex Sexual Relations and Same-Sex Marriage[16]

	Agree with same-sex couples' "right to marry" (acceptance)	Disagree with same-sex couples' "right to marry" (rejection)
Same-sex sexual relations are "wrong only sometimes" or "not wrong at all" (affirmation)	affirmation-acceptance	affirmation-rejection
Same-sex sexual relations are "always wrong," "almost always wrong" or "don't know" (objection)	objection-acceptance	objection-rejection

TABLE 4.1B. Toleration, 2006–2014

	Acceptance	Rejection
Affirmation	42.7% (41.2–44.2)	5.7% (5.0–6.4)
Objection	8.5% (7.8–9.3)	43.2% (41.7–44.7)

TABLE SOURCE: General Social Survey. N = 6419. Results are weighted by year and by the GSS weight variable WTSSALL. Numbers in parentheses represent the 95% confidence interval.

The social classes differ markedly in these combinations, yet not always in expected ways. Affirmation-acceptance is the dominant position among elites, objection-rejection prevails in the working class, and the middle class shows a balance between the two. On the matter of toleration, however, there are no significant class or class fraction differences save one. The single standout is higher professionals, who are remarkably the least tolerant class fraction of all. Less than 5% express objection-acceptance opinions (see table 4.2, panel A). Granting that such low levels of "toleration" are in part a consequence of high levels of affirmation, a more meaningful test of class toleration is to look strictly at those who are candidates for toleration in the first place, namely those with objections to homosexuality. By this definition higher professionals are surprisingly still the least tolerant of all. When restricting analysis only to those who are actually candidates for toleration, less than 10% express objection-acceptance opinions (see table 4.2, panel B).

What if, however, same-sex marriage is not a meaningful object and measure of toleration? If it explicitly or implicitly affirms same-sex sexual relations, same-sex marriage lacks the essential objection component of toleration—and there are strong reasons for thinking exactly that. U.S. courts ruling in favor of same-sex marriage consistently lauded the institution of marriage for the unique approval it conveys. In his famous 2010 decision overturning California's Proposition 8, Federal District Court Judge Vaughn Walker observed that "marriage is the state recognition and approval of a couple's choice to live with each other, to remain committed to one another and to form a household."[17] In the majority *Windsor* opinion in 2013, Supreme Court Justice Anthony Kennedy recognized that "the State's decision to give this class of persons [i.e., same-sex couples] the right to marry conferred upon them a dignity and status of immense import."[18] What more need be said?

State policies that convey acceptance without affirmation are the appropriate gauges of toleration. Thankfully the GSS has been measuring opinions of just such policies toward homosexuality for decades. Three questions have been asked repeatedly since the 1970s:

- whether "a man who admits that he is a homosexual" should be allowed to make a speech in the local community;
- whether the same man should be allowed to teach in a local college or university; and
- whether this man's book "in favor of homosexuality" at the local public library should be removed.

If this man is allowed his speech, in each case the state need not express any explicit or implicit opinion on the content of that speech. Unlike same-sex marriage policy, here the state is (potentially) truly neutral. And unlike same-sex marriage opinion, here Americans are largely united. In the GSS data over the same 2006–2014 period, 86% of respondents believed that

TABLE 4.2. Views on Homosexuality and Same-Sex Marriage by Class Fraction, 2006–2014

(Panel A)	HM	HP	LP	LM	I	SB	LST	SR	R	TOTAL
Affirmation-acceptance	50.0% (42.2–57.7)	53.7% (49.9–57.5)	49.4% (46.1–52.7)	46.7% (41.9–51.5)	43.1% (39.1–47.2)	39.7% (34.5–45.2)	28.8% (25.0–32.9)	32.4% (28.7–36.3)	32.8% (28.5–37.4)	42.5% (41.0–44.0)
Affirmation-rejection	6.5% (3.2–12.8)	9.0% (7.1–11.3)	4.5% (3.4–5.9)	4.7% (3.0–7.3)	4.3% (3.1–5.9)	4.7% (2.8–7.9)	7.4% (5.1–10.7)	4.7% (3.2–6.7)	7.3% (5.3–10.1)	5.8% (5.1–6.5)
Objection-rejection	34.4% (27.1–42.4)	33.7% (30.2–37.4)	38.1% (35.1–41.2)	39.5% (35.2–43.9)	43.6% (39.6–47.6)	46.2% (40.8–51.6)	52.6% (48.0–57.2)	50.8% (46.6–55.0)	52.9% (48.1–57.7)	43.2% (41.7–44.7)
Objection-acceptance	9.2% (5.5–15.0)	3.6% (2.4–5.4)	8.0% (6.3–10.0)	9.1% (6.7–12.2)	9.0% (7.2–11.4)	9.4% (6.6–13.2)	11.2% (8.7–14.2)	12.1% (9.8–14.9)	7.0% (4.9–9.9)	8.6% (7.8–9.4)
TOTAL	100%	100%	100%	100%	100%	100%	100%	100%	100%	100%

(Panel B)	HM	HP	LP	LM	I	SB	LST	SR	R	TOTAL
Objection-rejection	78.9% (67.2–87.2)	90.3% (85.9–93.5)	82.7% (78.7–86.1)	81.3% (75.7–85.8)	82.8% (78.6–86.3)	83.1% (76.7–87.9)	82.5% (78.0–86.2)	80.7% (76.4–84.4)	88.3% (83.6–91.8)	83.4% (81.9–84.9)
Objection-acceptance	21.1% (12.8–32.8)	9.7% (6.5–14.1)	17.3% (13.9–21.3)	18.7% (14.2–24.3)	17.2% (13.7–21.4)	16.9% (12.1–23.3)	17.5% (13.8–22.0)	19.3% (15.6–23.6)	11.7% (8.2–16.4)	16.6% (15.2–18.1)
TOTAL	100%	100%	100%	100%	100%	100%	100%	100%	100%	100%

TABLE SOURCE: General Social Survey. Panel A, N = 6143, p = 0.0000; Panel B, N = 3172, p = 0.0421. Total percentages here differ slightly from those in table 4.1 due to some respondents lacking a class fraction designation and thus not appearing in the totals here. Results are weighted by year and by the GSS weight variable WTSSALL.

TABLE 4.3. Views on Homosexuality and Speech, 2006–2014

	Allowed to speak (acceptance)	Not allowed to speak (rejection)	Allowed to teach (acceptance)	Not allowed to teach (rejection)	Not favor removing book (acceptance)	Favor removing book (rejection)
Same-sex sexual relations are "wrong only sometimes" or "not wrong at all" (affirmation)	48.1% (46.6–49.5)	1.0% (0.7–1.3)	47.4% (45.9–48.9)	1.7% (1.3–2.1)	46.2% (44.8–47.7)	2.8% (2.4–3.3)
Same-sex sexual relations are "always wrong," "almost always wrong," or "don't know" (objection)	37.8% (36.5–39.1)	13.2% (12.3–14.1)	36.1% (34.8–37.4)	14.9% (13.9–15.9)	32.6% (31.4–33.9)	18.3% (17.2–19.5)

TABLE SOURCE: *General Social Survey. N = 7043; 95% confidence intervals are listed in parentheses. Only respondents who answered all three questions are included in the results. Results are weighted by year and by the GSS weight variable WTSSALL.*

an "admitted homosexual" should be free to make a speech in the local community, 84% agreed that he should be free to teach in a local college or university, and 79% maintained that his prohomosexuality book should remain in the local public library. Compare this to the 51% who supported same-sex marriage over the same period. Setting the marriage and book shelving questions next to one another is especially telling. While the speech and teaching scenarios imply no affirmation of homosexuality at all, the actions of a public library may do so in that the book's contents are specified and the library has used limited public resources to (possibly) present one opinion over another. Yet even here 28% more Americans supported a "freedom to shelve" than a "freedom to marry." If we restrict analysis to only those who hold objection opinions regarding same-sex sexual relations and thus are candidates for toleration in the first place, we find 74% of respondents are tolerant of speech, 69% of teaching in a college or university, and 62% of retaining a prohomosexuality book in the public library. The toleration rate for same-sex marriage is a mere 14%.[19]

When broken down by social class, we do find that elites are more tolerant than the masses. For example, among all managers and professionals who hold moral objections to same-sex sexual relations, 80% are tolerant on public speech. Among all middle class respondents the figure is 72%, and working class respondents are at 67%. On teaching in a local college or university, elites are also more tolerant, although not by much: 78% among elites, 69% among the middle class, and the working class at 64%. On the library book question there is a similar separation by class: 71% of elites, 61% of those in the middle class, and 56% of working class respondents are tolerant by any meaningful definition.[20] Notably the number of tolerant respondents outweighs the number of intolerants in each of the three classes on each of the three GSS toleration questions.[21] While it is fair to say that elites are more tolerant of homosexuality than the masses, the masses are rather tolerant themselves.

This evidence strongly challenges a common charge against opponents of same-sex marriage. In his *Windsor* decision, which overturned section 3 of the Federal Defense of Marriage Act in 2013, Justice Kennedy strongly endorsed the claim that opposition to same-sex marriage is animated primarily, and perhaps even solely, by a "desire to harm," "demean," and "humiliate" LGBT persons and their children—in short, by naked "animus."[22] Putting same-sex marriage in a wider context, a more honest conclusion is that its opponents do not and never did view same-sex marriage as a matter of civil rights. When the state simply refrains from suppressing speech, it expresses no opinion on the value of that speech. When the state brings same-sex couples into the institution of marriage, however, it confers social approval upon same-sex sexual behavior. Not only a clear majority of Americans but a clear majority of federal judges as well understand it as such.

What truly differentiates elites from the middle and working classes is not their superior commitment to toleration. It is instead their commitment to go beyond tolerance. This was always implicit in elite opinion if one listened carefully enough. Recall the hopes of Massachusetts Supreme Judicial Court Justice John Greaney in his concurring decision in the 2003 *Goodridge* case quoted in chapter 1. Because supporters of same-sex marriage had already moved beyond tolerance, Greaney wanted opponents to do so as well. For him opponents' "grudging acknowledgement of the court's authority" was not enough. He wanted "full acceptance" of same-sex coupling as normatively equal to opposite-sex relationships. Scholars recognized clearly that the *Goodridge* majority "reached well beyond the jurisprudence of tolerance." But had they done so because "by 2003 Massachusetts had moved beyond the politics of tolerance"?[23] The claim is doubtful. Three months after the *Goodridge* ruling Massachusetts lawmakers convened a constitutional convention to consider overturning the court's decision. By constitutional rule a joint session of the state legislature in two consecutive sessions is required to approve any proposed constitutional amendment before it can go to the voters. Lawmakers passed a marriage amendment in 2004 but defeated it in the required second vote the following year, killing any chances of a referendum. After simply refusing to vote at all on a second proposed amendment in 2006, the legislature passed it in early 2007 only to defeat it yet again in a second ballot later the same year. The leadership of the Massachusetts Democratic Party spent nearly four years actively obstructing popular attempts to hold a marriage referendum in the state. It's safe to say that elected officials were far from convinced Massachusetts voters had moved beyond tolerance. What does seem beyond doubt, however, is that by 2003 Massachusetts elites had abandoned toleration for a very different political and cultural project.

Elites and the Contact Hypothesis

Why did elites leave behind the toleration of homosexuality for its affirmation? A popular argument claims that elite evolution beyond tolerance has been a response to LGBT persons coming out of the closet, living openly, and forming personal relationships with heterosexuals. This in turn is said to stimulate social learning and moral transformation in those capable of empathy.[24] Historian George Chauncey, an expert witness in both the *Hollingsworth* and *Windsor* Supreme Court trials, is an exemplar of the genre. He claims the process of coming out "succeeded in humanizing lesbians and gay men for many outsiders, making the demonization of homosexuals less persuasive and less acceptable, and rallying many heterosexuals to support the rights of people they now realized were not alien pariahs but often among those they most loved and respected."[25] Putting aside all subtlety, Chauncey asserts that personal connections between LGBT persons and "millions of heterosexuals who cherish their gay nephews, sisters, friends, and teachers, and for whom justice, compassion, fairness, and equality are fundamental moral values" are the most powerful cause of normalization.[26] Unsurprisingly the elite press embraces this same theory. In the words of the *New York Times* editorial board, "There are lots of theories to explain these more tolerant attitudes. Our own guess is that as more and more gays have acknowledged their sexual orientation, straight Americans have come to see that gays are not deviants to be feared, but valued friends, neighbors and colleagues who are not much different from anyone else."[27]

This empathetic theory of normalization is certainly plausible—not to mention highly flattering of those who subscribe to it—but does it have any empirical support? The evidence in favor is essentially the finding that personal knowledge of LGBT persons is strongly correlated with support for normalization and same-sex marriage.[28] This is a version of the well-known "contact hypothesis" in social psychology, which finds that, under specified conditions, interpersonal contact generates positive attitudes and cooperative behavior between groups. Research shows, however, that simplistic versions of the "coming out as a political act" argument have significant shortcomings.[29] First, personal acquaintance with LGBT persons may not cause political opinions so much as be an effect of them. That is, one's support for normalization and same-sex marriage may cause one to build personal bonds with LGBT persons rather than vice versa. LGBT persons may also be more likely to come out to those they think are likely to affirm them, also making contact an effect rather than a cause. Second, research shows that many factors strongly mediate the relationship between contact and opinion. For example, older Americans, political conservatives, Southerners, Evangelicals, strong Republicans, and even white Christians in general have all been found to be far less influenced in their views of same-sex marriage than others through contact with LGBT persons. Some groups are not influenced at all, while increased contact with gays and lesbians actually *reduces* support for normalization and same-sex marriage among strong conservative Evangelicals and persons with large numbers of conservative religious friends and family. One scholar observes that "increasing personal contact with LGBs accounts for 5–10 percentage points of the rise in support for LGB rights—an important but not overwhelming share."[30] "Not overwhelming" indeed.

We can be confident in saying that the broadest claims of the "coming out as a political act" argument are false. Why then do so many elites place such confidence in it? The contact hypothesis does have good empirical support for liberal, highly educated, nonreligious, non-Southern Americans. Since these are precisely the kinds of people overrepresented among the country's professionals and managers, it isn't surprising that the argument has more than an air of plausibility for them. Moreover the contact hypothesis contains a strong moral undertone that flatters precisely those persons who have changed their opinions through contact with LGBT persons—or who believe as much about themselves. They have become better than they were before and can enjoy their moral growth even more in comparison to those who remain blinded by "moral obtuseness."[31]

This moral growth has been rather uneven, however. While elites may practice a "politics of humanity" toward LGBT persons "that combines respect with curiosity and imaginative engagement,"[32] they continue to harbor their own biases and prejudices. We can measure them thanks to the American National Election Studies (ANES) and its "feeling thermometer" questions. Since the 1960s the ANES has asked American voters every two or four years to rate how "warm" or "cool" they feel toward prominent political, economic, and cultural figures and groups. Using a scale of 0–100, ratings between 51 and 100 signify favorability or warmth while ratings between 0 and 49 signify unfavorability or coolness. A rating of 50 indicates either equanimity or indifference, and the further away from 50 in either direction, the stronger the feeling. Unlike the GSS, the ANES does not provide sufficiently detailed occupational information to assign respondents to one of the nine social class fractions or three broad social classes with confidence. Each respondent's level of education can stand in as a rough proxy, however.

The 2008 ANES provides feeling thermometer readings for twenty-one social groups in the United States defined by race/ethnicity, social class, religion, cultural ideology, and several other identities. Relativing and normalizing the readings makes meaningful comparisons possible across all the survey's respondents (see appendix C for the full methodology). For fifteen of the twenty-one groups there is no significant difference between persons with and without a bachelor's degree.[33] The list includes many relatively unpopular groups including feminists, people on welfare, Muslims, atheists, and illegal immigrants. As educated opinion expects, those with a bachelor's degree or more have significantly warmer feelings than those without such education toward three groups: Asian-Americans, Jews, and gay men and lesbians. The latter two are of course classic reference groups in the toleration literature. Yet there are also three groups toward which the less educated are warmer than the better educated: the working class, the poor, and Christian fundamentalists. Of these six groups where a difference of opinion by class seems to exist, four actually have positive thermometer ratings from both sides of the education divide. That is, even the less warm group is still warmly disposed relative to their feelings about all other social groups.

Only gay men and lesbians and Christian fundamentalists have negative ratings from each educational group that are significantly different. As expected, many without a bachelor's degree are quite cool toward LGBT persons. Over 15% of such respondents in 2008 rate them at 0 degrees, the coldest possible response, while 25% rate them at 30 degrees or less. At the same time we see similar readings among the highly educated toward Christian fundamentalists. While only 6% of those with a bachelor's degree or higher give them a rating of 0 degrees, 22% put them at 30 degrees or less. Figure 4.1 shows the raw thermometer scores for each broad educational attainment group. The two panels are nearly mirror images of each other. For those with a bachelor's degree or more, Christian fundamentalists outnumber gay men and lesbians at thermometer ratings below 50 degrees while gay men and lesbians outnumber Christian fundamentalists above 50 degrees. The opposite is true for those without a bachelor's degree. When respondents are broken down into five categories of educational attainment, there is a clear negative relationship between level of education and feelings toward Christian fundamentalists. Those with less than a high school education are even warm toward them (this group's strongest negatives are toward Muslims, gay men and lesbians, and atheists). Those with a high school diploma or some college are moderately negative while those with a bachelor's or advanced degree are strongly negative. Apparently intense dislike is an equal opportunity emotion across the classes.

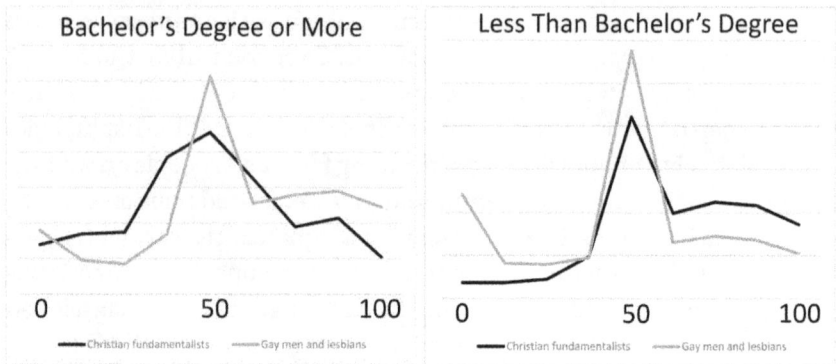

FIGURE 4.1. Feeling Thermometer Ratings by Educational Group

SOURCE: *Author's analysis of the 2008 American National Election Studies.*

Moral Change within the Elite

The philosopher Alasdair MacIntyre tells the following story.[34] In 1777 on the Pacific island archipelago of Tonga the British explorer Captain James Cook became the first European to encounter the Polynesian concept of "taboo." To Cook's eyes taboo involved inexplicable social prohibitions on physical contact with certain objects and people. It was especially rigorous around food. For example, it was forbidden for Tongans to eat in the presence of a higher-rank relative, to touch the food of such a relative, or to feed themselves if they had touched the dead body of a chief. Taboo infused all of Polynesian culture. Yet when Cook and his crew pressed the Tongans on the meaning of their taboos and the reasons behind them, they were "unable to get any intelligible reply." Over time, increasing contact with European culture and technology further eroded the taboo system throughout the far-flung Polynesian islands. Just forty years after Cook first visited Hawaii, the taboos there met a dramatic end. In 1819 Kamehameha II, son of the king who united the islands, ascended the throne. Among his first acts was to abolish the entire taboo system in his kingdom, which he did with impunity and ease. A Western eyewitness, the missionary Artemas Bishop, tells the dramatic tale:

> The king rose up and said to Mr. Young, "Cut up the fowls and the pig," which being done, he suddenly started off and went to the women's table, where, seating himself by the queen, he began to eat with a fury of appetite, requesting them to partake with him. The whole assembly

was struck with consternation at the sight, and looked to see him fall down dead. But no harm to the king ensuing, they at length cried out with one voice, "The taboo is broken, the eating taboo is broken."[35]

MacIntyre draws an important conclusion. Not only did Cook and other Europeans not understand Polynesian culture. The Polynesians themselves didn't understand it. By the early nineteenth century taboos had lost all meaning. They could be abolished with little trouble or opposition because the larger framework into which they had once fit had dissolved in the solvent of cultural change.[36]

The collapse of a strictly opposite-sex definition of marriage in early twenty-first century America is much like the collapse of the Polynesian eating taboos in the nineteenth. Same-sex marriage not only makes sense to tens of millions today but is profoundly obvious in their view. Yet coming to such a belief is far from obvious. Americans could have embraced normalization and same-sex marriage when they were first proposed in the 1970s but did not. While normalization is an integral part of progressive thought in the 2010s, it was far from being so a generation ago. Despite the many efforts of queer theorists to advance a radical theory of homosexuality and the family, instead a rather conservative version ordered toward marriage has prevailed.

Normalization has been socially constructed over time, enabled by the collapse of a culture that gave intelligibility to strictly opposite-sex marriage. Only two generations ago, the overwhelming cultural presumption in America was that marriage, sex, and reproduction enjoyed a special unity. Down to the mid-twentieth century, marriage was the singular socially endorsed setting for sexual relations and childbearing. Extramarital sex was, if not rare, then certainly proscribed. Contraception was stigmatized and in some states illegal as late as 1972. Cohabitation was virtually unknown outside the country's underclass. This unity was solemnized by the country's religious bodies with an eye toward forming and sustaining procreative families. And these norms were largely lived out. From the mid-nineteenth century divorce and cohabitation were practiced by fewer than 5% of the population. From at least 1930 to as late as 1968, less than 10% of all American children were born to unmarried parents.

Today that normative unity is in disarray. The statistics are well known. By the late 2000s, 14% of U.S. women ages 15–44 had been divorced and 11% were currently cohabiting.[37] The U.S. marriage rate for all women was less than half what it was in the 1890s or 1930s and barely over one-third the level of the 1950s.[38] Every year since 2008 more than 40% of American children have been born to unmarried parents.[39] Less well-known are the dramatic class differences in these patterns. In 2011 some 60% of women with a bachelor's degree or more were married, while among women without a high school diploma the figure was under 30%.[40] In 1995, among women ages 22–44, 46% of those without a high school degree cohabited as a first union compared to 34% of those with a four-year degree or more. By 2006–2010 the figure for the most educated had grown to 47% while for the least educated it had swelled to 70%. The highly educated tend to turn cohabitation into marriage while the least educated do not. At three years from the formation of first union, 53% of cohabiting college educated women had married while only 39% of high school graduates had done so and just 30% of women lacking a high school diploma. A pregnancy during cohabitation is especially likely to transition the most educated women in America to marriage but is not likely to transition the least educated.[41] No wonder that in 2011, 57% of children born to women without a high school diploma had unmarried mothers. For high school graduates the figure was 49%, and even among women with some college the unmarried birth rate was 40%. For women with a college degree or more, however, the figure was a mere 9%—the unmarried birth rate for the entire country in 1967.[42]

As unwed childbearing has become normal among the country's working and increasingly middle classes, opinion has changed as well. The GSS shows that in 1988, 73% of Americans agreed with the statement "people who want children ought to get married." By 2012 the figure had fallen to 61%. The most dramatic part of the decline was the portion that "strongly agree" with the statement, dropping from 35% in 1988 to a mere 18% in 2012. While support for the unity of marriage and procreation has declined across all classes, the fall has been especially steep among the working class. While in 1988, 16% of them disagreed with the premise that only married people ought to have children, a quarter century later more than 26% openly rejected the norm.

The normative separation of children from marriage goes even deeper than this. In 1982 the European Values Study conducted a survey in which it asked Americans what in their view "make[s] for a successful marriage." Not surprisingly the survey found that 93% said "faithfulness" was "very important." It occupied the top spot. A "happy sexual relationship" was considered "very important" by 76% of respondents. Children were rated so by 60%. Fewer than half considered things like good housing or sharing household chores to be at the same level. In 2007 Pew Research polled

Americans on the same battery of questions and found some dramatic changes of opinion in twenty-five years. Of the nine questions asked in both polls, faithfulness didn't move at all and remained in the top spot. Agreement on politics was also unchanged and remained at the very bottom. The place of children within a "successful marriage," however, changed dramatically. While 60% of respondents thought children "very important" in 1982, only 41% did so in 2007. No other response changed as much or fell as far. This remarkable plunge was mirrored by a surge in the importance of sharing household chores. This element of marriage rose in "very important" estimation from 45% in 1982 to 62% in 2007. Every response save one saw as many or fewer respondents claim "not very important." The sole exception was children. While 15% thought them "not very important" to a successful marriage in 1982, fully 28% said so in 2007. "Not very important" responses to sharing household chores, on the other hand, dropped from 17% to a mere 6%.

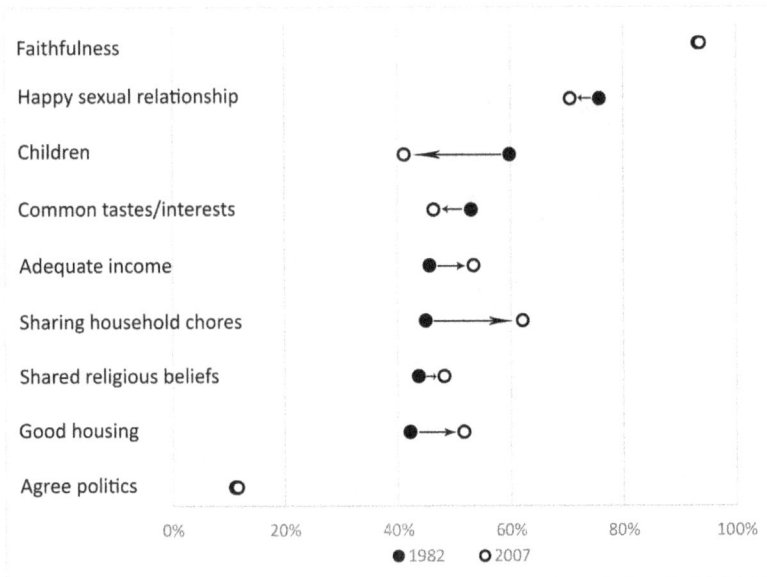

FIGURE 4.2. Percentage of Americans Saying "Very Important" for a "Successful Marriage," 1982 and 2007

SOURCES: *European Values Study, Survey 1981; Pew Research Center, February–March 2007 Social Trends, March 2007. N = 2242 (1982). N = 1845 (2007). Answers of "don't know" were removed from the 2007 results as no such option appeared in the 1982 survey. Results are weighted using the EVS weight variable "weight_g" and the Pew Research Center weight variable "weight."*

Not surprisingly a notable class difference exists regarding the value of children in marriage. While the 1982 data does not include any way of measuring class, the 2007 Pew survey contains information on respondents' level of education, which can serve as a rough approximation of social class. A strong negative relationship exists between educational attainment and the importance of children for marriage. While 60% of persons without a high school diploma felt that children remain "very important" to a successful marriage—the same as American society at large reported in 1982—a mere 29% of those with advanced degrees felt the same. In fact for those with the highest level of educational attainment, most characteristic of the upper professional class fraction, a plurality viewed children as "not very important" in marriage.

The Sexual Revolution reconfigured the connections between sex, marriage, and childbearing differently across the social classes. For the working and middle classes, marriage ideally remains an institution connected to children even as the experience of marriage becomes less typical and less stable. For elites, however, marriage has become centered on

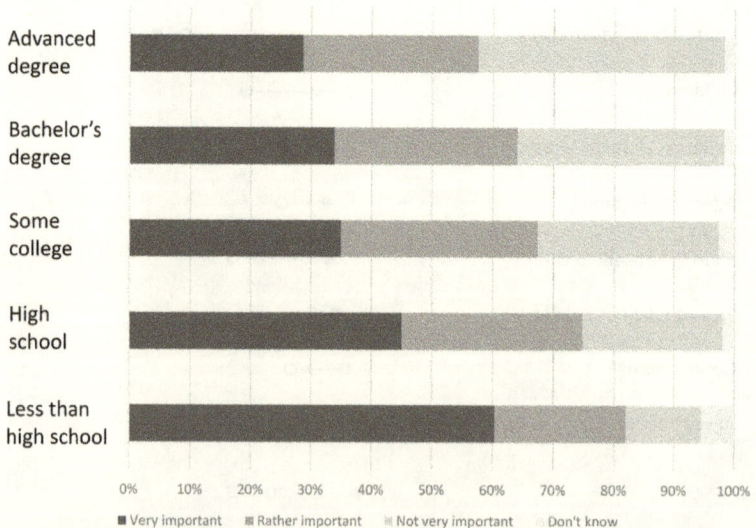

FIGURE 4.3. Importance of Children to a "Successful Marriage," by Education Level

SOURCE: Pew Research Center, February–March 2007 Social Trends, March 2007. N = 2011. "High school" includes persons with technical, trade, or vocation school after high school. "Some college" includes persons with a two-year degree.

the couple. Children, should they exist at all, come to adorn the couple rather than seal the marriage.[43] Such a cultural understanding of marriage is the premise of the sweeping words of the *Goodridge* court: "It is the exclusive and permanent commitment of the marriage partners to one another, not the begetting of children, that is the sine qua non of civil marriage." Justice Kennedy offered a hyperromantic version of this view in his *Obergefell* opinion: "Marriage responds to the universal fear that a lonely person might call out only to find no one there. It offers the hope of companionship and understanding and assurance that while both still live there will be someone to care for the other." In light of American divorce law and American divorce rates, one has to take the invocation of permanence and assurance as either intentional dishonesty or clever dissembling. The emphasis on "commitment," no matter how fleeting, however, does tap something fundamental in the contemporary American way of marriage.

Most every other of marriage's characteristics has been eroded in culture and eliminated in law. By definition, the advent of same-sex marriage removes sexual difference from the fundamental premises of marriage. We have seen above that procreation has largely been removed from elite cultural understandings, and the courts enjoy repeating the observation that childbearing has no necessary relationship to marriage. Even gender—not a synonym for biological sex but a belief in sex roles and the complementarity of the sexes—has gone by the wayside. In overturning California's marriage amendment Judge Vaughn Walker boldly pronounced that "gender no longer forms an essential part of marriage; marriage under law is a union of equals."[44] Pew's finding of the high importance of sharing household chores in a successful marriage lends cultural support to the legal assertion. The one remaining premise of marriage having any relationship at all to sex seems to be sexual intercourse. After all, "faithfulness" and a "happy sexual relationship" remain central to the vast majority of Americans' definition of a successful marriage. And how else can we make sense of so many states' eagerness to maintain traditional rules of consanguinity for same-sex couples?[45]

While the Supreme Court in *Obergefell* ultimately settled on a liberty-based argument for the constitutional right to same-sex marriage, it is liberty hemmed in by a deep cultural premise. While Western science and law once knew only sexual behavior and sexual desire, today both are subsumed under the umbrella of sexuality. Sexual identity or orientation now so dominates discussions of sexual behavior and desire that few outside academia realize how novel this cultural concept really is. The word "homosexuality" is less than 150 years old. Its widespread usage in Western European (particularly German-speaking) psychiatry and law dates back only to the 1880s, and in the United States it is even more recent. "Heterosexuality" is yet newer still, coming into its present usage only in the 1920s. Despite all this, American elites are convinced that sexuality—a unity of sexual behavior, desire, and identity—owes nothing to culture because it is the very essence of our species and individually every member of that species. Thus the *Obergefell* ruling says that sexual orientation is "immutable" and that the case's petitioners have an "immutable nature." Many studies have found that belief in a genetic origin to homosexuality is strongly associated with support for normalization and same-sex marriage.[46] And such beliefs have grown markedly over time. In the 1970s and 1980s less than 20% of Americans believed in a biological account of homosexuality while roughly half believed sexual orientation was a product of society. Even in the 1990s upbringing and environment outstripped birth by ten percentage points. Throughout the 2000s the figures were roughly even and remained that way down to 2011. By 2013, however, "born that way" had advanced significantly. Today nearly half of Americans think that a homosexual orientation is given at birth while only one-third believe it develops later.[47]

Those with higher levels of education have greater confidence in the immutability of sexual orientation. A 2012 Gallup poll showed that 59% of respondents with a graduate degree agreed that homosexuality is "something a person is born with," compared to just 45% of high school graduates. Because of the nature of the survey, it is not possible to be confident that differences of belief in the "born that way" hypothesis are not simply by chance. However, differences over a social theory of sexual orientation are significant. While 46% of high school graduates and 45% of people with some college thought that being gay or lesbian was "due to factors such as upbringing and environment," just 24% of postgraduate degree holders did likewise. Interestingly this is a break from the patterns of the 1970s and 1980s when no differences existed across levels of education.

Belief in an immutable sexuality, whether heterosexual or homosexual, diverges sharply from the arguments of radical queer theorists.[48] It also contradicts the scientific evidence on the fluidity of sexuality, particularly among women.[49] It has provoked strange debates over whether bisexuality really exists[50] and whether pedophilia should or shouldn't be considered an orientation.[51] Despite all this a strong cultural will to believe in unalterable nature persists. While belief in the naturalness of sexual orientation is today strongly associated with support for normalization and same-sex marriage, there is no necessary reason this should be the case. Many studies demonstrate that a belief in biological determinism is associated with more *negative* views of racial and ethnic outsiders, gender egalitarianism, and the mentally ill.[52] Typically it is opponents of equality who invoke genetic theories of difference while proponents of equality advance social theories. Sexual orientation seems to be the exception crying out for explanation.

5

NORMALIZATION AND THE FAMILY

The Mommies Wars

If the 1969 Stonewall riots in Greenwich Village were the start of the modern American gay rights movement, the 1977 Save Our Children campaign in Dade County, Florida was the beginning of the backlash. A wave of pronormalization social and legal change swept the country between these two events. The American Psychiatric Association declassified homosexuality as a mental illness. Nineteen states enacted partial or total repeals of their sodomy laws. Some forty cities passed local sexual orientation nondiscrimination ordinances. A rather typical example was the ordinance passed by the Metro-Dade County (FL) Commission in January 1977 outlawing discrimination in housing, public accommodations, and employment on the basis of "affectional or sexual preferences." Quite untypical, however, was the tremendous political reaction that followed.

Hundreds of residents turned out to speak for two-and-a-half hours, mostly against the proposed ordinance, in an open forum. Nearby Evangelical churches bused members into the city to protest. While the commission voted 5–3 in favor of the nondiscrimination ordinance, this proved a short-lived victory for gay rights. An organized countercampaign headed by well-known singer and local resident Anita Bryant began immediately. Its goal was to force a referendum on the ordinance and thereby repeal it through a popular vote. While housing and public accommodations were important aspects of the law, Bryant and her campaign focused exclusively on employment, and within employment almost exclusively on the employment of teachers in the county's schools. They named their organization "Save Our Children," and Bryant spoke tirelessly on the supposed dangers of LGBT teachers acting as "role models" for the community's children, warned of gay teachers' efforts to "recruit" to their identity, and promoted the campaign's ultimate goal, to "save our children from homosexuality."

Emphasizing the relationship between adult LGBT persons and children proved a smart political move. Dade County voters turned out in record numbers for a special election and supported repeal of the non-discrimination ordinance by an overwhelming 70%–30% margin. The matter of children in the care of LGBT persons clearly tapped a deep cultural anxiety. Over the next year similar ordinances fell by referenda in cities in Minnesota, Oregon, and Kansas. While gay rights advocates won a major battle defeating California Proposition 6 in 1978, the question of LGBT adults and children remained a major cultural flash point throughout the late 1970s and 1980s.

Overcoming first the presumed danger and then the presumed inferiority of LGBT parenting became an essential project for proponents of normalization. In turn any research demonstrating that gay individuals or same-sex couples are equal to straight individuals or opposite-sex couples in raising children became a cause for celebration. Whether in the initial burst of studies responding to the anti-gay rights victories of the late 1970s or the slow trickle of research following through the early 1990s, all indicated that no differences existed between gay and heterosexual parents. With the dam break in public opinion in the early 1990s, a new flood of research reiterated these findings. The social science foundations of the "as good as" narrative became so politically and socially important that in 2005 the American Psychological Association issued an 82-page "brief," *Lesbian and Gay Parenting*, summarizing sixty-seven academic studies on the topic over the previous quarter century. The country's leading psychologists concluded from this review,

> Not a single study has found children of lesbian or gay parents to be disadvantaged in any significant respect relative to children of heterosexual parents. Indeed, the evidence to date suggests that home environments provided by lesbian and gay parents are as likely as those provided by heterosexual parents to support and enable children's psychosocial growth.[1]

This was not the end of research on LGBT parenting, however. No sooner had social scientists coalesced around "as good as" than a new academic narrative rose to challenge it. In 2008 the *New York Times* summarized a "growing body of evidence [that] shows that same-sex couples have a great deal to teach everyone else about marriage and relationships." Why? Because same-sex relationships are "far more egalitarian" than opposite-sex relationships. Thanks to this equality, they enjoy "more relationship satisfaction" and use fewer "controlling and hostile emotional tactics." Among same-sex couples, "the ability to see the other person's point of view appears to be more automatic."[2] The *Times* followed up in 2013 with social science findings that same-sex couples report "higher levels of happiness," "far less conflict," and "higher levels of intimacy" than opposite-sex couples.[3] Such positive adult relationships translate into superior parenting. A 2009 *New York Times Magazine* piece reported social science research showing that the children of gay parents not only "do just fine" but in fact have the best outcomes. Girls raised by lesbians aspire to be doctors and lawyers while girls raised by opposite-sex parents want only to be nurses and teachers. Both sons and daughters of same-sex couples are "less conventional and more tolerant," while their adult children gravitate more to jobs "in the fields of social justice." This is all due to same-sex parents being "more equal in parenting" and less likely to "impose gender-based expectations" on their children.[4] In 2012 the *Huffington Post* reviewed a number of studies that agreed that gay parents were "more motivated, more committed than heterosexual parents." In turn their children were "more open-minded and empathetic" and "less stymied by gender stereotypes." One quoted academic was even allowed to speculate that gay men "will be the best parents" of all.[5] In 2013 the *Atlantic* ran a 10,000 word article demonstrating the superiority of same-sex marriages. When it comes to children, same-sex parents are "more cooperative and mutually hands-on." Lesbian mothers show "greater pleasure in parenting." Gay fathers can teach straight dads how to be more "emotionally accessible" and "logistically capable." They can also demonstrate to heterosexual wives the joys of a "genderless marriage" in which heterosexual husbands, just like gay men, can "get their act together and have a household and cook dinner and raise a child, without a woman doing all the work."[6]

The power of the new "better than" consensus showed most clearly in the elite reception of a 2014 Australian paper on LGBT parenting billed as "the largest study of its kind internationally."[7] In the summer of that year a team of researchers published the results of a survey of 315 Australian same-sex-attracted parents—nearly all women—of minor children in a relatively obscure British public health journal.[8] Based on parent reports of their children's well-being, the team found that "children in same-sex parent families had higher scores on measures of general behavior, general health and family cohesion" compared to the general population while there were "no differences between the two groups for all other scale scores."[9] While the journal might have been obscure, press coverage was anything but. Stories on the research appeared in the *Washington Post*, *Boston Globe*, CBS News, NBC News, *Time*, and *New York Daily News*, with a mention in a *New York Times* opinion column. Every outlet reported how children in same-sex parent families "fare better," "are happier and healthier," and enjoy "closer" families. The liberal news commentary website *Vox* summed up the findings vividly: "Largest-ever study of same-sex couples' kids finds they're better off than other children."[10]

University of Texas sociologist Mark Regnerus entered this social and academic environment like a skunk at a garden party. In 2012 he published the first prominent academic study contrary to received opinion.[11] Based on a nationally representative sample of over 15,000 young Americans ages 18–39, Regnerus found that "when compared with children who grew up in biologically (still) intact, mother-father families, the children of women who reported a same-sex relationship look markedly different on numerous outcomes, including many that are obviously suboptimal." Regnerus found that gay parenting produced children who were worse-off, whether in receiving public assistance, being unemployed, having an affair, being depressed, using drugs, or being sexually promiscuous. Such a claim was not simply in open dissent from established research. It was downright seditious, and—for the environs of elbow-patch academia—all hell broke loose.

Media attention to Regnerus and his research ran high. The *New York Times*, CBS News, ABC News, and the science news wire service LiveScience immediately ran stories on his study. Yet the nature of this attention differed dramatically from the media's usual practice in reporting same-sex parenting research. Normally the press simply relayed the findings along with a quote or two from the author. In Regnerus' case the news devoted as much space to his critics as to the author and his research. More unusual was that the vast majority of mainstream media coverage appeared on the opinion, not the news, pages. Readers of the *Economist*, *Boston Globe*, *Los Angeles Times*, *Chicago Tribune*, even *Scientific American* and *Psychology*

Today, found coverage strictly in op-eds. The only thorough news stories on the controversy appeared in the conservative opinion magazines *National Review* and the *Weekly Standard*. The *New York Times* did eventually run a more in-depth story several months later, but in its religion column where the focus was not on Regnerus' research but on his faith.

Controversy over the study was hardly unexpected. The editor of the journal that published Regnerus' paper commissioned three separate responses and printed them alongside the article in the same issue. The intensity of outrage, however, seemed to have caught all parties by surprise. Under considerable professional pressure, the journal editor agreed to submit himself and the entire publication process to an internal audit. The results were published four months later as part of a forty-page special section on the controversy in which the auditor judged Regnerus' paper a "non-scientific study." He described it more colorfully in a media interview as "bullshit." The auditor also condemned the journal's reviewers for "not do[ing] a good job," accused the original published responses of being "milquetoast critiques" by conservative cronies of Regnerus and his funding agency, and castigated the editor for trying to gin up attention for the journal by posting Regnerus' paper free online.[12]

The journal's editor wound up being sued by a journalist seeking public release of all documents associated with the decision to publish Regnerus' work. The editor later admitted he was "not prepared for the nastiness and vituperation that quickly ensued, much of it directed at me personally."[13] Regnerus himself faced an especially dire situation. He quickly became infamous in LGBT rights circles. The Human Rights Campaign established an entire website with its own URL dedicated to critiquing the study and maintained it for four years.[14] A special panel at the 2013 American Sociological Association conference was dedicated to condemning both Regnerus' work and him personally. Regnerus' employer even took up a formal investigation of his research under a charge of "scientific misconduct." This included sequestering all Regnerus' data on his work computer, including all emails and documents; forming a university inquiry panel; hiring an independent outside consultant to monitor the investigation; and formally interviewing Regnerus with transcriptions by a court reporter. Although cleared of all charges in the end, Regnerus reported finding the entire episode "worse than I ever could have imagined."[15]

Why did academia and the media react so very differently to the Australian study compared to the Regnerus study? The Australian study's "better than" judgment was received with great respect and acclaim while the Regnerus study's "worse than" judgment was widely rejected and even condemned as morally bankrupt. Many claimed the difference was simply a matter of science, pointing out a number of methodological flaws in Regnerus' work.[16] At the same time, the Australian study suffered from its own shortcomings.[17] More to the point, liberal Princeton professor Douglas Massey is certainly correct in noting that "papers based on questionable data and methods get published all the time," as is conservative Simon Fraser University professor Douglas Allen, who said, "If the Regnerus study is to be thrown out, then practically everything else in the field has to go with it."[18]

While science certainly played some role in the dispute, much of the difference in reception was political. A handful of socially conservative websites offered criticisms of the Australian study, but none gained any media traction. On the other hand, gay rights groups were well prepared for the Regnerus paper's release. Just one day after it was published online, four major LGBT rights organizations, including the Human Rights Campaign, condemned the study in a press release and began marshaling supporters through electronic and social media. Excellent preparation and organization helped an already sympathetic mainstream print and electronic press to cover the controversy as much as or more than the findings.

A simple political story doesn't quite do this episode justice, however. In the wake of the Regnerus affair, several writers in both academia and the press lamented the growing politicization of science. Yet how could this not be the case? Both politics and science exist in a cultural context. Particularly today it is impossible for "what are the effects of gay and lesbian parenting?" to be a strictly scientific question delivering a narrowly scientific answer. Same-sex parenting and the status of the family are cultural questions first and foremost. Science must fit within the confines culture sets.

Family Valued

America's culture wars have always been about the family. Before lesbian mothers became a cultural flashpoint, working mothers and single mothers stood in the spotlight. As the "traditional" American family eroded throughout the 1970s and 1980s, reaction to its disintegration defined a major cleavage between the country's two major political parties. While Democrats chose feminist values, Republicans championed "family values." The strategy peaked during the 1992 presidential race. During a speech at the San Francisco Commonwealth Club, Vice President Dan

Quayle famously criticized the television sitcom character Murphy Brown for "mocking the importance of a father" and for praising single mother-hood as a "lifestyle choice." At the Republican National Convention, failed presidential candidate Patrick Buchanan accused Bill and Hillary Clinton of advancing "radical feminism." An entire night of convention speeches was dedicated to family values. Televangelist Pat Robertson highlighted Bill Clinton's "radical plan to destroy the traditional family." Second Lady Marilyn Quayle spoke of the joys of being a homemaker, insisting that "most women do not wish to be liberated from their essential natures as women." In his acceptance speech at the convention, Vice President Quayle condemned those who insisted that "every so-called 'lifestyle alternative' is morally equivalent" and highlighted the "cultural divide" between the two parties. The family values theme became so shrill that Republican moderates sought desperately to tone down the rhetoric. No attempt was more vacuous than that of First Lady Barbara Bush who insisted, "However you define family, that's what we mean by family values."

To be fair, Bush's line was not quite as empty as it sounds out of con-text. Before this conclusion the first lady offered a list of practices—from teaching children "integrity, strength, responsibility, courage, sharing, love of God, and pride in being an American" to "putting your arms around each other and being there"—which she believed were characteristic of the American family regardless of its form. Behind this rhetorical moderation was a radical premise, however. Amid a Republican Party convention busy defining the family in structural terms, Bush drained it of structural qualities altogether. In her seemingly witless phrase, the first lady was really saying, "Regardless of family structure, practices are what we mean by family values."

Of course none of the practices mentioned, separately or collectively, are peculiar to the family. And we cannot flee from structure so easily. Structures bias and even create practices. A wealth of social science evi-dence tells us that different family structures generate different family practices around child educational attainment, father involvement, child abuse, poverty, age of first sexual intercourse, attitudes toward marriage, and more.[19] The "better than" literature on same-sex couple parenting in fact claims exactly this—structure matters.

For over a century, from the mid-1800s down to the 1970s, Ameri-cans shared a common structural vision of the family, how its members were supposed to interact, and what its role in the larger society should be. This was the "bourgeois" family centered on marriage and a "cult of

domesticity" in which nurturing and educating (especially young) children was the family's primary work. Men and unmarried women worked
outside the home while married women—exercising the "moral prestige
of the wife as mother"—dominated the domestic sphere.[20] Evangelical
Christianity played an important ideological role in supporting this family ideal among the middle class and promoting it to the working class.
Industrial unions responded in kind, fighting for a "family wage" so that
the working class, too, could emulate the bourgeois ideal.[21]

This model of the family was the premise and goal upon which the
American welfare state was constructed. "Maternalists" under Franklin
D. Roosevelt crafted New Deal legislation to encourage a family model
characterized by "the bread-winning father, the stay-at-home mother, and
children enjoying a true childhood" and to protect it from social forces
associated with industrialization and urbanization. Work relief programs
such as the Federal Emergency Relief Act, the Civil Works Administration,
the Civilian Conservation Corps, and the Works Progress Administration
openly discriminated in favor of married men both in employment and
in wages. The relatively small numbers of women hired through such programs were channeled into traditionally female occupations tied to domestic skills such as sewing and food preparation. The New Deal's hallmark
program, Social Security, was structured to support the bourgeois family
model by privileging full-time industrial labor and incorporating women
into the system primarily through spousal benefits, survivor's benefits,
and mother's pensions.[22] While this family ideal may not have dominated
the thinking and behavior of American blacks as much as whites, it was
nonetheless embraced even across the country's stark racial line.[23]

Second wave feminism, the Sexual Revolution, economic stagnation,
deindustrialization, and globalization all contributed to the demise of
this unifying social ideal. Married women began to enter the workforce.
Divorce rates shot upward. Fertility rates plummeted. Courts eliminated
the privileged legal status of husbands and fathers within the family, and
of children born within marriage as opposed to outside it. Legislatures did
away with laws against adultery. No-fault divorce became nearly universal.

Two rival family ideals emerged to replace the old unifying model.
Legal scholars Naomi Cahn and June Carbone call them the "red family"
and the "blue family."[24] The red family is a socially conservative ideal and
the most direct descendant of the old bourgeois family. Its foundation is
a prescriptive unity of sex, marriage, and procreation. Sexual relations
should be confined to committed couples. Their commitment should be

authoritatively regulated by the institution of marriage. All children should be born to such committed couples, who then act as their primary caregivers. Early marriage and childbearing are prescribed. Beyond these basics, the red family ideal also sees the sexes as complementary. Thus gender roles and gender difference—although never defined in exactly the same way across space and time—are central to the model. Religion acts as the primary source authorizing these norms.

The blue family, on the other hand, is a socially liberal ideal less directly descended from the old bourgeois model. Instead of a unity of sex, marriage, and procreation, the blue ideal values the equality of partners as the center of the family. Marriage is ordered primarily toward companionship. The sexes are not viewed as complementary, and gender roles are either suspect or banished. Sexual behavior is governed by the principles of individual autonomy balanced by individual responsibility. Long periods of education capped by successful employment are a typical manifestation of that responsibility. Sex outside of marriage is perfectly acceptable as long as it, too, is responsible and "safe." Like the red model, the blue paradigm frowns on childbirth outside marriage. Yet here contraception and abortion help manage sexual behavior. Religion plays little if any regulatory role.

These are not the only family models in the contemporary United States. Both the red and blue ideals are strongly associated with particular social classes and regions. The blue family is a coastal elite paradigm based on college education and secure employment for both partners, while the red model largely describes the country's small-town and suburban middle class. What of working class blacks in the Northeast who may vote blue but rarely live in blue families, or working class whites in the South who may vote red but whose lives are usually a long way from the red ideal?

The Swedish sociologist Göran Therborn describes an alternative "Creole" family system characterized by traditional matriarchy, father absenteeism, weak parental control over children, unstable sexual unions dominated by men, nonmarital births, and high fertility. Practiced historically in the United States mainly by blacks and Hispanics, data suggest this model has spread far into the country's white working class as well.[25] Is the Creole family more than just a collection of behaviors? Is there a Creole ideal? Ethnographic research tells us that there is.[26] Although the family lives of American working class women and men of all races and ethnicities seem beset by multiple failures to approximate any ideal at all—unemployment, criminal behavior, incarceration, drug and alcohol abuse, domestic violence, extremely low social trust, sexual infidelity—interviews with people at the bottom of the American social hierarchy show that many values and ideals animate their families. Children are highly valued, and the parent-child bond is considered the strongest and most precious of all social ties. Delaying parenthood beyond the age of thirty is nearly incomprehensible. Contraception has an ambivalent status, while abortion is largely viewed as immoral. Nonmarital sexual relationships carry no social stigma, and nonmarital childbearing carries little. Adherents of the red and blue ideals might see these practices and values as irresponsible, yet those within the Creole model see them as embracing responsibility—accepting the consequences of their actions (mostly among women) or meeting the challenges of fate (mostly among men). The Creole family is strongly matriarchal. Children "belong to" mothers who in turn regulate fathers' access to them. A strong and ongoing relationship with one's family of origin is more valuable than a bond with a partner. In-laws, whether formal or informal, are of little social importance. Both men and women value highly their economic, emotional, and behavioral autonomy. Despite the near-disappearance of marriage as a social practice in the Creole model, it continues to have normative prestige. Marriage is not viewed as a commitment mechanism for shaping future behavior, however. Instead it is seen as a luxury good or a symbol of past behavioral success and thus plays a minor role in the family.

Even with three models of the American family, we are still leaving out a significant number of people who do not live in a family and may not even aspire to a family ideal. In 2016 among persons between 15 and 50 years old—those most capable of forming some type of family—29% of households were nonfamily, while 19% of all households (66% of nonfamily households) were single persons living alone. Many family households were childless—28% of all married couples and 56% of all cohabiting couples in this age group had no minor children in the household—and thus lacked what many consider a signature feature of the family. Over 10% of all Americans age 18 and over were living in the household of one or more parents, a figure that includes 20% of males ages 25–34.[27] These multiple nonfamily living arrangements are by now familiar parts of the American social landscape.

All four models—red, blue, Creole, and nonfamily—answer central cultural questions for their adherents. They define the proper expression of sexual desire, the proper understanding of gender, and the proper relationship between the sexes. In this way they are also central in defining the meaning of homosexuality. A vision of the family strongly disposes one toward a compatible understanding of normalization and same-sex marriage. The absence of any family ideal even more strongly affects such opinions.

Testing Family Models

The importance of family models in influencing views on normalization and same-sex marriage can be demonstrated empirically using a statistical method known as "multiple correspondence analysis" (MCA). MCA uses survey data on a particular subject of interest to create a "field," a structured space of social relations. It plots survey responses and respondents in the social space of the field and measures their relative positions. The results of an MCA can then be read like a map. Positions close to one another "go together," while positions far from one another do not. For example, if two responses are positioned near each other in a field, this indicates that individuals offering one response tend to offer the second as well. If they are far apart, on the other hand, individuals offering the first response rarely if ever offer the second. A "cloud of categories" results, and lines may be drawn showing different concentrations of categories (subclouds) within the larger cloud. A "cloud of individuals" can also be projected onto the same space. By isolating different subgroups—creating subclouds of individuals by social class, for example—we can literally see how they differ in their responses by how they take up different positions in the field.

Fields with multiple dimensions are a complicating factor in multiple correspondence analysis. Each dimension is a measure of variance between categories. The first dimension captures the most variance within the dataset, the second dimension captures the second most variance, and so on until the analysis accounts for 100% of the variance. Dimensions can easily run into the dozens. While a two-dimensional projection is standard for obvious reasons, it is important to remember that often many more dimensions exist that can be important for describing the full set of relationships in the field.

The interest here is the field of the American family, created using data from the 2011–2013 National Survey of Family Growth. This survey was devised and administered by the National Center for Health Statistics, part of the U.S. federal government's Centers for Disease Control and Prevention. The survey collects information on behaviors and opinions regarding sex and family life from over 10,000 women and men ages 15–44. It is the only large-scale contemporary survey on the family in the United States that covers both behaviors and opinions. The field is created using responses to fifteen questions regarding sex, procreation, and marriage: eight on behavior and seven on opinion. These questions are listed in table 5.1. Because of the limited experiences of most young Americans in forming families, the analysis here is limited to the almost 4,600 women and men ages 30–44 at the beginning of the survey. This captures people born in the years 1967–1983, America's "Generation X," which pioneered the normalization of homosexuality and currently defines most family formation in the country.[28]

TABLE 5.1. Questions Used to Create the Field of the American Family

Behavior	N.OutWed	Number of respondent's biological children born out of wedlock
	P.OutWed	Portion of respondent's biological children born out of wedlock
	N.Cohab	Number of cohabitations
	N.Partners	Number of sexual partners (both opposite-sex and same-sex) in lifetime
	FirstBaby	Respondent's age at first live childbirth
	FirstCohab	Respondent's age at first cohabitation
	FirstMar	Respondent's age at first marriage
	N.SSPartners	Number of same-sex partners in lifetime
Opinion	ChildSingle	Okay for an unmarried woman to have and raise a child
	ChildCohab	Okay for a cohabiting couple to have and raise children
	Sex18	All right for unmarried 18 year olds to have sex if there is strong affection
	Sex16	All right for unmarried 16 year olds to have sex if there is strong affection
	NoCohab	A young couple should not live together unless married
	SameSex	Sexual relations between two same-sex adults are all right
	GayAdopt	Gay adults should have the right to adopt children

TABLE SOURCE: *Centers for Disease Control and Prevention, National Center for Health Statistics, 2011–2013 National Survey of Family Growth.*

Multiple correspondence analysis indicates a field of three dimensions that together explain 87% of the variation in the data. The first two explain 50% and 23%, respectively, and therefore are the primary focus in the discussion that follows. We can have considerable confidence that ignoring the fourth and higher dimensions will make very little difference in the interpretation of the results.

Figure 5.1 plots sixty "modalities" in the first two dimensions. These are all sixty possible responses to the fifteen questions in table 5.1. Modalities related to behavior are represented by circles, while those related to opinion are represented by triangles. All modalities that contribute more than the average amount of variance to the first axis (depicted along the x-axis) are labeled and in bold, while those contributing less than the average are shown in gray without labels. This shading helps focus attention on the modalities that most define the field.

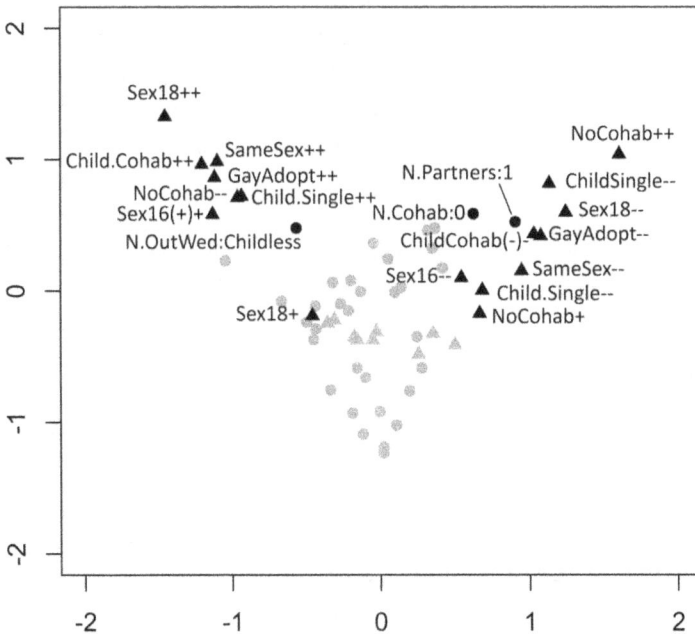

FIGURE 5.1. Field of the American Family, Dimensions 1 and 2 (Dimension 1 Modalities Highlighted)

KEY FOR FIGURES 5.1, 5.2, AND 5.3: ++ = strongly agree; + = agree; – = disagree; – – = strongly disagree; (+)+ = combination of strongly agree and agree; (–) – = combination of strongly disagree and disagree. NOTE: Two responses are combined for some questions due to very low numbers for one of the responses.

The complete cloud of categories in figure 5.1 is shaped like the letter V. Two subclouds, one in the upper left of the field and another in the upper right, are immediately apparent. These two clusters and the distance between them reflect the greatest distinctions in American family behavior and opinion. Both are made up mostly of opinions. This is an interesting result indicating that Americans (of this generation) differ much more in their opinions than in their behaviors. The subcloud in the upper left is a cluster of sexual progressive modalities. The seven opinions there strongly endorse the views of the Sexual Revolution. We see strong agreement (represented as "++") with the moral acceptability of teen sex and with procreation outside marriage, as well as strong disagreement ("- -") with the statement "a young couple should not live together unless married." Strong support for normalization (the moral acceptability of same-sex sexual relations and of gay adoption) is also a component of the sexual progressive subcloud. The subcloud in the upper right is its opposite, a cluster of sexual traditionalist modalities. The nine opinions there strongly endorse "red family" morality, a union of sex, marriage, and procreation. We see disagreement ("-") and strong disagreement with teen sex and procreation outside marriage, as well as both agreement ("+") and strong agreement with the normative status of marriage over cohabitation. Strong opposition to the normalization of homosexuality is also present.

In sum, figure 5.1 shows that views on homosexuality are part of a larger set of opinions on sexual behavior and the family in general. Those who most strongly believe in the moral acceptability of same-sex sexual relations and gay adoption are the same people who most strongly endorse sexual liberty. Those who most strongly oppose normalization hold to the red family ideal in strongest opposition to sexual progressivism.

Although the two subclouds in figure 5.1 are made up almost wholly of opinions, three behaviors make a significant contribution to axis 1. Among those holding progressive opinions, the single most characteristic family behavior is childlessness. Recall that the responses of young Americans under age 30 are not used to create this field. Thus this result is not a function of teens and twenty-somethings yet to enter parenthood. While it is obviously possible for people to procreate for the first time after age 30, many such persons are already included in these results. Moreover, since becoming a parent for the first time after age 45 is very rare, we shouldn't expect that the absence of such people from the data would make any notable difference in the results. Among those holding sexual traditionalist opinions, on the other hand, two behaviors are distinct: no history of cohabitation and having only one sexual partner over a lifetime. Again it is important to recall that these are the behaviors of 30–44-year-olds, not of young Americans yet to enter into sexual relationships. For both sexual progressives and sexual traditionalists, these are behaviors consistent with professed beliefs, evidence for "the practical operation of habitus."[29] Traditionalists holding to an ideal unity of sex, marriage, and procreation are actually more likely to carry out those ideals in their behavior. In turn, sexual progressives holding to a sex and family model hostile to the stability of family life are less likely to have a family in the first place.

Figure 5.2 shows the very same cloud but highlights the second dimension of the field, foregrounding the modalities that contribute a greater than average amount of variance to the second axis (depicted along the y-axis). Three subclouds result. Like the first dimension, the second is defined (in

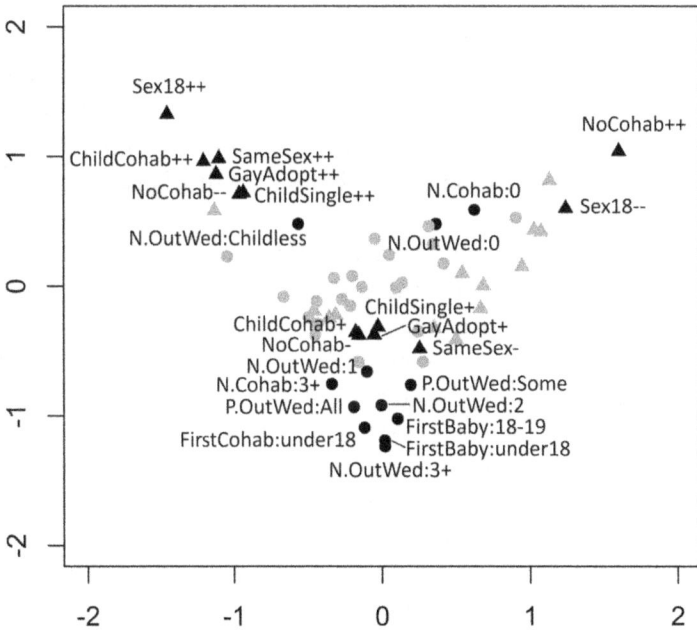

FIGURE 5.2. Field of the American Family, Dimensions 1 and 2 (Dimension 2 Modalities Highlighted)

KEY FOR FIGURES 5.1, 5.2, AND 5.3: ++ = strongly agree; + = agree; – = disagree; – – = strongly disagree; (+)+ = combination of strongly agree and agree; (–) – = combination of strongly disagree and disagree.

part) by differences between progressives and traditionalists. However, most of the difference is accounted for by a cluster mainly of behaviors in the bottom center of the field characteristic of the Creole model.

The bottom of the Creole cluster sits furthest from the center of the overall cloud and thus most defines the cluster. Here are behaviors associated with early childbearing, such as a first birth before age 18 and a first birth at ages 18–19. Also here is a track record of cohabitation, including a first cohabitation under age 18 and three or more cohabitations over a lifetime. Finally, the subcloud also contains all the surveyed behaviors associated with childbearing outside marriage. Not surprisingly, the opinions in the cluster lend moral support to these behaviors. Persons engaging in early nonmarital cohabitation and childbearing agree that it is okay for both cohabiting couples and single women to bear and raise children but disagree with the claim that a young couple should not live together outside marriage. The Creole model also incorporates its own distinct views of homosexuality. First is disapproval of same-sex sexual relations. Yet the Creole model combines this moral opposition with support for gay adoption. The wording of the question makes this combination difficult to interpret. In asking about "gay adults" rather than "gay couples," the survey may have biased respondents' answers in a pronormalization direction. That being said, dimension 2 does show that the Creole family model exists and has a distinct view of homosexuality based upon its own moral and social reasoning.

The sexual progressive subcloud appears in figure 5.2 much the same as it did in figure 5.1. This repeat appearance in both of the first two dimensions is an indication of just how strongly distinct this cluster is. The traditionalist subcloud also appears on axis 2 but in greatly diminished form. One interesting difference between the traditionalist cluster in figure 5.2 versus 5.1 is the appearance of the behavior modality "zero children born out of wedlock." As this response includes only women and men who have had at least one biological child, it further reinforces the connection between traditionalist opinion and traditionalist behavior.

Dimensions 1 and 2 together account for nearly 75% of all variation in the field. Yet where is the blue family model? The fact that it cannot be found in the first two dimensions indicates that this elite model contributes relatively little to differentiating family models from one another. Only in the third dimension, which accounts for only 14% of the total variance in the data, does it appear. In the lower center of figure 5.3 is a subcloud of two behaviors and five opinions. The two behaviors are

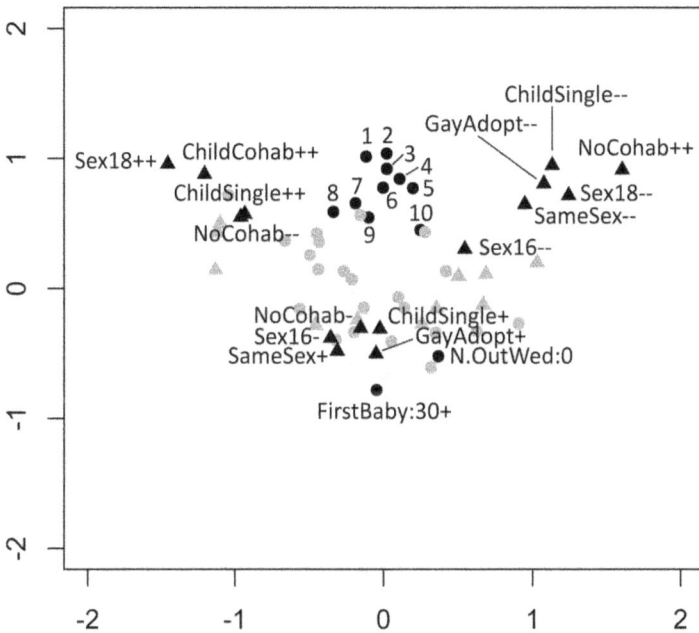

FIGURE 5.3. Field of the American Family, Dimensions 1 and 3 (Dimension 3 Modalities Highlighted)

KEY FOR FIGURES 5.1, 5.2, AND 5.3: ++ = strongly agree; + = agree; – = disagree; – – = strongly disagree; (+)+ = combination of strongly agree and agree; (–) – = combination of strongly disagree and disagree. KEY TO NUMBERS: 1. First Cohab:under 18   2. First Baby:under 18   3. N. Out Wed:3+   4. First Baby:18–19   5. P. Out Wed:Some   6. N. Out Wed:2   7. P. Out Wed:All   8. N. Cohab:3+   9. N. Out Wed:1   10. First Baby:20–24

classically blue: zero children born outside marriage and a first child born when the respondent was thirty or more years old. The cluster of opinions is true blue. Cohabitation and homosexuality pose no moral problems, sex between sixteen-year-olds does, and all opinions are moderately held. One exception seems to be a moral acceptance of single motherhood. This should probably be interpreted as an instance of nonjudgmentalism rather than endorsement. While blue family adherents may not condemn single motherhood, they certainly don't practice it.

A survey question on level of education allows some traction toward where social classes lie in the field of the American family. Figure 5.4 projects the nearly 4,600 survey respondents as five education level sub-clouds in the same social space already constructed through the prior MCA in the first two dimensions. A concentration ellipse with its center is drawn on top of each subcloud. Each ellipse contains about 85% of the individuals of the relevant subcloud, and the center of the ellipse represents the mean value of all the relevant points.[30] All the ellipses and center points without their subclouds are depicted in a final panel. Several interesting relationships can be seen. Each increase in level of education moves the mean strongly upwards and slightly to the left. This is movement away from the Creole model toward sexual progressivism. Furthermore the angles of the ellipses' major axes change noticeably as education increases. For the subcloud of individuals with less than a high school diploma, the ellipse is tilted with its major axis running from the lower left to the upper right. As education increases the ellipses become much more horizontal with the angle of the major axes eventually sloping gently from the upper left to lower right. Finally the length of the ellipses grows and extends ever leftward as education level increases. Thus what the MCA shows is the predominance of the Creole family model at the lowest levels of education with some inclusion of red family respondents. As education increases, fewer Creole family adherents but more red family members and sexual progressives are included. The move toward tradition-alism in the upper right part of the field is slight, however. A small step in that direction occurs when moving from a high school diploma to some college, but otherwise there is little differentiation by level of education. On the sexual progressive side of the field, however, the ellipses extend steadily outward with each advance in education. The distance between the "less than high school" ellipse and the "advanced degree" ellipse in the upper left quadrant is in fact remarkable. The most educated Americans are most distinct not for their adherence to the blue family model but instead for their commitment to sexual progressivism.[31]

What Are Men for?

Each family model is a cultural collection of opinions and practices regarding gender, sex, marriage, and procreation. Views on same-sex sexual relations are not only part and parcel of these models. In the current American cultural environment have become symbolic expressions of the models themselves: thus the sexual progressive model strongly endorses normalization as an expression of its commitment to sexual liberty. The blue family endorses normalization more moderately as a reasonable manifestation of the equality of partners and controlled fertility. The Creole family's ambivalence toward normalization is rooted in its primary commitment to the parent-child bond. The red family strongly opposes

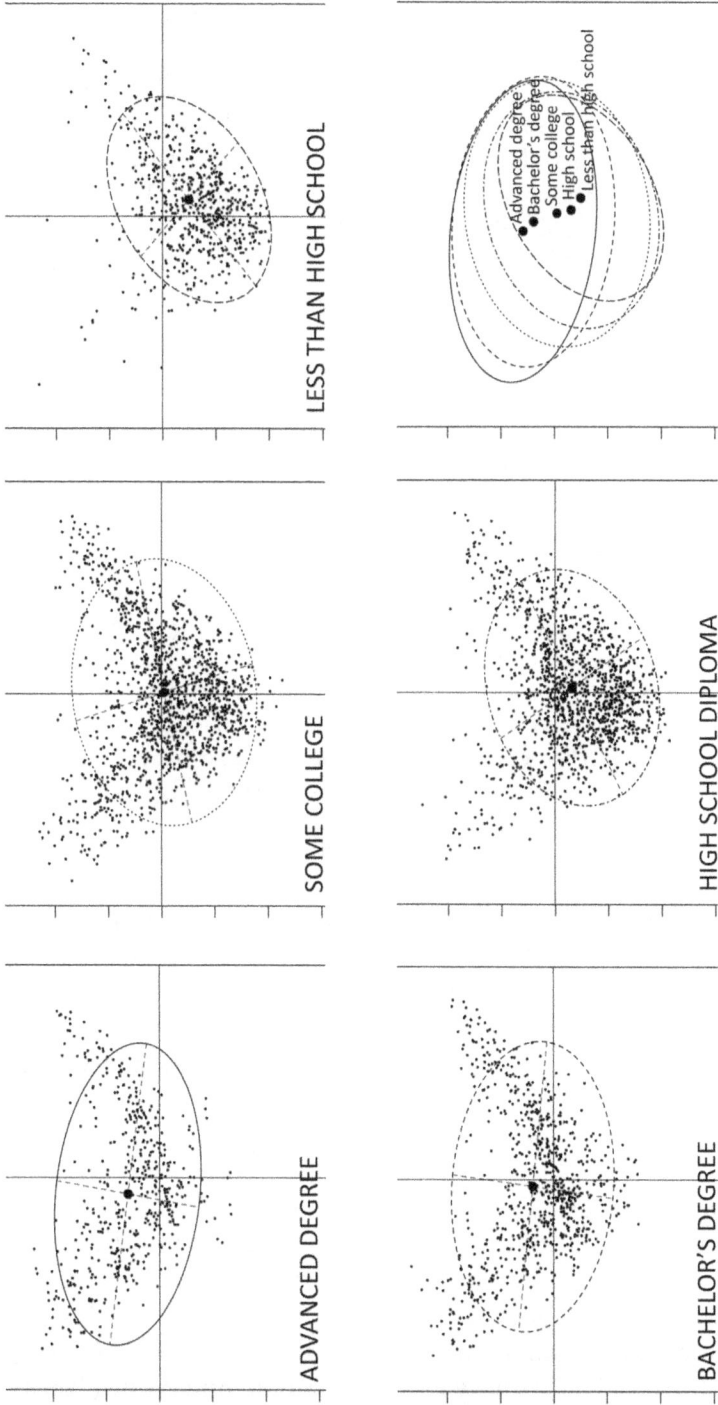

FIGURE 5.4. Clouds of Individuals by Level of Education Projected onto Field of the American Family, Dimensions 1 and 2

SOURCE: National Survey of Family Growth 2011–13. NOTE: "Some college" includes respondents with an Associate's Degree.

normalization due to its emphasis on gender roles and its reinforcement of the practices and norms widely ascribed to patriarchy.

The argument from patriarchy is common. From a feminist perspective the red model's attempt to control female fertility is most telling. Its opposition to premarital sex and abortion combined with support for early marriage and childbearing is patriarchy's essence.[32] The fact that red family proponents willingly refer to husbands and fathers even today as "patriarchs"—even if only "soft" ones—seals the case.[33] According to America's "gay bishop" V. Gene Robinson, the former Episcopal Bishop of New Hampshire,

> This battle over homosexuality is as much about the end of patriarchy as anything else. . . . What we're seeing is the beginning of the end of patriarchy. For a very long time, men—mostly white, educated, Western, heterosexual men from the Global North—have been making all the decisions for the world. People of color have demanded a place at that decision-making table, and so have women. Now that lgbt people are claiming a place too, the system of patriarchy, out of which all of our Abrahamic religions developed, seems to be starting to unravel. No wonder there's so much resistance! That's why the conservatives are right in saying this is such a big deal. It's not because gay and lesbian people are any different than others who have demanded equality, but because for religious bodies and for the culture, the full equality of gays and lesbians strikes at the very heart of the patriarchy.[34]

There is good empirical evidence to support Robinson's Manichean clash between normalization and "the rule of the father and the rule of the husband."[35] Married women's naming practices remain one of patriarchy's few cultural vestiges, and they maintain a revealing connection to views on homosexuality. In 2004, 93% of all native-born married women in the United States shared their husband's last name. Giving up a maiden name remains standard practice even among the most highly educated women. For those with a bachelor's degree, 92% shared a last name with their husbands, and 85% of women with an advanced degree did the same.[36] Unsurprisingly, feminists are much less likely to bow to this symbolic shadow of male prestige. A small 2012 study of self-identified feminist women found that only 65% of those who were married took their husband's name. Moreover a significant difference exists between married feminists with and without children. While 70% of mothers changed their name, only 49% of nonmothers did the same.[37] A small 2006 survey found that fertility is negatively correlated and feminist self-identity positively correlated with ideological support for women keeping their own name after marriage. Most interesting, however, are the relationships between name change beliefs and cultural attitudes more broadly. The highest correlations with beliefs about name changes are not with feminist identity, political identity, or religious beliefs. They are with attitudes toward homosexuality. Those most opposed to women taking their husband's name are generally those most supportive of same-sex sexual relations, of defining gay and lesbian couples as a family, of same-sex couple adoption, and of same-sex marriage. Vice versa, those most supportive of married women taking their husband's name are the least supportive of normalization.[38]

Differential fertility rates are also seen as a lingering effect of patriarchy. Feminist scholars and demographers both argue that high fertility is a product of the power of husbands to restrict and control their wives. Low fertility in turn is a product of female empowerment to pursue life goals beyond the household.[39] Second wave feminism, for example, contributed significantly to the most rapid and largest decline in the American fertility rate in the country's history.[40] International development policy today is premised on lowering the fertility rate precisely through educating girls and expanding women's employment.[41]

Thus fertility becomes the fulcrum around which family models turn. We can see as much by projecting fertility rates onto the field of the family. Figure 5.5 projects fertility subclouds with their concentration ellipses and mean points onto the same social space as in figure 5.4. Just like level of education, fertility has strong and clear connections to family models. As the number of children increases, the means move steadily from the upper left of the field to the lower right. This means that each step increase in the number of children moves the subcloud ever away from sexual progressivism and toward both the traditionalist and the Creole family models. The angles of the ellipses' major axes also rotate nearly 90 degrees as fertility grows, and the ellipses themselves become much more elongated to take in the farthest reaches of the traditionalist and Creole models as we move from lowest to highest fertility.

In turn, increasing fertility is also a move away from normalization. This is clear in both the red and Creole ideals' negative views of same-sex sexual relations. Thus, not surprisingly, fertility is negatively correlated with agreement to the statement, "Sexual relations between two adults of the same sex are all right." Only the childless have a mean score above neutrality. While we can't have confidence that the means at low levels

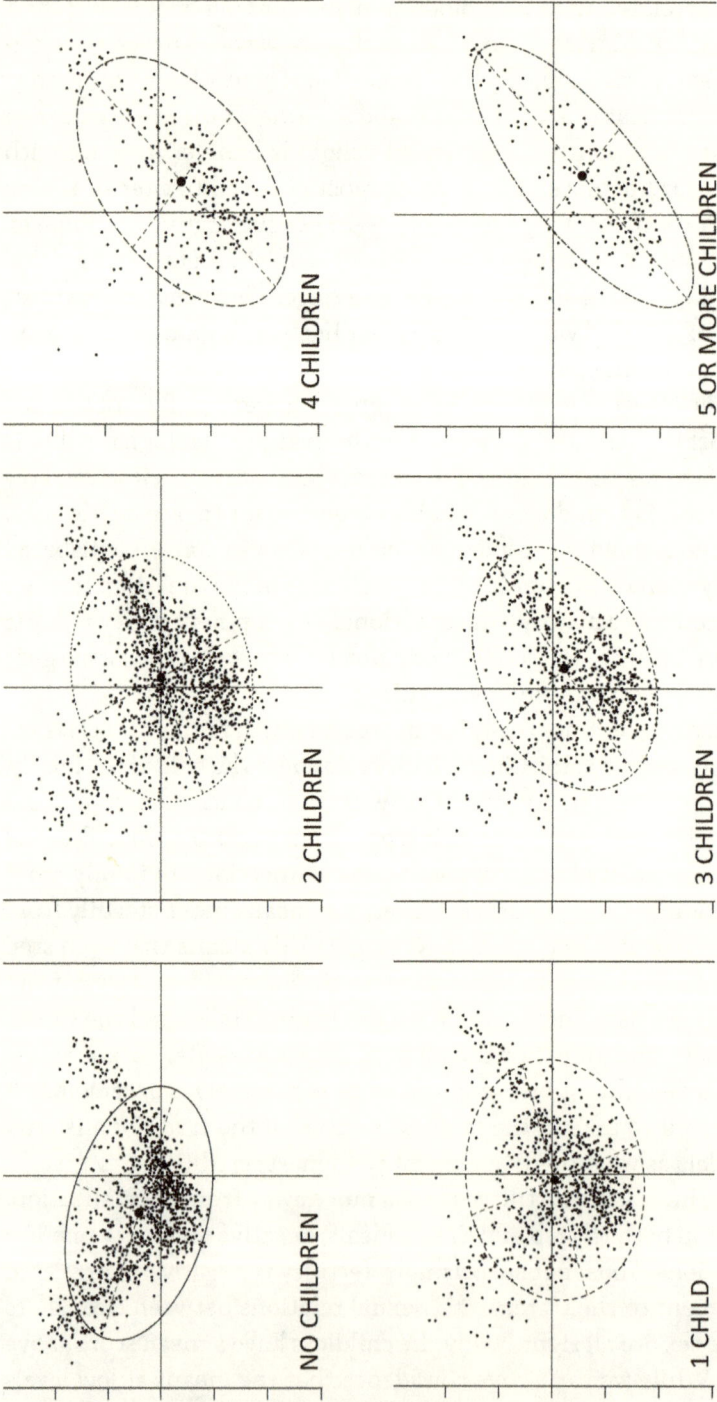

FIGURE 5.5 PANEL A. Clouds of Individuals by Number of Children Projected onto Field of the American Family, Dimensions 1 and 2

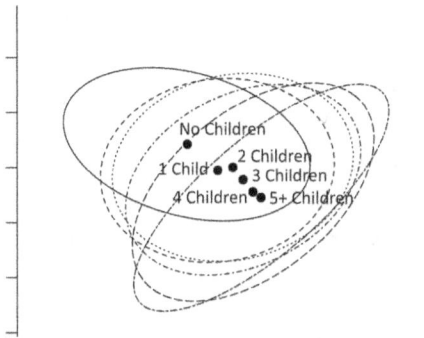

FIGURE 5.5 PANEL B. Clouds of Individuals by Number of Children, Concentration Ellipses Only

of fertility (1–3 children) are different from one another, we can be sure that respondents with four or more children have more negative views than respondents with one child. Groups with the highest levels of support for normalization—the young (59%), highly educated women (72%), those with no religion (75%), the voluntarily childless (80%)—are also the groups with the lowest fertility.[42] The connection between fertility and views on normalization is especially strong among men. First, it is already well known that women approve of homosexuality more than do men. In the National Survey of Family Growth (NSFG) data among 30–44-year-olds, for example, 55% of women either strongly agree or agree that same-sex sexual relations are "all right" while only 46% of men do. Moreover, men's weaker support erodes immediately with increasing fertility. By level of fertility, the only group of men who on average support normalization are the childless. This contrasts with women, a group in which childless women and women with one child do so. Only women with four or more children are definitively negative on same-sex sexual relations, whereas all fathers on average oppose normalization (see tables A.5A and A.5B in appendix D).

Why would this be the case? Higher fertility creates patriarchs, men who understand themselves as attached to the family of which they are the head—even if only in a symbolic or nominal sense. Patriarchy is one of human society's methods of inducing the domestication of men. After all it is far from every man's goal to marry and raise children. Down through history, war, athletics, fraternal clubs, sexual promiscuity, and philosophy stand as common rival male visions of the good life. A wife and children have at times been so unattractive that taxes on bachelors and legal penalties for childless married couples have been tried (and largely failed) to induce men to take on the role of husband and father.

Positive social inducement tends to work better. Through patriarchy men are honored by state, society, wives, and children in their domestication, for playing their social roles. Ideally they become attached to the family and the home, contributing their economic and cultural capital to the formation of the next generation. This is not to say that patriarchy is the only social order able to attach men to their biological children and those children's mothers. The blue family is an obvious alternative. That being said, the blue family may not be able to reproduce itself in the most literal sense, while patriarchy—despite the negative qualities pointed out and largely overturned by feminists in the past fifty years—does have a successful track record on this score.[43]

Understanding patriarchy in this way helps explain the fertility effect on views of normalization, and particularly its differential strength by sex. The normalization of homosexuality does indeed "strike at the very heart of patriarchy" by rejecting the normative status of male domestication. Consider that gay men are less likely to marry than either lesbians or heterosexual men.[44] They are also much more likely to incorporate sexual liberty into their committed relationships.[45] Gay men are very unlikely to be fathers. While 31% of American lesbians are mothers, only 16% of gay men are fathers.[46] Moreover 28% of lesbian couples live with minor children at home while just 13% of gay male couples do. The figure for opposite-sex couples is 40%.[47]

In turn same-sex marriage also strikes against patriarchy by eliminating the normative status of fathers and challenging the very concept of fatherhood. The most common gay family is a lesbian couple. Thanks to same-sex marriage and the state's presumption of paternity being extended to the wives of lesbian birth mothers, today the children of such couples lack not only social fathers but even recognized biological fathers. Adoption, single motherhood, and sperm donors all predate same-sex marriage, of course. Yet each of these in its own way disguised, replaced, or anonymized the father. None presumed his nonexistence. State enforcement of child support payments could even reveal a hidden father or open a pathway for a biological father to become a social father. Now that two women are listed on a *birth* certificate as a child's two parents, the complete separation of biological from both legal and social fatherhood is not only possible but necessary. While the Creole family model normalized the father's absence, same-sex marriage normalizes his absolute nullity.

Perhaps American men will trade in their desire to be a father for a desire to be an unsexed parent. Or perhaps they will instead lose interest in children altogether. Before the financial crisis and the Great Recession the United States had one of the highest fertility rates of any economically developed country. In 2007 the total fertility rate (TFR)—a statistical projection of the number of children who will be born to all currently living women by the end of their fertility—in the 28 countries of the European Union was 1.54. That is, every European woman alive in 2007 was projected to bear just over one-and-a-half children on average in her lifetime. The TFR in Canada was slightly higher at 1.66 while Japan's was an exceptionally low 1.34. In the United States, however, the total fertility rate stood at a robust 2.12. This made the United States one of only two wealthy countries at the time with a rate above replacement, a common marker of population stability and demographic health. The U.S. annual fertility rate had even been growing steadily across all racial and ethnic groups for ten years prior to the Great Recession.[48] For twenty years the country had been an exception to the general rule of low fertility in rich societies.

All that came to an abrupt halt in 2008. By 2015 America's total fertility rate had dropped to 1.84, its lowest level in over thirty years. Between 2007 and 2013 the annual fertility rate fell 10%. In 2015 it tied 2013's all-time low of just 62.5 births per 1,000 women ages 15–44. This strong fertility undertow has pulled down the birth rates of younger men in particular. Since 2007 the number of children born to men ages 15–19 (-43%), 20–24 (-32%), 25–29 (-21%) and 30–34 (-6%) has collapsed.[49] All this portends fewer children and smaller families in the United States into the future, as well as an increasing paucity of patriarchs. That being the case, it also indicates a bright future for the progress of homosexuality's normalization.

6

DIVERSITY WITHOUT TEARS

A Great Deodorant

Former National Football League coach John Madden is famous for many things: his victory in Super Bowl XI, his membership in the NFL Hall of Fame, his thirty years of sports broadcasting, his popular *Madden NFL* video game franchise. He is also well known for dispensing pearls of sports wisdom. During the 1993 season longtime NFL coach Buddy Ryan was working as defensive coordinator for the Houston Oilers, in charge of the team's defense and second in command behind only the head coach. In the waning minutes of the first half of the final game of a successful season leading to a playoff berth, Ryan lost patience with the play calls of his colleague, Oiler offensive coordinator Kevin Gilbride. Rather than run the ball to kill the clock and give Ryan's defense much needed rest and protection from injury, Gilbride insisted on passing. This often led to incomplete passes, a stoppage of the game clock, and a return of the defense to the field in pointless game situations. Two star members of Ryan's defense had been injured just two games earlier following Oiler turnovers, and Ryan blamed Gilbride personally. Passions intensified on the sideline. Words were exchanged. Suddenly Ryan threw a punch at Gilbride. Before the fight could escalate, players separated the two coaches, but it was all captured live on national television.

While attacking a coworker is generally cause for dismissal in most occupations, things are often different in sports. As the Oilers prepared for the playoffs and sought to put the fracas behind them, Madden observed, "Winning is a great deodorant. Winning covers up everything. That's the harsh reality of sports. And if they win, they'll give Buddy a parade."[1] In the end the Oilers didn't win. The team lost its first round playoff game, and Ryan didn't get his parade. That said, he arguably got something better—promotion to head coach of another team.

Things are often different in politics as well. For most of his long political and legal career, superlawyer Ted Olson had been *persona non grata* on the left. Although he served in both the Ronald Reagan and the George W. Bush justice departments, his choice of clients in his private legal practice made Olson especially toxic among liberals. He served as Reagan's personal counsel during the Iran-Contra scandal in the late 1980s. Along with Robert Bork, he prepped the attorneys for Paula Jones in her private sexual harassment lawsuit against Bill Clinton in the late 1990s. In 2000 he served as lead attorney representing George W. Bush before the Supreme Court in *Bush v. Gore* and delivered the oral argument against restarting the Florida presidential vote recount. Worst of all, in 2010 Olson represented the conservative advocacy group Citizens United and successfully argued its case before the Supreme Court. Olson's victory led to virtually unlimited spending in federal election campaigns and provoked especially caustic political reactions from Democrats. Barack Obama himself tarred the *Citizens United* decision with the words, "I can't think of anything more devastating to the public interest."[2]

While this trail of misconduct should have made him permanently repellent to liberals, Olson instead applied a powerful deodorant that changed everything. In 2009 Olson and his *Bush v. Gore* rival David Boies agreed to represent gay rights activists seeking to overturn California Proposition 8 in federal district court. While Boies focused on examining witnesses, Olson delivered the plaintiffs' opening and closing statements. Both lawyers stayed with the case for three years: through its initial victory before Judge Vaughan Walker; to the three-judge federal district court panel; to the California Supreme Court; and ultimately before the U.S. Supreme Court. There Olson alone presented and defended the argument for the constitutional right to same-sex marriage. Along the way both he and Boies jointly collected the American Bar Association's ABA Medal, the highest honor the country's legal profession can bestow. When the Supreme Court refused in June 2013 to overrule the decisions of Judge

Walker and the federal circuit court, effectively invalidating Proposition 8 once and for all, Olson was hailed as a hero. Partially tongue-in-cheek, this cofounder and literal card-carrying member of the law establishment's "hard core of the extreme right" reflected on his newfound acceptance by the left.[3] "I had no idea how popular I would be on law school campuses. . . . All of [a] sudden, the monster I was from *Bush v. Gore* and *Citizens United* is gone."[4] Putting a high gloss on John Madden's pearl of wisdom, in 2014 the California gay rights organization LA! Pride honored Olson, Boies, and the two plaintiff couples in the Proposition 8 case as Community Grand Marshals for its annual festival in West Hollywood. Unlike Buddy Ryan, Ted Olson got his parade.

Managing Pluralism

Diversity is the reigning social and political ideal of our age.[5] It is the public ideology of the country's most powerful institutions. In his 2016 State of the Union address, Barack Obama even identified it as the essence of American national identity.

> Our unique strengths as a nation—our optimism and work ethic, our spirit of discovery, our diversity, our commitment to rule of law—these things give us everything we need to ensure prosperity and security for generations to come. . . . The world respects us not just for our arsenal, it respects us for our diversity and our openness and the way we respect every faith. . . . When politicians insult Muslims, whether abroad, or fellow citizens, when a mosque is vandalized, or a kid is called names, that doesn't make us safer. That's not telling it what—telling it like it is, it's just wrong. It diminishes us in the eyes of the world. It makes it harder to achieve our goals. It betrays who we are as a country.[6]

Among American elites, diversity stands alongside liberty, equality, progress, and family as obvious goods no sane person could oppose. "The word wears a halo."[7]

The American cultural, economic, and political project known as "diversity" traces its ancestry back to the black civil rights and women's movements of the 1950s, 1960s, and 1970s. First blacks and then women began to organize and pressure state and society with demands for equality. Struggles took place in nearly every social arena, from housing to public accommodations to religion to sport. Conflict was especially pointed in employment and education, the country's key avenues of upward social mobility. The Civil Rights Act of 1964 stands as the signature legal culmination of those demands, and its Titles IV and VII set forth society's new norms on "equal opportunity" in both arenas. By ensuring equal access to university admissions, job training, the professions, and corporate management positions, supporters hoped that over time equal outcomes would result, the power of prejudiced white men would be curtailed, and the skills of blacks and women would expand. Underprivileged individuals would benefit, but so, too, would the country as a whole.

While the social intent of the Civil Rights Act was clear, the legal definition of this new equality norm was not. What would the government consider evidence of discrimination? How much activity counted as a good faith effort toward equal opportunity? Was it possible to pursue too much equality? America's largest, most dynamic, and most profitable firms in aerospace, computers, communications, and heavy manufacturing, as well as its largest and most prestigious universities, blazed the trail that all others—even the state—followed. Elite institutions in business and education eventually defined nondiscrimination and equal opportunity as "affirmative action." Concretely this meant an expanding set of bureaucratic practices including written nondiscrimination policies, targeted recruitment, targeted financial aid, special managerial training programs, formal grievance and disciplinary procedures, performance evaluations, affirmative action officers and offices, and an end to job tests. Over time these "best practices" created the country's legal benchmark for compliance. They also created hundreds of thousands of managerial best practitioners. From the early 1970s to the dawn of diversity in the late 1980s, the number of large U.S. firms with a personnel office nearly doubled. The number with an equal opportunity office quadrupled. Those with an affirmative action officer grew five-fold.[8]

By the mid-1970s the rapid spread of affirmative action policies met its backlash. "Reverse discrimination" was coined and even appeared on the cover of *U.S. News and World Report*. By the late 1970s affirmative action became caught up in the country's broad reaction against regulation and the bureaucratic state. Ronald Reagan's victory in the 1980 presidential election institutionalized the backlash. Regulators curtailed enforcement. Administration lawyers sided with affirmative action's opponents in court. New judges reinterpreted old laws.

The backlash was largely a white middle class revolt, however. Support for affirmative action never flagged among elites. In fact, most of the country's largest corporations opposed Reagan's efforts to dismantle affirmative action practices. Despite regulatory relief, nearly all Fortune 500 firms continued to pursue or even expand efforts to recruit and employ more racial minorities and women.[9] Elite universities remained strongly committed as well. Their resolve was demonstrated in 1977 when the U.S. Supreme Court agreed to hear the reverse discrimination case of Allan Bakke. Three years earlier Bakke had brought suit against the University of California, Davis for twice rejecting his application to its medical school. Despite his having test scores well above average for the school's applicant pool, in addition to four years of service in the Marine Corps and a seven-month tour in Vietnam, UC–Davis refused Bakke admission. The School of Medicine justified this in part because of his age—such discrimination being both socially acceptable and perfectly legal at the time—and in part because of the manner in which he blamed his first rejection on the School's affirmative action policy. Beginning shortly after its founding in 1968, the Davis medical school operated a quota system for racial minorities in which around 15% of its admission slots were reserved for nonwhite students. Congress believed its Civil Rights Act banned quotas in employment, and the Department of Labor under President Nixon clearly forbade them. Colleges and universities, however, had been using various types of admissions quotas for decades and were committed to continuing them.

Bakke's suit claimed he was denied admission because of the medical school's special admissions program and that the university was therefore guilty of violating his rights under the Fourteenth Amendment, the California Constitution, and the 1964 Civil Rights Act. In 1976 the California Supreme Court found in favor of Bakke, but the decision was quickly stayed to allow the U.S. Supreme Court to hear the case in turn. It took nearly two more years before the highest court in the land issued its famously scattered *Bakke* ruling. The nine justices issued six separate opinions, none gathering a majority. Justice Lewis Powell's idiosyncratic opinion, however, garnered enough partial support in places that it stood as the judgment of the Court. In a victory for affirmative action opponents, it ordered Bakke to be admitted to the Davis School of Medicine and barred the use of racial quotas. Yet in a victory for affirmative action supporters, the Court also agreed that some alternative system of racial preferences could pass constitutional muster. It is precisely here that the ideology of diversity entered mainstream American thought and practice.

Justice Powell argued that "a diverse student body" was a worthy goal of any university that allowed consideration of race in admissions. He justified this neither on the grounds of racial justice nor the amelioration of past or present discrimination. Instead he claimed that racial and ethnic diversity advanced the core intellectual mission of American higher education, namely "speculation, experiment and creation," "the interplay of ideas and the exchange of views," and an encounter of differing "ideas and mores of students as diverse as this Nation of many peoples." This claim hardly originated with Powell, of course. He was simply repeating the collective views of Harvard, Columbia, Stanford, and the University of Pennsylvania as stated in their joint brief to the Court in defense of affirmative action. According to the country's most elite private universities, diversity in all its forms—race, region, social class, field of interest, occupational life plan (although neither sex nor age)—is a precondition for the best educational experience possible.[10]

Powell's endorsement of the "Harvard plan" as a constitutionally permissible and even preferable equal opportunity practice spread diversity throughout American higher education and the elite business sector. Equal opportunity officers and consultants morphed into diversity officers and consultants. New diversity categories expanded older affirmative action mission statements. Diversity training replaced race relations workshops. Culture audits burst onto the scene. By the early 1990s, diversity had conquered Corporate America.[11] The same is true in elite higher education. The University of Michigan was a pioneering if eventually quite typical case. It took up diversity as a central social and educational mission in the 1980s as affirmative action receded into the background of the school's public image. University President Harold Schapiro (1980–1988) spoke of diversity as encompassing race, ethnicity, and religion, and praised diversity's contribution to "freedom of thought, innovation, and creativity." His successor James Duderstadt (1988–1996) went further, asserting that the university had received a "mandate . . . to build a model of a pluralistic, multicultural community" as the "key to the future strength and prosperity of America."[12] Although Duderstadt named his diversity strategy the "Michigan Mandate," it was never quite clear who had given the university its marching orders. No mass electorate was clamoring for its flagship public university to take on the project. No state legislature was ordering such steps. All Duderstadt could do was appeal to the university's "heritage of leadership" and its internal organizational values.[13] One could be forgiven for mistaking this public university official for the head of a Fortune 500 firm.

Since that time the country's higher managerial class has embraced its opportunities to demonstrate commitment to diversity. In California (1996), Houston (1997), Washington state (1998), and Michigan (2006), policies barring consideration of race, ethnicity, and sex in the public sector went to referendum. In each case the largest corporations in the area—Exxon, Enron, Boeing, Microsoft, General Motors, Ford—were among the strongest opponents. In 2003 the U.S. Supreme Court revisited its *Bakke* decision in the case *Grutter v. Bollinger*. General Motors and a collective of sixty-five Fortune 500 firms filed separate passionate and influential defenses of diversity before the Court.[14] Race/ethnicity-based university admissions policies appeared yet again before the Court in *Fisher v. University of Texas*. In 2012 and again in 2015, forty-five Fortune 100 firms argued that diversity is essential both for individual "success in the corporate world" as well as "business success" in "country and world economies that are increasingly diverse." Diversity in higher education management is today so hegemonic that it stands as an orthodoxy against which only the most foolhardy (or cantankerous) now speak.[15]

Firms would have us believe their embrace of diversity practices and ideology is a straightforward matter of efficiency, productivity, and profitability. In their 2015 *Obergefell* brief, the "379 Employers and Organizations" supporting a constitutional right to same-sex marriage pointed to "rigorous analyses" that demonstrated "the business value of investments in diversity," including "significant returns for our shareholders and owners." A 2013 survey of four hundred executives conducted by the consulting and recruitment firm Korn Ferry found that a stunning 96% believed "having a diverse and inclusive workforce can lead to higher employee engagement and improved business results."[16] The "business case for diversity" couldn't have been stated more clearly than in the Fortune 100 firms' brief to the Supreme Court in the *Fisher* case. For these largest globe-spanning firms "to succeed in their businesses," American higher education must develop "university-trained employees [who] have had the opportunity to share ideas, experiences, viewpoints, and approaches with a broadly diverse student body. . . . This is a business and economic imperative."[17]

But is there really a business case for diversity? While most firms are true believers, social science gives a decidedly mixed answer.[18] That being said, the academic debate over diversity's impact on the bottom line is largely, well, academic. Managers embraced diversity long before any meaningful evidence existed for its positive effects. The first systematic academic study of whether diversity policies even produce diversity, much less profitability, was not published until 2006.[19] Business and educational elites certainly are not waiting around for academics to tell them what to do now. Higher education administrators are in a similar position. Universities claim the case for diversity is an educational one, an argument their most elite representatives pioneered decades ago. Yet academic debate continues, particularly over the degree to which diversity improves students' cognitive skills and tendencies.[20] Whether diversity admissions practices even help their targets remains a matter of controversy.[21] Despite all this uncertainty, higher education displayed total unity of purpose in the *Fisher* case. Briefs supporting the University of Texas were filed by seventy-five universities and colleges as well as by the American Association of College Registrars and Admissions Officers, the Association of American Medical Colleges, and the Association of American Law Schools. Not one college, university, or educational organization filed in support of Abigail Fisher.

Plenty of cynical arguments exist to explain managerial enthusiasm for diversity. Critical race theorists in particular claim diversity is little more than propaganda designed to sideline discussions of racial justice and to legitimate the power of managers.[22] No doubt an element of self-interest is behind the promotion of any ideology. Managerial elites supported affirmative action in the 1960s and 1970s in part out of a fear of black riots. Creating a black managerial elite was thought to counter the frustration that supposedly motivated urban unrest.[23] As personnel initiatives, both affirmative action and diversity created managerial employment opportunities particularly for women. Evidence suggests that white women have in fact benefited more than any other group from corporate diversity initiatives.[24]

Such arguments have notable problems, however. They fail to grapple with clear evidence that many managers show genuine enthusiasm for diversity. They ignore the contentious social and political debate over the merits of diversity and thus the contradictory, even ironic, effects of the ideology on elite legitimacy. Most importantly, they overlook diversity's deeper class aspects. As an ideology and associated set of practices, diversity is attractive to managers and administrators because it is a particular version of the broader ideology of managerialism. Unlike capitalism or socialism, managerialism is not a household word. Yet it should be thought of alongside these more famous "-isms." Capitalism of course places the business entrepreneur at the center of society and emphasizes her role in social development. Socialism elevates the worker to this status and places labor at the foundation of society. Managerialism, too, is a coherent and complex account of society and a program for creating social order. Not surprisingly, it places the manager at the center of that order and assigns her the key role in producing it.[25]

Managerialism sees society as a collection of organizations. Those organizations are themselves made up of smaller organized groups down to the basic group units of society. Not only does each group require internal management to realize its goals; the entire society does as well. Any positive order reached spontaneously through the interactions of individuals and groups is either impossible or inefficient. Positive order must be intentionally produced through expert managerial technique. In fact, this is the way all organizational goods are realized. Thus, within diversity, pluralism is not simply a social fact of American society. It is its deepest truth. This makes pluralism an inescapable problem. Because of cultural differences across lines of race, ethnicity, sex, sexual orientation, and the like, diverse groups of different individuals have problems interacting in peaceful and productive ways. Bigotry and prejudice compound the negative effect. Yet pluralism offers a shining promise as well. If differences are reconciled, new pinnacles of cooperation, creativity, productivity, and social harmony can be achieved. Because this process is neither natural nor automatic, skilled managers are essential for the good society to be realized. In a managerial society all enjoy the fruits of greater efficiency, creativity, and productivity as society's opportunities for advancement are more effectively distributed. No human capital will go to waste. Bureaucracy becomes the pathway to progress.

Managerialism's ideal is a society in which every individual has an equal chance to develop, realize his merit, and be rewarded by society for it. This is a process of individual transformation and empowerment. Networking and mentoring programs thus are thought to build personal skills toward increasing personal value, self-affirmation, and self-realization. Diversity training is claimed to be a transformative educational experience that both explores the self and creates cultural competencies. Even white men can gain marketable interpersonal skills and realize multicultural character ideals through diversity.

Symbolic Power

Normalization began in earnest at the very same time diversity was securing its position as the country's dominant public ideology. One can even pin down 1993 as the cultural Rubicon. Diversity peaked as a topic in the professional management literature the same year that media coverage of homosexuality experienced "an explosion."[26] This was no coincidence. Diversity and normalization share a deep symbolic and ideological affinity.

Today the rainbow is the ubiquitous symbol of the gay rights movement. This was not always the case, however. Throughout the 1970s and 1980s the pink triangle stood as the preferred symbol of the LGBT community, a marker originally affixed to gay men in the Nazi concentration camps.[27] Like the pink triangle, the rainbow, too, long predates the gay rights movement. Its traditional association is with multiracialism and cosmopolitanism. In the years before the First World War, J. W. van Kirk, an American Methodist minister and advocate of the gospel of "Worldism," incorporated a rainbow into his flag for a future world federation. Van Kirk explicitly chose the rainbow to represent the diversity of mankind's "nations, races, languages, and sects."[28] He popularized his flag on speaking tours and through a self-published pamphlet titled "The Rainbow: A World Flag for Universal Peace." His efforts bore fruit in 1913 when the Universal Peace Congress meeting in The Hague adopted the symbol as the official "world peace flag." Prior to World War II the rainbow was so associated with the cause of multiracialism and cosmopolitanism that the popular 1929 speculative fiction novel *The Red Napoleon* depicted an invasion of the United States by an international Soviet-led army marching under a rainbow "banner of race equality" to establish global socialist unity through interracialism.[29] The rainbow remained popular with the international peace movement after World War II and particularly so in Europe, where it became a favored symbol in nuclear disarmament demonstrations. In the United States, however, its association remained primarily with multiracialism. In the mid-1980s Jesse Jackson formed the National Rainbow Coalition as a multiracial civil rights and social justice organization to continue the work of his failed 1984 presidential campaign. Around the same time the clothing retailer Benetton Group began its famous "United Colors of Benetton" line and associated advertising campaign linking the brand to multiculturalism and multiracialism.

All this symbolic meaning was intentionally transferred to the gay rights movement. San Francisco artist, flag-maker, and activist Gilbert Baker designed and sewed the first LGBT rainbow flag in 1978. Symbolism was first and foremost in his mind. Baker wanted to create a flag for gays and lesbians, a symbol appropriate to "a people, a tribe." He wanted parallel horizontal stripes in imitation of the American national flag as well as of the World Peace Association's multiracial "brotherhood flag," then popular among his hippie friends. Baker settled on the colors of the rainbow in part because they were "beautiful," especially in comparison to the pink triangle's association with the Nazi death camps. Yet Baker also recognized the rainbow as a symbol of diversity. "The colors represented all of who we are as a diverse people," he said in a 1994 interview. Nearly twenty years after first creating his flag, Baker recalled that the "rainbow came to mind almost instantly as an obvious expression of diversity and acceptance."[30] The rainbow flag's big coming out party was the 1994 Gay Games in New York City, coinciding with the twenty-fifth anniversary of the Stonewall riots. To celebrate and commemorate the occasion, organizers and volunteers constructed and then paraded a mile-long rainbow flag through the city's streets. This proved another serendipitous event at the dam break in American popular opinion on homosexuality and the crystallization of diversity as an ideology. The gay rights movement quite literally wrapped itself in the flag of diversity and thus unified the two.

In this way homosexuality has come to symbolize diversity itself. The cultural logic seems to go like this: Unlike race and sex, sexual orientation is invisible to casual observation. As living "in the closet" is peculiarly attached to LGBT persons, so, too, is publicly declaring one's identity—the act of "coming out." In combination with reigning cultural beliefs in the biological innateness of sexual orientation, homosexuality has therefore become peculiarly attached to individual authenticity. Gay intellectuals and social movements have fostered this symbolic association. First an LGBT person must accept and embrace her "true self." Only then is she able to create social change for others.[31]

Individuality and its associated characteristics—originality, uniqueness, creativity, authenticity—also lie at the heart of diversity. As an ideology, diversity tells us the world is defined by differences that go well beyond the affirmative action categories of race and sex. Thus Harvard's interest in the 1970s—which has since become standard in elite American college admissions offices—in both the black boy and the white boy, rich and poor, Christian and Jew, Anglo and Hispanic, rural and urban, West Coast and East Coast, jock and nerd, scientist and musician. While everyone is called upon by diversity to represent the culture of their groups, the multiplicity of groups and the crosscutting group identities within each individual are the bases of individuality and creative self-realization.

Homosexuality aptly symbolizes this heart of diversity: urban, edgy, hip, fashionable, successful, and, above all, cosmopolitan. Advertisers feature LGBT persons because "they hope to construct an association between image products and gay people to suggest a particular kind of well-being for gay consumers and, by association, for the heterosexual majority who want to cash in on gay cachet."[32] Homosexuality is a prestige category not only in advertising and entertainment but in all of society.[33] Race may remain the "modal category" of diversity practices and thought,[34] but homosexuality represents its ideal.

Here are just seven examples from the 2010s, each from a Forbes Global 2000 corporation. Frito-Lay introduced rainbow-colored Doritos chips in partnership with the gay pride education project It Gets Better. Frito-Lay's corporate marketing director endorsed the new design with the observation, "Time and again, our consumers have shown us, there really is nothing bolder than being true to yourself and living life to the fullest."[35] The Gap featured a young male couple in a print ad campaign promoting its T-shirts. The photo appears with the words "Be One" and "Be Your Own T." The Gap subsidiary Banana Republic included a male couple in its "True Outfitters" print ad campaign to express "authenticity and cultural awareness."[36] Target used a same-sex couple and the phrase "Be Yourself, Together" in promoting its wedding gift registry.[37] Tylenol placed a lesbian couple at the head of the family dinner table in a reproduction of Norman Rockwell's famous "Freedom from Want" painting with the phrase "Family is what you make it out to be."[38] Ray-Ban, a brand of the Italian firm Luxottica Group, used a 1942 photo of a smartly dressed gay male couple (neither wearing sunglasses) walking down a Manhattan street holding hands under its longtime advertising slogan "Never Hide." This was thought to fit well the campaign's theme of "Having the courage to express your true self, your thoughts and your personality genuinely, to stay faithful to the values of authenticity and uniqueness."[39] Burger King launched its new "Be Your Way" slogan to create an image of the company "centered around self-expression" and its belief that people "can and should live how they want anytime." It was an obvious next step to introduce a gay pride Whopper at one of its San Francisco restaurants and post a video about it to YouTube. According to the company's president of global brand management, "it shows how we, as a brand, believe in self-expression."[40]

Even sweetened breakfast cereals seek cultural cachet through a symbolic attachment to homosexuality. In June 2013 Fortune 500 firm General Mills used the rainbow marshmallows of its well-known Lucky Charms cereal as the centerpiece of an LGBT-themed advertising campaign directed at the cereal's "diverse younger adult audience." Consumers were encouraged to post photos of themselves to the corporation's Tumblr site together with an explanation of why they are "#LuckyToBe." Why did General Mills executives think homosexuality was an attractive theme for selling breakfast cereal? Because it symbolizes the intangible inner essence of the ad campaign and of millennial consumers. Lucky Charms' young adult consumers are a "diverse, creative, artful and self-expressive group," and social media sites like Tumblr offer them an "open, dynamic platform for self-expression."[41] The following year a brand marketing director insisted that, through #LuckyToBe, "we are celebrating everyone who is proud to live life on their own terms and love every second of it."[42] In 2015 the campaign produced an accompanying video in which both LGBT and heterosexual young adults finished the "lucky to be . . ." prompt. The first three adjectives presented were "creative," "original," and "free."[43]

Understanding homosexuality as a powerful symbolic brew of authenticity and prestige helps makes sense of the peculiar explosion of support for same-sex marriage across social media on the day the *Obergefell* decision was handed down. Within the first hour after the Supreme Court announcement, Facebook counted nearly four million postings mentioning same-sex marriage. Within four hours of the decision, Twitter counted over six million tweets on the subject, and more than ten million by 9:00 pm EDT. While several hashtags were popular in the early hours, including #MarriageEquality, #EqualityForAll, and #Pride, the heavyweight champion proved to be #LoveWins. At 12:30 pm the tag was appearing on 21,000 tweets per minute, and within 24 hours #LoveWins became the most used hashtag in history, appearing on 6.2 million tweets. Notably #LoveWins was the hashtag President Obama himself chose in a tweet from his personal account just ten minutes after the decision was announced. That night the president's staff lit the White House in rainbow colors, livestreamed the visuals over the internet, and invited the world via Twitter and Facebook to watch. The hashtag? #LoveWins, of course.[44]

The country's largest corporations were not to be left out. Thirty-four of the Fortune 100 firms tweeted support on the day of the *Obergefell* decision, twenty-three under #LoveWins. A pattern of support seemed to exist. Manufacturing firms (in aerospace and defense, construction and farm machinery, food production, motor vehicles, petroleum refining, pipelines) ignored the celebration while most "new economy" corporations (in commercial banking, computer software and hardware, internet services) stormed social media to endorse love. It is probably no coincidence that firms selling retail goods and services to newlyweds (airlines, general merchandisers) as well as firms selling services often accessed through marital status (health care, life and health insurance) were also vocal supporters. While this may express a measure of self-interest, anyone content with that understanding will fail to appreciate the power of a symbol and the desire to be publicly attached to it.

Consider a counterfactual. Despite the popularity of the television drama *Big Love* (2006–2011) and the reality series *Sister Wives* (beginning in 2010), both showcasing fundamentalist Mormons, the diversity of lifestyle portrayed therein has not led corporate and academic elites to embrace an association with polygamy. Neither have other possible diversity categories such as disability or body size or physical attractiveness gained the prominence of sexual orientation. Unlike the polygamous, the disabled, the obese, or the unattractive, gays and lesbians symbolize success—thus the deep affinity with diversity. An obvious and yet almost wholly overlooked fact is that diversity is all about elites. It is a project to reshape the professional and managerial class. Organizations engage in diversity programs to identify "promotables," develop their leadership skills, and cultivate the human capital necessary for elite status competition in a pluralistic world.[45] Outside a handful of nonelite government jobs such as firefighting, diversity bypasses the middle and working classes because, quite frankly, it has nothing to do with them. In her study of the pseudonymous "Starr Corporation," sociologist Ellen Berrey observed,

> Diversity management—the programming, the numbers, the culture—was for and about *exempt* employees [that is, exempt from the federal Fair Labor Standards Act, specifically its rules on minimum wages and overtime pay. Functionally the term refers to a firm's salaried, nonunionized workers in executive, administrative, professional, and outside sales roles]. This was taken for granted among diversity personnel in the company headquarters, so much so that it was almost never mentioned. When diversity personnel or other Starr executives and managers mentioned "diverse employees" at the company, they normally meant exempt women and people of color. They spoke and acted as if the exempt workforce *was* the workforce, or at least the workforce that mattered.[46]

No corporation or university seeks to develop a diverse secretary pool, a diverse kitchen staff, a diverse shipping department, or a diverse landscaping crew. These jobs are not opportunities for the cultivation of individuality, merit, and success. Neither are they opportunities for exciting expressions of cosmopolitanism. While Fortune 500 firms and ranked universities recruit nationally and even globally for students, managers, professors, advertising executives, and physicians, they draw strictly from the local job market when filling middle and working class positions outside the professional and managerial ranks. In this way diversity has a built-in cosmopolitan flavor that defines what forms of diversity are most and least welcome: "yes" to the urban, mobile, networked, new, universal; "no" to the rural or small town, static, self-contained, traditional, national (and especially ethnonational). Contrary to the laments of progressive sociologists, diversity has not made every form of difference equal. Those who best represent cosmopolitan values are the most "diverse" of all.

Diversity without Tears

The urban policy scholar Richard Florida has made a career of tracking and advocating the rise of what he has dubbed the "creative class."[47] This group of highly educated, highly skilled, socially intelligent postindustrial managers and professionals is, according to Florida, the key to local economic prosperity in the twenty-first century. Rather than work to attract economic capital, urban political leaders, planners, and developers should be attracting human capital. Florida's research and his lucrative associated consulting business aim to show them how to do it.

In Florida's view, timeworn appeals to mobile firms advertising low taxes, cheap land, good schools, and an advanced transportation infrastructure are policies belonging to a bygone age. In a postindustrial economy driven by high technology, cities must offer creatives what they truly want: an "integrated ecosystem or habitat" that revolves around their cultural interests and values.[48] Creatives love high population density. They love nightlife. They love art and music. They love technology. They love higher education. They especially love diversity. In fact, diversity cropped up so often in Florida's creative class focus groups that the concept is the most encompassing yet most compact descriptor of elite culture.[49]

Florida's definition of the creative class is nearly identical to the rough U.S. Census Bureau and Department of Labor definition of managers and professionals.[50] His research involves constructing different spatial measures of diversity at the metropolitan level and comparing them to the geographic location of the creative class.[51] By uncovering what kinds of diversity elites really like, Florida in turn recommends that city planners cultivate just such diversity so as to attract creatives to their cities.

One measure is the "Melting Pot Index," which Florida later renamed the "Foreign-Born Index." This is quite simply a measure of the immigrant population as a percentage of total residents in a particular metropolitan area. Florida finds a strong correlation between the relative economic size of the metropolitan high technology industry and the prevalence of immigrants, but "there is no significant statistical relationship between the Melting Pot Index and the Creative Class." The correlation value between the two was so low and unreliable that Florida more or less dropped the index from the second edition of his pioneering book.[52]

If creatives show little spatial overlap with immigrants, they seem to express actual aversion to certain forms of racial and ethnic diversity. Managers and professionals are whiter and much more Asian than the general American population, and they show no inclination to live out their diversity values among blacks and Hispanics. Florida finds "a troubling negative statistical correlation between concentrations of high-tech firms and the percentage of nonwhite population."[53] Subsequent research by others finds a very small (<0.1) positive but statistically insignificant correlation between the creative class and the black percentage of a metropolitan area's population, and an outright negative (but insignificant) correlation between a city's creative class and the Hispanic percentage of the population.[54]

We should be careful of any conclusions drawn from such correlations, however. While we know that metropolitan areas with relatively large numbers of immigrants, blacks, and Hispanics also have relatively small numbers of managers and professionals, we don't know from these indices that creatives wall themselves off from what limited racial and ethnic diversity does exist in "creative cities." In fact they may embrace it. To explore this possibility, Florida and his coresearchers forged a new "Integration Index" in the 2010s to measure the level of creative class spatial segregation at the census tract level within a metropolitan area. Florida found that creatives in fact segregate themselves (being elites, they are hardly the objects of segregation by others) most in large, dense cities with high levels of ethnic and racial diversity. Particularly high positive correlations exist between creative class segregation and a metropolitan region's prevalence of both immigrants (+0.59) and Hispanics (+0.45). There is also a large negative correlation between elite segregation and the percentage of whites (−0.51).[55] More immigrants, blacks, and Hispanics means a more spatially segregated creative class within the city. More whites, however, means less spatial isolation of the creative class. None of these data speak well of elites' supposed enthusiasm for diversity.

A rare study of Florida's thesis at the neighborhood level amplifies this conclusion. Two geographers at the University of Nebraska–Omaha tested Florida's diversity claims with census tract-level data for the Chicago metropolitan area. They found a small statistically significant *negative* relationship between creative class locations and racial diversity, and no correlation at all between racial diversity and the class's "super creative core." As a proxy for immigrants, they also measured linguistic diversity and found no spatial relationship with the creative class here, either.[56] While American elites may choose to live in racially and ethnically diverse metropolitan areas, evidence strongly suggests they like such diversity at arm's length—and perhaps even further away.

When diversity is defined as sexual orientation, however, everything changes. Of all his diversity indices, Florida's "Gay Index"—a measure of the relative prevalence of partnered same-sex households in a metropolitan area—shows the strongest positive results. He finds a large number of same-sex households to be the best diversity predictor of high-technology industry location and growth. It is also positively associated with the relative size of the creative class in a metropolitan area and negatively associated with the prevalence of the working class.[57] Other researchers have found similar spatial correlations between the creative class and the LGBT population, nearly twice as large as the correlation with immigrants and statistically significant as well.[58] In addition, the more spatially segregated the creative class is from other classes in a metropolitan area, the more same-sex households.[59] Yet unlike with immigrants, blacks, and Hispanics, spatial overlap between gays and elites exists at the neighborhood level. In the previously mentioned study of Chicago, researchers found a small but positive and statistically significant correlation at the census tract level between the presence of gay households and the prevalence of both the creative class in general and the super-creative core in particular.[60]

According to Florida, the creative class likes to live near LGBT individuals, couples, and neighborhoods because of the latter's production of amenities associated with gentrification and urban redevelopment.[61] Creatives are also attracted to gay men and lesbians as symbols of creativity, cosmopolitanism, authenticity, toleration, and the reward of merit. These, of course, are precisely the values of diversity. As normalization is the "last frontier of diversity in our society," Florida says that a large number of visible gays and lesbians is the best indicator of "low entry barriers to human capital" and its bearers, the creative class.[62] In fact, Florida believes that LGBT persons exercise such a strong gravitational pull on the creative class that he once referred to "the legalization of gay marriage [as] one of the great talent attraction packages of the last hundred years."[63]

If this is diversity, however, it is an amazingly self-referential version. Persons with higher levels of education are more likely to express an LGBT identity.[64] Partnered gay men and, particularly, partnered lesbians are overrepresented at the highest levels of the managerial and professional class fractions.[65] At the same time, America's higher managers and higher professionals are the least racially and ethnically diverse class fractions in the country (see table A.2B). Privileging normalization rather than racial integration as a social ideal allows elites to have their diversity cake and eat it, too.

In the brave new world of Aldous Huxley's twenty-sixth century London, World Controller Mustapha Mond praises the hallucinogenic drug soma as the ethical foundation of a truly happy society. Soma is "Christianity without tears." Patience, temperance, courage—all the virtues— require "no great effort" nor "years of hard moral training." Instead they can be simply practiced through the medicine bottle.[66] While normalization is no managerial drug, it has a similar ethic. Few sacrifices need be made to integrate those already so similar to members of the class they are joining. Diversity without tears only demands that elites follow the logic of the beliefs they already have.

7

CLASS CULTURE WARS

Zero-Sum Game

A generation ago Walmart was known as one of the most culturally conservative firms in America. Its origins in Bentonville, Arkansas and its
anchor in the small cities and military towns of the Upland South lent
the company a distinct ethos and image associated with populist values
and the cultural style of rural white Southerners. The firm cultivated this
image. It celebrated "Walmart Country" as a land of honesty, fair dealing,
hard work, thrift, service, neighborliness, family, and patriotism. In turn,
cultural conservatives adopted Walmart. The intertwining of the company
with its rising Evangelical customer base led Walmart to sanitize its merchandise. It became famous in the 1990s for censoring album covers and
lyrics as a condition for selling music in its stores, and for placing issues
of *Cosmopolitan* magazine under thick plastic covers. By 2000 it stood as
America's largest retailer of Christian books, videos, music, and general
merchandise. No wonder Christian Coalition head Ralph Reed said in
1995, "If you want to reach the Christian population on Sunday, you do
it from the church pulpit. If you want to reach them on Saturday, you do
it at Wal-Mart."[1]

It should be of little surprise then that Walmart traditionally scored
rather poorly on the Human Rights Campaign's annual measure of corporate policies regarding LGBT persons. In the first issue of the HRC's

Corporate Equality Index, released in 2002, Walmart was among a set of "particularly poor performers," scoring just 14 out of 100, the second lowest of the year. While scores improved from this inauspicious start, the company routinely ranked well below average throughout the 2000s and early 2010s. Individual Walmart executives even made prominent political stands against gay rights, including public support in 2008 for an Arkansas referendum question banning adoption and foster care by unmarried couples.

This is such a well-known and well-cultivated history that many casual observers were surprised—and many social conservatives shocked—when in 2015 Walmart CEO Doug McMillon announced the company's official opposition to the Arkansas Religious Freedom Restoration Act on the grounds of gay rights. The Christian entrepreneurial spirit of the company's earlier decades publicly gave way, in McMillon's own words, to the newer "spirit of inclusion" and "diversity" that truly "reflects the values we proudly uphold."[2] He called directly on Governor Asa Hutchinson to veto the bill.

Even though the Arkansas Senate passed the Arkansas Religious Freedom Restoration Act overwhelmingly in a 24–7 vote, followed by the Arkansas House in a similar 72–20 rout, the single vote from Bentonville proved more important than all the rest. Hutchinson was at first widely expected to sign the legislation. The morning after McMillon's statement, the governor instead called a press conference and announced his opposition. Unless the legislature scaled back the reach of the legislation, the governor promised a veto. That very evening the state Senate recalled its own bill and passed a new version amenable to Hutchinson. The state House followed in kind the next day. As there was no further public word from Walmart, the governor signed the amended bill into law.

With that, Arkansas became the twenty-first state to pass a religious freedom restoration act (RFRA). Such laws were uncontroversial, bipartisan, and roundly popular when they originated in the 1990s. Their explicit purpose was to overturn the Supreme Court's 1990 ruling in the case *Employment Division v. Smith*, which dramatically diminished the scope for the free exercise of religion under the First Amendment. Writing for the majority, Justice Antonin Scalia argued that "the right of free exercise does not relieve an individual of the obligation to comply with a valid and neutral law of general applicability." Criticism flooded in from all corners. The ACLU dwelled with the Christian Legal Society, and the National Association of Evangelicals lay down with the American Humanist Association.

The legislative response was the federal Religious Freedom Restoration Act of 1993, which markedly raised the bar on the government's legal ability to burden religious liberty. The bill was sponsored by two of the most liberal members of the Congress at the time, Senator Ted Kennedy of Massachusetts and Representative (later Senator) Charles Schumer of New York. It passed the Senate 97–3 and the House by a unanimous voice vote. President Bill Clinton happily signed the bill as an expression of the country's "shared desire here to protect perhaps the most precious of all American liberties—religious freedom. . . . Let us never believe that the freedom of religion imposes on any of us some responsibility to run from our convictions—let us instead respect one another's faith." After the Supreme Court ruled in 1997 that the federal RFRA did not bind state governments, a wave of state-level RFRAs followed. They came from all corners of the geographic and political map. Not only did most southern states pass RFRAs in the next decade, so did Pennsylvania in the northeast and Idaho in the west, not to mention Connecticut and Rhode Island prior to 1997. RFRAs also enjoyed overwhelming bipartisan support even in states under the control of liberal Democrats such as Illinois and New Mexico. This is not to say that religious freedom laws advanced unopposed everywhere. Some attempts to pass state-level RFRAs failed. Prison guard unions warned of prisoners' ability to command resources and threaten safety. Preservationists objected to the destruction of historic buildings. Child welfare professionals worried about empowering vaccine skeptics. Feminists opposed Christian employers who would enforce patriarchal policies on their employees. Many governors opposed opening any door on exceptions to generally applicable laws. By the early 2010s, however, this hodgepodge of concerns receded before a single overriding opposition on the grounds of LGBT rights.

In the religious freedom debate, the laser focus on homosexuality occurred almost overnight. In May 2013 the Arizona state legislature passed an amendment to its long-standing state-level RFRA originally passed in 1999. It was motivated by a judicial ruling in neighboring New Mexico that found that a Christian photographer had no right to refuse hire for a same-sex commitment ceremony on the grounds of religious liberty. Despite New Mexico's own RFRA, the state court ruled that the law only limited the power of the state, not the power of private citizens in the market. The Republican-controlled Arizona House and Senate sought to avoid a similar outcome. No national outcry ensued. The *New York Times* failed to run a single story on the legislation. Although Republican

Governor Jan Brewer vetoed the bill, she did so as punishment for the legislature refusing to take action on her legislative agenda rather than for any perceived problems with the bill itself.

What a difference nine months and a national media spotlight can make.

Arizona Republicans reintroduced their religious liberty bill into the state legislature the following January. Two changes were made for the 2014 version. Consistent with the spirit of the 2013 bill and the letter of the Code of Laws of the United States, the definition of a "person" entitled to religious liberty in the state was clarified to include all businesses regardless of legal form.[3] At the same time, a clearer statement of the standard for demonstrating an infringement of religious liberty was introduced. Otherwise the two bills were identical. Their political reception, however, was not. While national LGBT rights groups ignored the 2013 bill, they strongly attacked the 2014 version and marshaled a powerful business alliance behind them. The Human Rights Campaign was the first major national organization to speak out. The day after the bill was passed, it issued a statement demanding that the governor issue a veto. Significantly, the group's very first criticism was not that the bill was a violation of LGBT rights. Instead it led with the charge, "This bill is bad for business."[4] The theme quickly engulfed the state's Republican legislators. The day after the HRC's statement, a Saturday, the Arizona bill made the front page of the *New York Times*. Over the weekend the largest businesses in the state organized a coordinated campaign to pressure Governor Brewer to veto the measure. That Monday American Airlines, Apple, Marriott, Verizon, the Arizona Super Bowl Host Committee, the Arizona Chamber of Commerce, the Arizona Technology Council (of which AT&T is a member), and several other smaller business groups released separate letters or made phone calls to the governor herself criticizing the bill. They were joined by former Republican presidential candidate and sitting U.S. Senator from Arizona John McCain. Three Republican state senators even publicly recanted their votes that day. On Tuesday the *New York Times*' editorial board condemned the "noxious" bill as a "license to discriminate." In light of the planned 2015 Super Bowl in the state, the National Football League warned ominously that it was "following the issue." Former national Republican Party leaders Mitt Romney and Newt Gingrich both advised rejection. The writing on the wall couldn't have been clearer. Days before the required deadline, Brewer vetoed the bill.

The 2014 fight over Arizona's RFRA amendment suggested that religious freedom had become a destructive antiparticle to both business interests and LGBT rights. The 2015 fight over Indiana's RFRA crystallized the sentiment. Unlike most socially conservative states, Indiana did not pass a state-level RFRA in the years following the 1997 Supreme Court ruling and did not really consider one until 2014. That year Indiana social conservatives suffered two major defeats on same-sex marriage. A long-debated same-sex marriage referendum bill failed to pass the Republican-controlled state Senate in January, and, setting the whole question moot, a federal court overturned the state's existing opposite-sex-only marriage law in October. A RFRA was thus pitched as a secure place of retreat before the oncoming national forces of normalization.

With a unified Republican government and a strong Republican majority in both houses, the legislation was nearly guaranteed to become law unless public protest rose to stop it. The battle in Arizona four months earlier carried over to Indiana without a pause. Powerful corporations including Salesforce, Eli Lilly, Cummins, the Indiana Pacers, and the NCAA voiced opposition and urged Governor Mike Pence to veto the bill. Local businesses represented by the Indiana and Indianapolis Chambers of Commerce joined their protest. The Republican mayor of Indianapolis and the Obama administration added their voices to the chorus. The governors of Connecticut, Washington, Vermont, and New York as well as the mayors of Seattle, Portland, San Francisco, Oakland, and Washington, D.C. banned all publicly funded travel to Indiana. Washington Governor Jay Inslee was especially blunt, proclaiming, "We are open for business, and open to all people." The Human Rights Campaign called the bill a "super-RFRA" that enabled "religion to be wielded as a sword of discrimination."[5] The *New York Times* editorial board ramped up its rhetoric, titling its first of two editorials on Indiana's RFRA "Religion as a Cover for Bigotry." The ACLU even formally renounced its support for all RFRAs on the grounds of the laws becoming "a sword to discriminate against women, gay and transgender people."[6]

Thus the national battle over the public status of homosexuality morphed into a national battle over the public status of religion. At some level this development was inevitable. As far back as 2006, Georgetown Law School Professor (and later Barack Obama's Commissioner of the Equal Employment Opportunity Commission) Chai Feldblum observed that religious liberty and LGBT rights were trapped in a "zero-sum game." Any pretense to mutually beneficial compromise between the two was impossible, and state neutrality between them a charade. As long as religious conservatives hold same-sex sexual behavior to be morally suspect and LGBT persons and their allies hold it to be natural and moral, every action and inaction of the state is a choice to recognize one side against the other.[7] The history of RFRAs and Supreme Court decisions since then have been so many battles in this larger and inescapable cultural and legal clash.

The changing religious landscape of American society has intensified this conflict. The collapse of mainline Protestantism reduces institutional support for religious claims. The rapid rise of the "nones"—not atheists or agnostics, but rather those who claim no religious affiliations or views at all—since the early 1990s makes religious rights seem particular rather than universal. This is especially so among young adults, more than one-third of whom now claim no religious affiliation.[8] The concentration of "anti-fundamentalist" voters in the Democratic Party adds partisan conflict to the mix.[9]

Four days after Governor Pence signed the legislation and just one day after he appeared on the Sunday morning talk shows to defend it with the words, "I stand by this law," nine CEOs from Indiana's most prominent employers sent a hand-delivered one-page letter to the governor and the leaders of the state House and Senate demanding "new legislation" that would prevent anyone from filing a religious liberty claim in cases of "sexual orientation or gender identity"—precisely the category that motivated the RFRA in the first place. The very next day Pence called for the state legislature to "clarify" the new law. Within two days—one week exactly after Pence signed the original Indiana RFRA—he put his name to what become widely known as the RFRA's "fix." Through it Indiana explicitly banned religious freedom as a permitted legal defense—never mind whether the defense might or might not succeed—to anyone (outside narrowly construed religious organizations) refusing goods or services on the basis of a customer's sexual orientation or gender identity. A reasonable conclusion is that this "clarification" constituted nothing less than "a wholesale repeal of the Indiana Religious Freedom Restoration Act."[10] Moreover, through the whole battle the status of religious freedom itself suffered a major blow in elite opinion. Consider that the phrase "so-called religious freedom" appeared in American newspapers more times in 2015 than in the previous twenty-two years since the passage of the federal RFRA combined.[11] For the first time since the founding of the republic, the entire subject of religious freedom had shifted from the category "taken for granted" to that of "up for grabs."[12]

Class(ification) Struggle

From the very beginnings of the culture wars, the number one critique of them has been that they are a distraction, manufactured for the purpose of division, even "bogus" and "fake." From this perspective, the proper focus of politics is material: employment, income, taxes, the distribution of wealth, the use of police and military force. Any turn to the symbolic is a betrayal of "reality."[13]

A basic premise of cultural sociology is that human beings do not simply perceive or misperceive social "reality." They construct it in the very process of perceiving it. Tremendous power exists in symbolic acts, in the words of Pierre Bourdieu, in "all the forms of benediction or malediction, eulogy, praise, congratulations, compliments, or insults, reproaches, criticisms, accusations, slanders, etc. It is no accident that the verb *kategoresthai*, which gives us our 'categories' and 'categoremes,' means to accuse publicly."[14] Symbolic acts differentiate and define. They create groups and position them on the field of society.

Yet Bourdieu goes even further. He argues that "the class struggle" is "the classification struggle." While material interests are clearly important and should not be minimized, classification is for "individuals and groups . . . their whole social being, everything which defines their own idea of themselves, the primordial, tacit contract whereby they define 'us' as opposed to 'them.'"[15] Distinctions between groups arise naturally in society all the time without any explicit intent to distinguish. Yet in perceiving differences, a spontaneous and meaningless distinction can through symbolic acts become a "sign of distinction (in all senses of the phrase)."[16]

In the nineteenth and early twentieth centuries, the consumption of alcohol stood as a prominent sign of distinction in American society. One didn't simply have a personal view on temperance. One was a "Wet" or a "Dry," identities that encompassed far more than just an attitude toward drinking. For nearly a century abstinence was a marker of superior status in America, membership in the native white Protestant preindustrial middle class and commitment to its values. From the Second Great Awakening around the turn of the nineteenth century down to the Civil War, conservative Protestants dominated the country's institutions of higher education, science, law, and publishing, not to mention the state. Their morality was taught in the public schools. Their churches were central institutions of socialization. Their clergy played prominent roles in the moral life of the country, and nearly all cultural and intellectual debate took place within the contours of conservative Protestant sensibilities. All the great social movements of the time were theirs, including the wave of foreign missions that spread their way of life around the world. Beginning in the 1870s, however, the influence of this Protestant establishment began to wane. A new secular university model, supported by the rising titans of industrial capitalism, emerged and focused on research rather than forming character. New professions such as psychiatry and social work rose wholly separate from, and usually rival to, churches and their ministers. Conservative Protestants morphed into "fundamentalists." The famous Scopes trial of 1925 over the teaching of evolution in the public schools was their ultimate Pyrrhic victory. By the Great Depression, conservative Protestants had completed a "great reversal" from the halls of power. Among elites, conservative Protestant culture and institutions had ceased to exercise any meaningful authority. The repeal of Prohibition in 1933 was the final ignoble symbol of their rout.[17]

Liberal Protestants (supported by Jews and secular intellectuals) became the core of a new elite. From the 1930s to the 1970s the "main line" of American Protestantism supplied the country with its leading hospitals, social service organizations, civic groups, national youth organizations, architectural touchstones, and political elites. Their institutions commanded tremendous prestige.[18] In 1930 John D. Rockefeller Jr. built Riverside Church in Upper Manhattan for the prominent antifundamentalist Baptist minister Harry Emerson Fosdick so he could lead a self-consciously interdenominational congregation with a modernist theology. Rockefeller placed it directly next to Union Theological Seminary, the country's first independent seminary and a leader of Protestant ecumenism and the social gospel movement. Rockefeller's money also enabled the National Council of Churches, an ecumenical Christian organization born from the social gospel movement, to begin construction on its famous Interchurch Center across the street. In 1958 President Dwight Eisenhower himself laid the building's cornerstone in a ceremony attended by the president of the United Nations General Assembly. Executive staff of all the mainline Protestant denominations took up residence in what was quickly billed as "the Protestant Vatican" or, thanks to its high modernist style, the "God box." By the early 1960s over 40% of all Americans were members of a mainline denomination.[19]

In this era the Catholic Church stood as liberals' primary antagonist. Whether in religion, language, ethnicity, region, political party, or social class, the liberal Protestant elite differed greatly from what looked like not simply the new immigrant masses but a rival power structure. Contraception turned into a powerful sign of distinction. Small planned families had long been a hallmark of mainline Protestant life. The Episcopal Church first endorsed birth control in 1930, followed quickly by the Federal Council of Churches (predecessor to the National Council of Churches) in 1931. After World War II, all American elites were rallying behind contraception as both a liberal cause for freedom at home and a technological fix for rapid population growth abroad. Association with contraception, sterilization, and eventually abortion became the height of respectability. Former presidents Dwight Eisenhower and Harry Truman cochaired a Planned Parenthood fundraising committee. America's only Catholic president, John Kennedy, endorsed family planning as a component of U.S. development assistance. In the early 1970s every mainline Protestant church began to adopt a prochoice position on abortion. The *New York Times* plausibly identified the Supreme Court's 1973 ruling in *Roe v. Wade* as a "final and reasonable resolution of a debate that has divided America too long."[20]

Yet already the country's liberal Protestant elite was becoming exhausted. Urban riots, stagflation, ecological fears, and new revolts against American power abroad all undermined their authority. Conservative Protestants returned from their long, self-imposed exile in the guise of "Evangelicals" and began to (re)occupy some positions of influence in government, science, and media.[21] Elite prep school and university admissions quotas on Jews and Catholics fell away. The expected rapprochement with a liberalized Catholicism stopped in its tracks with the election of Karol Wojtyła as Pope John Paul II in 1978. The class distinction of contraception also disappeared. At home the moral acceptability of birth control became nearly universalized. Abroad its hard edge suffered from the developing world's backlash against population control.[22] The liberalization of abortion law reoriented social debate without producing a definitive prochoice class culture.

Yet liberal Protestantism did not suffer the same kind of defeat it inflicted upon conservative Protestantism half a century earlier. One might have expected as much considering its post-1960 demographic and institutional freefall. From the early 1960s to the mid-1990s the percentage of Americans in mainline denominations was nearly halved and

Catholics began to outnumber them. In 2010 the Supreme Court entered a seven-year period in which it had not a single Protestant member, mainline or otherwise. An ignoble milestone was reached in 2013 when the National Council of Churches abandoned the Interchurch Center and took up life as a full-time lobbying organization in Washington, D.C. Yet even as mainline institutions withered and faded, the ethos of liberal Protestantism conquered the larger culture. The twin ideals of the authority of individual experience and a commitment to pluralism, toleration, gender equality, and social criticism came to dominate American universities, entertainment, and media. By winning society's leading cultural institutions, liberal Protestantism made its own churches and congregations redundant.[23] Thus to see the contemporary American elite as the most secular or irreligious in two hundred years is to miss the social and cultural continuity between the liberal Protestants of the mid-twentieth century and the post-Protestants of the early twenty-first.[24]

The continuity between the former and the current elite helps explain the prominence of homosexuality in today's class(ification) struggle. Post-Protestants have the same cultural enemies—Evangelicals and (conservative) Catholics—as did liberal Protestants in their heyday. By the 1990s, contraception's cultural charge had all but run out, and the country even became somewhat more conservative on abortion after that point. The time was ripe for a new elite to cultivate a new sign of distinction.

The Opposite of Gay Is Fundamentalist

In the 1960s many Western countries entered into what demographers call the "second demographic transition." During the 1940s and 1950s, North Americans and Western Europeans stormed into early marriage, high fertility, low rates of divorce and cohabitation, and what has come to be called "family values." In the mid-1960s, however, the tide began to go out on the "traditional" family and the society organized around it. Quite suddenly, in fact, divorce rates skyrocketed, marriage was delayed, extramarital childbearing became normal, and fertility rates collapsed.[25] Not surprisingly, a values shift was part and parcel of these behavioral changes. Individual autonomy, self-expression, aesthetics, and other "postmaterial" values displaced older commitments to patriotism, religious authority, and social order. Secularization and the Sexual Revolution progressed hand in hand.[26] There is no inherent or necessary reason why this had to be so. After all, liberal Protestants and liberal Jews have accepted or even embraced most aspects of the Sexual Revolution. Officially atheist communist states, on the other hand, have ruthlessly repressed homosexuality. Yet that is the route they have taken in Western countries and particularly in the United States.

The role the Sexual Revolution plays as the Other to conservative values and identity is well studied and well known (recall the discussion of the "authoritarian personality" in chapter 4). The importance of religion and religious authority as the Other of the Left should not be overlooked. Conservative Christians emerged in 1992 as a key "negative political referent" for a large number of Americans and continued to play this role afterward. Many Americans dislike what they call "fundamentalists" on the grounds of that group's supposed intolerance, subjugation of women, low intelligence, homophobia, irrationality, and political threat to liberal values. Such "antifundamentalist voters" tend to be much more educated, rich, white, urban, politically attentive (e.g., they are regular news consumers, possessing correct factual knowledge of candidate positions), and secular than average—a profile highly like that of the professional and managerial class—and they concentrate their votes on Democrats.[27] They have also become a significant percentage of the population. In 2012 nearly one-third of all voters harbored "relative animosity" toward Christian fundamentalists.[28]

Does a positive political referent exist on the Left to stand as the symbolic opposite of conservative Christians? Analysis of surveys from the American National Election Studies' (ANES) "feeling thermometer" reveals its existence (a full discussion of the methodology appears in appendix C). Comparing recent ANES respondents' thermometer readings for thirteen common racial, religious, and cultural groups, one finds that in 2008 the strongest correlation between any two groups was the negative one between views of Christian fundamentalists and views of gay men and lesbians (–0.42). This means that the strongest combination of sentiments surveyed is "warm" feelings toward one and "cool" feelings toward the other. In 2012 the correlation remained strong (–0.37) although weaker relative to three of the other seventy-eight pairs as well as to its 2008 value. That being said, the strongest correlation by a wide margin for feelings toward gay men and lesbians remained feelings toward Christian fundamentalists. It seems unlikely that this strong negative relationship is due to Evangelicals' unusually hostile attitudes toward gays and lesbians. In a 2007 study of the American population, a similar percentage of the groups "Muslim" and "Evangelical" held negative views of homosexuality.[29] Yet the correlation in 2008 between feelings toward gays and lesbians and feelings toward Muslims was for all practical purposes zero. In 2012 it was small and actually positive. While warm feelings toward gays and lesbians were combined with cool feelings toward Christian fundamentalists, the public pressed similarly conservative Muslims into a dramatically different symbolic role.[30]

Standing as the symbolic opposite of gay men and lesbians today is an unenviable position. The stock of LGBT persons is rising dramatically while that of conservative Christians is falling. We can see this clearly in the ANES feeling thermometers. In 2012 the mean feeling thermometer reading for gays and lesbians surpassed that for fundamentalists for the first time. In both 2008 and 2012 views toward fundamentalists were the most polarized of any of the thirteen groups analyzed here, and the intensity of dislike for fundamentalists was surpassed only by animosity toward atheists. In fact, those who disliked Muslims or gays and lesbians the most—groups that are said to suffer tremendous stigma in the United States—disliked them less than people harboring animosity toward conservative Christians disliked that group.[31]

Fundamentalists' falling stock has implications going well beyond the most conservative expressions of Christianity. In both 2008 and 2012, attitudes toward Christian fundamentalists were highly correlated with attitudes toward Christians in general.[32] In a cultural context in which Americans strongly link their attitudes toward Christians to their attitudes toward Christian fundamentalists, Christians more generally face a potentially precarious future.

Culture Is the Form of Fighting before the Firing Actually Begins

The stakes in any cultural clash are high.[33] The class or class fraction that succeeds in defining its own culture and universalizing it gets to sit at the top of the social hierarchy. Its class ethos becomes society's ethic.[34] This is not simply the measure of what is right versus what is wrong, but also of what is elevated versus what is base, what is natural versus what is abnormal, what is unquestioned versus what is questioned, even what is rational versus what is irrational or even insane. The fight is over nothing less than who shall have the power to define reality.[35] All the combatants know as much. No wonder they fight so hard. To lose is not just to be consigned to the wrong side of history. It is to have the weight of the dominant culture pressed firmly against you, peeling away members and undermining the ability and willingness of the remainder to resist.

It is to be denied access to elite institutions and networks, and to all the material and social benefits they confer. It is even to have the force of law and thus ultimately the power of the state used against you.

Any culture war is fought both inside and outside. On the outside, a class or class fraction fights its rivals for power, seeking to elevate its own way of life and diminish that of others. However, the struggle also goes on inside a class (fraction). In fact the struggle on the inside is usually the more intense. It determines class distinctions and the class ethos, which is the act of defining the class (fraction) itself. It is the process of classification at the very heart of social life.

Higher professionals have always been the leading proponents of normalization in American society. In turn, their fields—especially those with the greatest interest in homosexuality—are especially important sites of class(ification) struggle. The mental health professions—psychiatry, psychology, counseling, social work—are at the top of the list. Psychiatrists and psychologists led the cultural fight for normalization within the elite and are, not surprisingly, the least religious of all professionals. A 2007 survey found that psychiatrists are markedly less religious than other physicians. Religious physicians seem to know this. The same study found that the more religious a physician, the less likely she is to refer a patient to a psychiatrist.[36] A 2006 survey found psychology professors to be the least religious of all American higher education faculty, with 61% holding atheist or agnostic views compared to 23% of all professors and just 4% of the general public.[37] A 2016 study found that only 6% of social workers define their political ideology as "conservative" and 45% "almost never" attend religious services.[38] Even in conservative Oklahoma, social workers strongly support same-sex marriage on par with their support for no-fault divorce, abortion rights, and minors' open access to birth control.[39]

Normalization has become an effective point of prosecuting the class(ification) struggle within these fields. As of mid-2017 nine states, the District of Columbia, and over a dozen cities have banned licensed mental health professionals from practicing so-called "conversion therapy" on minors.[40] Not a single government at any level had done so five years earlier. Each state law invokes the psychological harm of such therapies and defines their practice as unprofessional conduct. Practitioners are subject to discipline and penalties by government licensure boards. For good measure, Illinois and New Jersey even open up violators to prosecution under laws against consumer fraud and deceptive business practices—a treatment no other psychiatric, psychological, or counseling service receives. Each state also goes well beyond science to condemn not only conversion therapists but all those who object to normalization. The legislatures of California, New Jersey, Illinois, and Vermont use identical language in proclaiming that "being lesbian, gay, or bisexual" is "not a disease, disorder, illness, deficiency, or shortcoming." The Vermont legislature goes even further, adding "transgender" to the list. Vermont and Rhode Island declare all sexual orientations to be "part of the natural spectrum of human identity." While banning practices to change sexual orientation, these states explicitly endorse therapies that affirm an LGB orientation or identity. Using identical language, all ten (including D.C.) commend "acceptance, support, and understanding" as well as therapies that facilitate "coping, social support, and identity exploration and development."[41]

Social work counseling nips most such problems in the bud by dissuading or preventing opponents of normalization from entering the profession in the first place. The sole American social work accreditation body, the Council on Social Work Education (CSWE), defines "advanc[ing] human rights and social, economic, and environmental justice" as a "core competency" of the professional social worker. Any program hoping to be accredited must "provide a learning environment that models affirmation and respect for diversity and difference" and "affirm[s] and support[s] persons with diverse identities."[42] Social work faculty have carried out this charge in several high-profile clashes with Evangelical students.

In 2009 two social work graduate students at public universities, one in Michigan and the other in Georgia, were expelled from their programs for violating the American Counseling Association Code of Ethics. Their specific violations involved a refusal to counsel a client regarding a same-sex sexual relationship and a refusal to make up "professional deficiencies" incurred by negative classroom comments regarding homosexuality. Both students brought legal suits against their universities. While one won her case and the other lost, neither returned to their programs.[43] Missouri State University has been caught up in not one but two lawsuits brought by counseling students resisting professional ethics standards. In 2005 a professor in the university's School of Social Work leveled a formal grievance against an undergraduate student who refused to write a letter to the state legislature in support of LGBT foster parenting. The program called the student before a formal ethics hearing and threatened to withhold her degree for violations of "professional behavior." In 2014 the university's Counseling Graduate Program removed a student from an internship with a Christian counseling organization and eventually from the counseling program itself over the student's refusal to counsel same-sex couples.[44]

These are not isolated cases. Research suggests that social work programs exercise "systemic, profession-wide discrimination" against conservative Christian.[45] If there is inherent and perhaps irreconcilable tension between "social work values" and "Fundamentalist values,"[46] such cases are to be expected. In the words of the former chair of the American Psychological Association's Policy and Planning Board reflecting directly on two of these cases,

> Professions and the institutions that educate and train professionals cannot afford to fashion their ethics and curriculum around the individual personal beliefs of professionals or students in the profession. Students cannot be allowed to "opt out" of what the profession of psychology deems essential training, just as professionals cannot (and are not) allowed to selectively follow the standards in ethical codes—not when performing as a licensed professional. Not everyone is well-suited to the demands of multiculturally informed, ethical practice. We return to the vegetarian working at a sandwich shop. If he or she cannot make roast beef sandwiches for the customers of the shop, he or she should probably find a different line of work.[47]

The legal profession may not be far behind in the class(ification) struggle. Before the Supreme Court struck down the country's many defense of marriage acts in 2015, DOMA supporters were having increasing difficulty finding counsel willing to defend them. In 2009 California's attorney general and its governor both refused to defend the state's opposite-sex-only marriage law from legal challenge. In 2013 the U.S. Supreme Court ruled in *Hollingsworth* that, without a defense of state law marshaled by a state agency, no legal defense of any kind would be allowed. In 2011 the Obama Justice Department declared the federal DOMA unconstitutional and thereafter refused to defend it in court. With the blessing of former U.S. Attorney General Eric Holder, at least eight other state attorneys general likewise refused to defend their state DOMAs as the laws came under federal scrutiny in the early 2010s.[48] In 2014 the news organization Reuters reviewed over one hundred court filings on the subject of same-sex marriage. It found thirty of the country's largest two hundred law firms were representing challengers to state DOMAs. Not one Am Law 200 firm was representing state DOMA supporters.[49]

Over ten years earlier Supreme Court Justice Antonin Scalia claimed the American legal profession was dominated by an "anti-anti-homosexual culture." The passage of time seems to have only validated the charge. Judicial refusal to conduct same-sex marriages is considered a violation of professional ethics in nearly all states. Judges in Washington, Oregon, Alabama, Ohio, and Wyoming have been subjected to disciplinary procedures. In 2016 the American Bar Association revamped its Model Rule of Professional Conduct to define "conduct that the lawyer knows or reasonably should know is harassment or discrimination on the basis of . . . sexual orientation [and] gender identity" as professional misconduct.[50] At least one prominent supporter thought the new rule a "largely symbolic gesture" geared toward "educating the next generation . . . about other values besides First Amendment expression."[51] In a sign of moral unity, not a single delegate to the ABA annual meeting spoke against the measure from the floor and the reform passed on a voice vote.

The university may be the most important internal site of class(ification) struggle. It is here, after all, that professionals are created in the first place. When only a single U.S. state recognized same-sex marriage and under 40% of the public believed same-sex sexual relations were morally acceptable, a survey of American professors found that 80% of them held pronormalization attitudes.[52] A book on American academics' beliefs and behaviors published around the same time observed that "[p]erhaps most offensive to the beliefs of the vast majority of professors is the attack by some Republicans on homosexuality and homosexual rights." Its survey revealed that even the small number of self-identified conservative academics largely supported gay rights.[53]

While all forms of conservatism are rare on American college campuses, social conservatism is the rarest of all.[54] As befits their class status, most liberal professors are rather moderate on matters of taxation and government spending. Their liberalism is highly concentrated on social issues. Thus economic conservatives and libertarians fare relatively well in the academy. Even in the very liberal social sciences they find a home in economics departments and are well represented there, reporting little to no discrimination and almost never practicing self-censorship. The situation is quite different for cultural conservatives.[55] A 1999 survey found that being a practicing Christian is more damaging to one's prospects at an elite research institution than being a Republican or a woman.[56] A 2007 survey found that Evangelicals and Mormons are the least liked religious groups among American university faculty by a wide margin.[57] A 2008 survey revealed that Christian fundamentalists, Evangelicals, and Mormons were the most likely of twenty-seven social groups to experience discrimination in academic hiring. Across nine different fields in the humanities, social sciences, and physical sciences, both transgender and communist applicants faced better job prospects than fundamentalists or Evangelicals.[58]

The defeat of social conservatives in law has proved as complete as their defeat inside the professions. After Arizona's governor vetoed her state's RFRA in 2014, *New York Times* house social conservative Ross Douthat recognized the dimensions of his side's loss. Normalization had won the war. All that was left now was to receive "the terms of our surrender."[59]

The veto of RFRA bills in Arizona in 2014 and Georgia in 2016, the de facto veto in Arkansas in 2015, and the de facto repeal in Indiana the same year, are all indicative for two reasons. First, state religious freedom bills are popular ways in which social conservatives have sought to negotiate their "terms of surrender." RFRA defeats show the power of elites in general and Corporate America in particular to dictate rather than negotiate those terms. Second, these RFRAs have gone down to defeat in states with quite moderate levels of elite concentration. We shouldn't expect and in fact never do see RFRAs in the elite heartland at all.[60] That RFRAs are being defeated in the South Atlantic, the Midwest, and the Mountain West, however, indicates the power of elites and the weakness of religious conservatives. Only in elite deserts such as Mississippi and Louisiana have state RFRAs passed with a negotiation of terms.

Yet even in the place furthest removed from the professional and managerial heartland, resistance to the elite ethos is unlikely to matter beyond the social and cultural fringes. Recall that in 2004 Mississippi voters approved a constitutional marriage amendment in an 86% to 14% landslide, the largest margin of victory for any marriage referendum in the country. Ten years later that 800,000 vote gap was negated by one vote of a federal judge in the state capital. After the Supreme Court's *Obergefell* ruling in 2015, the Mississippi state legislature responded with a new religious freedom law designed to insulate religious conservatives from some of the implications of *Obergefell*. Despite its passing with nearly two-thirds majority support in both houses and receiving the governor's signature, the same federal judge who overturned the state's marriage law in 2014 proceeded to suspend the state's 2016 RFRA. Despite living in the country's most conservative state, Mississippi Democrats now embrace normalization. House Democrats opposed the state's final RFRA bill 40–1, and Senate Democrats voted against it by a 17–2 margin. Mississippi's

Democratic attorney general refused to defend the law, forcing the Republican governor to hire private attorneys to carry on in federal court a legal fight the state is likely to lose.[61] What will Mississippi conservatives do then? Experience suggests they will resign themselves to normalization. Earlier in 2016 a federal judge struck down the state's ban on same-sex couple adoption, the last one remaining in the country. Within a week same-sex couples began receiving children from state adoption agencies to no resistance.

Neighboring Alabama is also instructive. In 2006 voters approved an opposite-sex-only marriage amendment to the state constitution by an enormous 62% margin of victory. It was the third largest of any state marriage referendum in the country and the very largest for an amendment that refused legal recognition to any marriage-like union between same-sex couples, including domestic partnerships and civil unions. When the Supreme Court handed down its *Obergefell* opinion nearly nine years later, the state's elected Supreme Court Chief Justice Roy Moore defiantly ordered all judges in the state to continue to enforce state law. Four months later he was temporarily suspended from his position pending six charges, including defiance of a clear federal court injunction. Four months after that the Alabama Court of the Judiciary effectively removed Moore from office through a unanimous vote for a permanent suspension until the end of his term. The response from religious conservatives in the state? "From the pews, crickets."[62]

CONCLUSION
The Revolution beyond Tolerance

In the legal clashes between supporters of LGBT rights and supporters of religious freedom, the legal scholar Douglas Laycock seeks compromise. In his coauthored amicus brief to the U.S. Supreme Court in the *Obergefell* case, Laycock called the struggle between these two groups and their principles a "mostly avoidable conflict." Each is pursuing a wholly unnecessary and unreasonable strategy of total victory. Instead each should learn the art of compromise. If they will not, the Court should impose compromise on them. This Laycock calls "the American solution to this conflict . . . to protect the liberty of both sides." Thus he urged the court in strong terms both to declare a constitutional right to same-sex marriage and provide legal room to religious dissenters to "refuse to recognize those marriages" through religious freedom legislation.[1]

As a good liberal, Laycock believes deeply in the possibility of reasoned debate and peaceful compromise. For religious conservatives this entails accepting their cultural-cum-constitutional defeat in exchange for broad minority rights of dissent. If they refuse this compromise, conservatives will fall into the role of hopeless counterrevolutionaries who put the First Amendment itself at risk. Laycock sees same-sex marriage within the context of the Sexual Revolution as a whole and the normalization of not only same-sex sexual behavior but also of nonmarital sex, extramarital sex, nonprocreative sex, and pornography. In his view the Sexual Revolution is not the least bit metaphorical. It is as much a revolution as were the American or French Revolutions in their own times, drawn out over decades with dramatic and lasting political, social, and cultural implications. Laycock observes that religious freedom is dramatically more restricted in France than it is in the United States, a fact he ascribes to the very different relationships that organized religion had with the great revolutions in each country. The Protestant churches of eighteenth-century British America largely supported the American Revolution and were rewarded with a political culture of robust religious liberty. The Catholic Church of France in the late eighteenth through the mid-twentieth centuries, however, largely opposed the French Revolution and "permanently turned France to a very narrow view of religious liberty." Laycock draws a strong parallel between French Catholic monarchists of the nineteenth century and American religious conservatives of the twenty-first. The lesson he hopes to teach here is clear: "If you stand in the way of a revolution and lose, there will be consequences."[2] He who has ears, let him hear.

Even though Laycock was writing his brief to the Supreme Court as recently as 2014, the time of principled compromise around a stable cultural balance now seems long past—assuming it ever existed at all. The ever-expanding nature of the Sexual Revolution prevents any lasting compromise from forming. Once a moment of stability is seemingly reached, the ground shifts and the battle is rejoined at a new revolutionary frontier. Since the 2013 *Windsor* decision, that frontier is transgenderism.[3] The normalization of transgenderism has swept the highest echelons of elite culture as thoroughly as did the normalization of homosexuality but in just a quarter of the time. If we can step back and appreciate how stunning was the movement of homosexuality from mental illness to normal sexual orientation in two generations and same-sex marriage from fringe idea to constitutional law in a single generation, the acceptance of gender identity as a category wholly divorced from biological sex in only five years or so is truly mind-boggling.

That transgenderism has conquered the mental health professions should be obvious. Both the American Psychological Association and the National Association of Social Workers issued resolutions in 2008 calling for full societal normalization of transgenderism. The American Psychiatric Association followed in 2012 with a similar resolution. It also made the important symbolic step of removing "gender identity disorder" from its list of mental illnesses the same year. As with homosexuality, the legal profession has been slower to accommodate. That being said, in 2016 the American Bar Association prohibited discrimination on the basis of gender identity in its Model Rule of Professional Conduct for the first time. Religious bodies dominated by elites have followed their embrace of homosexuality with an embrace of transgenderism. The United Church of Christ (2003) and the Union for Reform Judaism (2015) have been in the vanguard with the most sweeping and encompassing resolutions. The Episcopal Church formally approved the ordination of transgender persons in 2012, the Evangelical Lutheran Church in America ordained its first openly transgender pastor in 2015, and Conservative Judaism's Rabbinical Assembly passed a full gender identity normalization resolution in 2016.

The rapid ascent of transgender normalization to pure conventionality is nowhere so stark and so dramatic as in Corporate America. Never mind the number of Fortune 500 firms with formal gender identity nondiscrimination policies (up from 50% in 2012 to 82% in 2017) or transgender-inclusive health care policies (from 19% to 50%) or official gender transition guidelines (from 208 to 387 "major employers").[4] Overlook the policies of retailers like Target, Starbucks, and Barnes & Noble that allow bathroom access based on gender identity rather than biological sex. Instead, witness the trials and tribulations of the infamous 2016 North Carolina "bathroom bill" for the effective unanimity of big business behind transgender normalization.

In February 2016 the Charlotte City Council in a 7–4 vote passed an expanded nondiscrimination ordinance that added "sexual orientation, gender expression, [and] gender identity" to its list of protected classes. The section on public accommodations drew the most controversy, particularly the removal of a former clause permitting sex discrimination (i.e., sex segregation) in "restrooms, shower rooms, bathhouses and similar facilities" as well as in "dormitory lodging facilities." To be crystal clear on the implications of its new ordinance, the city council explained on its website that public accommodations "may not refuse to provide the full and equal enjoyment of its facilities based on a protected characteristic, such as gender identity and gender expression. Restrooms, locker rooms, and other changing facilities are covered by the ordinance."[5] Within a month the North Carolina state legislature passed and the governor signed House Bill 2, better known as the "North Carolina bathroom bill." HB2 directly targeted Charlotte's ordinance, overturning the city's grant to transgender persons of free access to sex-segregated facilities of their choice. It also banned all local nondiscrimination employment ordinances that sought to "supersede and preempt" state nondiscrimination law.

Many North Carolina Republicans believed the Charlotte City Council passed the nondiscrimination ordinance as an intentional act of provocation. The year 2016 was a gubernatorial election year. Republicans charged the state Democratic Party with seeking to make transgender normalization in North Carolina a national political issue. That way Democrats could draw out-of-state money into the governor's race and also scare off out-of-state capital investment.[6] If this was true, Republicans in the legislature and Governor Pat McCrory—a former mayor of Charlotte himself—took the bait. Within a week of HB2's passage, the Human Rights Campaign had organized over eighty top executives from major firms like Goldman Sachs, Bank of America, Apple, and United Airlines behind a letter urging the governor to work toward a repeal of the law. Within a month of HB2's passage, PayPal publicly cancelled its plans to open a new global operations center in the state. Over the summer and fall the state's movie and television industries dried up; the NBA pulled its 2017 all-star game out of Charlotte; the NCAA removed seven championship tournaments from the state, including the first and second rounds of 2017 "March Madness" basketball; and the real estate research firm CoStar Group announced it had chosen Virginia over North Carolina for its new research operations center. *Forbes* magazine estimated that the bathroom bill had cost the state economy over $600 million in lost investment and revenue in only seven months.[7] If any major firms supported HB2, they kept it to themselves.

The Obama administration and the Democratic Party rallied against North Carolina. The administration's policy of full transgender normalization was formalized in 2016 by both the Department of Education and the Department of Justice, and was enforced with threats to withhold federal education dollars from noncompliant schools. One-third of the country's Democratic governors limited or banned state employee travel to North Carolina, including state university athletes. The Justice Department sued North Carolina in federal court. Attorney General Loretta Lynch drew an explicit parallel between HB2 and Jim Crow laws of the segregation era. She told transgender persons directly that her office would defend and protect "the lives you were born to lead."[8] The head of the Justice Department's Civil Rights Division stated definitively, "Here are the facts. Transgender men are men . . . transgender women are women." She reassured "every transgender individual . . . you belong just as you are."[9]

McCrory faced State Attorney General Roy Cooper in the gubernatorial election. Earlier that summer Cooper had embraced the opportunity to run against HB2, refusing to defend the law in federal court. Although Donald Trump comfortably won the state's presidential ballot by nearly 175,000 votes, McCrory lost to Cooper by 10,000, becoming the state's first sitting governor in nearly 170 years to lose reelection. On balance it appears the capital strike against North Carolina was effective. Primarily to get out from under the boot of big business—what former Forbes 400 entrepreneur Tim Gill calls a "punish the wicked" strategy—in March 2017 the Republican-led state legislature agreed to repeal HB2.[10]

All the familiar players from the cultural clash over homosexuality reconstitute their roles in the sequel on transgenderism. Does this mean transgender normalization is simply a continuation of the story line on homosexuality? Is gender identity simply a logical extension of sexual orientation? In some ways, the answer is clearly "yes." Their social constructions have been very similar. Both sexual orientation and gender identity advanced in America thanks to essentialist arguments. The assertion of being "born this way" has carried a great deal of cultural and political freight. This has been aided by building atop the country's cultural core of radical individualism and the sacred self, nowhere better expressed than in Justice Anthony Kennedy's 1992 majority opinion in *Planned Parenthood v. Casey*: "These matters, involving the most intimate and personal choices a person may make in a lifetime, choices central to personal dignity and autonomy, are central to the liberty protected by the Fourteenth Amendment. At the heart of liberty is the right to define one's own existence, of meaning, of the universe, and of the mystery of human life."[11]

Yet this is only part of the story of the normalization of homosexuality. The 1970s liberationist approach flopped culturally. Normalization was won as much through conservative appeals to social conformity in institutions like the family and the military as through liberal appeals to individual freedom. Homosexuality was first accepted and later embraced because of its symbolic expression of elite values and lived experiences in marriage, parenthood, gender equality, family planning, education, financial success, urbanity, and cosmopolitanism, as well as authenticity. Homosexuality—or the form of homosexuality eventually accepted as normal—synchronized with elite values and the professional-managerial class lifestyle. It endorsed elite authority.

Transgenderism offers no similar balance. First, there is nothing in transgenderism that resonates with the lived experiences of American elites. Its cultural project is not oriented toward the "blue family" model of gender equality, late marriage, low fertility, "safe sex," high education, and successful professional or managerial employment. Transgender persons are not overrepresented among elites. Transgenderism's relationship to feminism is, as academics like to say, "problematic." Recall that elite women were always the leading supporters of LGB normalization, and in light of the connection between normalization and the blue family model, this makes perfect sense. What in transgenderism, however, resonates with feminism?[12] When biological males become students at Wellesley and Smith Colleges, the former Martin Rothblatt is lauded as the highest paid female CEO in America, the former Roderick Cox is nominated for an Emmy Award in the outstanding guest actress category, the transgender boy Mack Beggs wins the Texas state girls' wrestling championship, the biological male Andraya Yearwood wins the Connecticut state girls' 100- and 200-meter dash championships, and the former Bruce Jenner is a *Glamour* magazine woman of the year, the equality gains of women—particularly elite women—are transferred to (former or current) men.

Second, transgenderism only weakly symbolizes diversity. Transgender people do maintain a culturally privileged connection to authenticity, and cultural conflict over their status further empowers managers to manufacture organizational culture, productive cooperation, and social harmony. At the same time, transgenderism lacks the symbolic connection to well-being and meritorious success. Even the National Center for Transgender Equality emphasizes the exceptionally high levels of violence, poverty, unemployment, homelessness, psychological distress, suicide attempts, and HIV infection among transgender persons.[13]

Third, transgenderism is not simply another useful stick with which to beat religious conservatives. It is a radical challenge to all external forms of authority and thus to the social and cultural foundation of elite rule itself. Transgenderism is the most radical form of individualism yet produced by the Sexual Revolution. Gender identity is self-authenticating in a far more extreme fashion than sexual orientation has ever been. Social expectations of medical intervention and "sex change" operations no longer exist. Neither do demands that transgender persons enact traditional gender roles or even mimic conventional biology. It is, of course, perfectly commonplace now to hear of men with vaginas who bear and nurse children and of women with full beards.[14] The legal authority of doctors and parents crumbles as gender identity becomes self-defined.[15] How do psychiatrists maintain plausibility when they endorse the existence of anorexia nervosa as an "eating disorder" or treat a desire to have one's own spinal cord severed as "body integrity identity disorder" at the same time treating a belief that one is a woman trapped inside a man's body (or vice versa) as a "dysphoria" on the way to normalization? As the controversial psychiatrist Paul McHugh observes, "Disorders of consciousness, after all, represent psychiatry's domain; declaring them off-limits would eliminate the field."[16]

The rapid normalization of transgenderism among elites is a symptom of a larger crisis. Elites are failing to exercise authority. Meritocracy's promise is deference to the superior technical knowledge of elites in exchange for efficient and effective social outcomes. Increasing numbers of Americans see that project as a failure. The evidence is all around. Confidence in all institutions—whether the state, the professions, or big business—drags along near forty-year lows. Only the military, the police, and small business enjoy majority support.[17] Homeschooling, "spiritual but not religious" viewpoints, alternative medicine, non-GMO foods, climate change denialism, and the antivaccination movement are all popular manifestations of a deep public distrust in claims of elite knowledge. The 2016 U.S. presidential election was in part a backlash against elites who now rightly fear an assault on their cosmopolitan values and way of life.

When Douglas Laycock analogized the Sexual Revolution to the French Revolution in order to teach and to warn American religious conservatives, he did so with little appreciation for the ebb and flow of history. The French Revolution never ran smoothly. Its most radical phase during the 1790s, which included state-invented alternative religions like the Cult of Reason, the Cult of the Supreme Being, and Theophilanthropy, not only failed but ultimately consumed its own leaders. Republicanism itself was overthrown three separate times in the country's history. The legal status of Catholicism remained unsettled until the 1950s, nearly 175 years after the storming of the Bastille.

A contemporary observer of the French Revolution insisted that "men do not lead the Revolution; it is the Revolution that uses men."[18] American elites today would do well to heed this historical lesson. They are no longer the vanguard conducting the revolution. The revolution is conducting them. The Sexual Revolution is a continuous cascade of cultural reconfigurations of sex, gender, marriage, and family. Like the universe itself, the Sexual Revolution has so far proven ever expanding, creating ever greater distance between where we stand today and where we stood just yesterday. Where its frontier will be tomorrow is anyone's guess.

The 2016 election of Donald Trump as President of the United States is proof positive that none truly know where history is leading nor where its "right side" lies. Trump's victory first in the Republican Party presidential primaries and then in the general election, much like the success of the Brexit campaign in the United Kingdom earlier in the year, seems like an archetype of the ancient Greek myth of Hubris and Nemesis. Elites and experts of all stripes embraced the inevitable expansion of international trade and finance, mass migration, cosmopolitan sensibilities, high technology, human rights, and global governance. Throughout the last weeks of the 2016 campaign, Barack Obama even proposed voting for Hillary Clinton as an opportunity to "bend the arc of history" a little further in its predetermined direction.[19] Such reckless self-confidence was destroyed in a moment by the vengeance of deplorables supposedly resigned to the ash heap of history.

Perhaps the Brexit supporter and the Trump voter truly are deplorable. Perhaps both Britain's departure from the European Union and four years of Donald Trump in the White House will prove to be as disastrous as elites predict. Nemesis is not a constructive force. It avenges and punishes. Yet by chastening excessive pride, it also restores balance between mankind and the gods.

APPENDIX A

Theory

The theoretical foundation of this project is the work of the eminent French sociologist Pierre Bourdieu (1930–2002). Bourdieu and his work are well known in sociology but much less so in political science. While they enjoy a small but growing presence in international relations, Bourdieu remains very little known among scholars of American politics and American political sociology.[1] This is an unfortunate shortcoming for fields so influenced and enriched by the work of two of sociology's founding fathers, Karl Marx and Max Weber. Bourdieu takes elements from both. In particular he picks up Weber's distinction between class and status group to elaborate a theory of class based on the interplay of what he calls "material systems" and "symbolic systems." From Bourdieu's perspective, both material goods and cultural goods structure societies. Power is exercised through not only property and police but through art, science, and even language. Thus the distribution of both material and symbolic goods is central to any adequate understanding of society.

While Bourdieu's theoretical framework is vast, his understanding of social class can be usefully summarized as a system anchored by the concepts of "capital" and "habitus."[2] Capital is the foundation of analysis. Any person's accumulation of three different forms of capital defines her position in the class structure. The first is the familiar economic capital.

Bourdieu takes a basic insight from Marx by incorporating the owner-
ship of property and one's relationship to the processes of production
as centrally important to the study of any capitalist society. Cultural
capital is a second form and Bourdieu's most influential and innovative
concept. The term refers to all culturally valued goods understood as
sources of social power. It includes not only objects (e.g., books) but also
social practices (e.g., patterns of speech) and social institutions (e.g., the
university). Third is social capital, one's social networks that allow one
to gain access to important individuals, families, and institutions.[3] In
his own empirical analyses, Bourdieu privileges economic and cultural
capital and uses different endowments of these two forms to differentiate class positions from each other. Professionals and managers are
distinguished from laborers by the large volume of capital they hold and
the low level of capital that workers possess. Professionals and managers can also be differentiated from one another by the types of capital
each holds. Professionals—particularly writers and artists—tend to have
large endowments of cultural capital and markedly less economic capital,
whereas corporate managers are in the opposite position. While economic
capital is always socially dominant for Bourdieu, the rise of the service
sector, educational qualifications, and class positions associated with
cultural capital over the course of the twentieth century encouraged him
to make cultural capital increasingly important in his analysis of social
relations and the exercise of power.

Bourdieu's concept of habitus is the subjective foundation of social
class. He chooses this term to suggest not only regularized social habits
but even more the mental "dispositions" of people. Such dispositions
structure thoughts and behaviors in ways that are largely nonrational.
What a person finds reasonable or unreasonable, possible or impossible,
valuable or valueless, are all outcomes of habitus. Each class is defined in
part by its distinctive habitus, and thus one can think of habitus as class
culture. It is produced and reproduced through social institutions such
as the school and the family that teach and enforce the cultural matrix
peculiar to a particular class. Bourdieu shies away from using the term
"culture" here because he wants to emphasize the practical agency of social
actors. Real people are not simply automatons following the dictates of
a culture identified by social scientists. They make real decisions about
how to engage their cultural prescriptions and how strongly to follow
class dispositions. At the same time they are not fully rational strategic

actors in pursuit of socially valued goods in the most efficient manner possible. Habitus structures and inclines action but does not dictate it.

The relationship between capital and habitus defines social class. For Bourdieu, a class is a social group whose members share similar distributions of capital, life chances, dispositions, and social practices, all of which correspond to one another. He sees considerable overlap between the material and symbolic dimensions of what Weber differentiated as class versus status group. Ultimately a materialist, Bourdieu argues that habitus legitimates class domination by mystifying class power. He goes so far as to claim that status groups are in reality social classes misrecognized. Similar to Marx, Bourdieu sees classes as entangled in perpetual struggle. Yet unlike Marx's conception, this is a struggle not only for material power but also for distinction, prestige, and even "the meaning of the social world."[4] In their struggle against one another, classes even create and define themselves. In Bourdieu's analysis, boundaries between classes are not fixed or given by the social scientist but are created historically by social actors themselves. In this way, the social definition of classes and their creation as real social actors is in a fundamental sense a symbolic process. To define one's own class is simultaneously to define other classes that are distinguished from it. Dominant classes use symbols to name and classify social groups, including themselves, and thus class habitus is constructed in opposition to the habitus of other classes.

The struggle between classes is carried out in what Bourdieu calls "fields." A field is a structured social space defined by the distribution of different types and amounts of capital, and is similar to the sociological concept "sphere" as a social arena in which actors operate under a distinct set of rules of interaction. Even outside social science we think of the social world in this way, segmented into politics, the economy, science, religion, literature and art, and the like. Social classes compete in these fields for valued social goods (i.e., capital) and for legitimation of their power. Bourdieu is committed to a strongly hierarchical understanding of society in which higher classes dominate lower classes. In his view the habitus of the working class, for example, is an expression of material necessity. Middle class habitus is defined as a pale imitation (constrained by limited capital) of dominant class habitus. The habitus of those at the top indulges in distinctions made possible only by large endowments of economic and cultural capital. For Bourdieu, all symbolic power flows from the top and is exercised by the dominant classes to no greater end than their own aggrandizement.

Bourdieu packs a theory of politics into his framework. This is clearest in his concept "symbolic violence" and the ways in which he uses it to explain class relations. For Bourdieu all power is a form of domination. He follows Weber in a belief that all values are ultimately arbitrary and nonrational. Since there is no such thing as truth, no value can be defended or legitimated by means of reason. In turn, every exercise of power is self-serving and every claim of authority is nothing more than an act designed to mystify domination. Such misrecognition is critical because it is the means by which the dominated classes accept their domination. Yet it is also crucial for the dominant class, which has an interest in not knowing its own role in the processes of domination.

Bourdieu's theory is a compelling one, and this book is built atop it. At the same time it has distinct shortcomings. I part ways from Bourdieu at three points in particular. First, Bourdieu goes too far with his concept "symbolic violence." His insistence on the necessary violence of culture is a consequence of his undefended premise that social inequality requires scientific explanation and social legitimation while social equality, being somehow primitive or natural, does not. To Bourdieu, every distribution of social goods is fundamentally arbitrary in that it is created through history and legitimated by nothing more than mystified power. If equality is natural and the only morally defensible value around which a good society might organize itself, then power clearly can only take the form of "violence" and "domination." For all his appreciation of the inherent social creation of the human being, Bourdieu fails to appreciate the positive and constructive aspect of power. He does not see how power is necessary for the realization of any human value at all, even equality. The philosopher Yves Simon shows how authority (simply the legitimation of domination according to Bourdieu) is not the opposite of freedom but grows along with it and is necessary for it.[5] Authority enables us both to participate in and benefit from acts of social cooperation through which we realize our own good and our own freedom. If social cooperation can be nonexploitative at least in principle, then so, too, can authority.

Second, Bourdieu's belief in the strongly hierarchical nature of society drives him to see agency as a function of structural position. Being at the bottom of the pyramid, the working class in particular lacks nearly all capacity for meaningful action. Recall that in Bourdieu's thinking, class habitus is a function of distance from material and social necessity. For example, he argues that working class households are decorated with "trinkets and knick-knacks," which accomplish a large quantity of decorating at a small price. Dominant class homes, on the other hand, are decorated, according to Bourdieu, "to suggest with the fewest 'effects' possible the greatest expenditure of time, money and ingenuity."[6] While the working and middle classes certainly live closer to "necessity" than do managers and professionals, they nonetheless engage in their own acts of distinction rather than simply strive to imitate elites through vulgar knock-offs. This takes place through the consumption of positional goods such as pickup trucks or Thomas Kinkade paintings, not because such goods are cheap but (in part) because they are rejected by elites. In a similar way, lower classes can emphasize "traditional" values in religion, political ideology, or sexual behavior as a means of intentionally distinguishing themselves from their supposed social betters and those betters' "cosmopolitan" values. Precisely this social agency explains a significant portion of the appeal and growth of Pentecostalism around the world today. In these ways, lower classes can and do exercise far more control over their own habitus than Bourdieu allows.

Third, Bourdieu equates society and its class structures with the boundaries of the nation-state. Just as he defines class as a position within a homogeneous and hierarchical social space, so, too, does he define society as a location in a state-defined geographical space. This should not be surprising in light of his empirical focus on France, one of the most centralized countries in the world, oriented toward a single demographic, political, cultural, and economic capital. In the United States, however, power is much more geographically dispersed, and class and class relations are much more strongly mediated by region, city, and even neighborhood. National homogeneity should be a historical and spatial variable, not a theoretical premise.

Methodology

The methodological foundation of the class analysis in chapters 3 and 4 is the National Statistics Socio-economic Classification (NS-SEC) schema used by the United Kingdom Office of National Statistics (ONS). The NS-SEC was developed from the work of Oxford University sociologist John H. Goldthorpe and adapted by the ONS on the basis of a thorough *ex ante* validation process. The NS-SEC schema can be shown to have a causal influence on a range of socioeconomic outcomes of interest to social scientists.[7]

The theoretical foundation of the NS-SEC is "employment relations and conditions." The schema makes two basic differentiations. The first is a person's relationship to the buying and selling of labor in the market. "Employers" buy labor, "employees" sell labor, and the "self-employed" neither buy nor sell labor. This is the most basic means of differentiating social classes. The NS-SEC separates employers into two categories, those in small organizations (fewer than 25 employees) and those in large organizations (25 or more employees). It then incorporates the former into the self-employed group, doing so because small employers rarely delegate managerial functions and thus are more similar to the self-employed in terms of employment relations and conditions.

The vast majority of occupations in contemporary Western societies involve selling labor. These "employees" are differentiated from one another based on their employment relation. The NS-SEC identifies two main relationships. The first is the "service relationship" between employer and employee characterized by an employee salary, job security, and clear lines of career advancement. Since the service relationship involves indirect links between effort and pay, employers grant a relatively high degree of autonomy to such employees. Skills are usually high in these positions. Employers in large organizations are incorporated into the category of employees with a service relationship because there are so few of them in society and thus they rarely appear in surveys. Moreover, chief executive and financial officers of major publicly held firms are similar enough to the owners of large private firms to justify their amalgamation. The second employer-employee connection is the "labor contract relationship" involving more direct links between effort and pay. Such positions are characterized by a wage, limited autonomy, and close direction by managers and supervisors. Skills are usually lower in these positions. The NS-SEC also defines a third "intermediate" employer-employee relationship that combines some aspects of both the service relationship and the labor contract relationship. In addition both service and labor contract employment relations can exist in varying strengths.

Through these steps the NS-SEC defines eight "analytic classes," one of which is subdivided into two. It also identifies three residual nonoccupational categories.

TABLE A.1. NS-SEC Analytic Classes

	Class name	Employment relations and conditions
1.1	Large employers and higher managerial occupations	Employers in large organizations (large employers [L1]); service relationship involving general planning and supervision of operations on behalf of employer (higher managerial [L2])
1.2	Higher professional occupations	Service relationship in a professional occupation regardless of employment status [L3]
2	Lower managerial and professional occupations	Attenuated service relationship involving planning and supervision of operations on behalf of employer under direction of senior managers (lower managerial [L5]) or involving formal and immediate supervision of intermediate occupations (higher supervisory [L6]); attenuated service relationship in a professional occupation except if employer in a large organization (lower professional and higher technical [L4])
3	Intermediate occupations	Combined service and labor contract relationship involving clerical, sales, service, and intermediate technical occupations that do not involve general planning or supervisory powers [L7]
4	Small employers and own account workers	Employers in small organizations (small employers [L8]); self-employed involving nonprofessional trade, personal service, semiroutine, or routine occupations with no employees other than family workers (own account workers [L9])
5	Lower supervisory and technical occupations	Modified labor contract relationship involving formal and immediate supervision of lower technical, semiroutine, or routine occupations (lower supervisory [L10]); modified labor contract relationship in lower technical and related occupations (lower technical [L11])
6	Semiroutine occupations	Slightly modified labor contract relationship in which the work involved requires at least some element of employee discretion [L12]
7	Routine occupations	Basic labor contract relationship in positions with the least need for employee discretion [L13]
8	Never worked and long-term unemployed	Available for work but experiencing involuntary exclusion from the labor market [L14]
*	Full-time students	Persons over age 16 engaged in full-time courses of study [L15]
*	Occupations not stated or inadequately described	[L16]
*	Not classifiable for other reasons	[L17]

TABLE A.1 NOTE: "Functional operational categories" names and codes appear in parentheses. This is the second-highest NS-SEC level of aggregation.

I use this basic structure of classification with some minor rearranging of the "functional operational categories" in table A.1. To suit my interests in elites and better detect value differences among them, I differentiate managers from professionals in both higher and lower instances. The NS-SEC more or less does this already at the higher level. I also eliminate analytic class 8, "never worked and long-term unemployed" and do not use the three "not classified" categories. The result is the classification scheme of nine social classes presented in table A.2A and table 3.1.

TABLE A.2A. Modified NS-SEC Analytic Classes

Abbr.	Title	Functional operational categories
HM	Higher managerial	Employers in large organizations (L1) Higher managerial occupations (L2)
HP	Higher professional	Higher professional occupations (L3)
LP	Lower professional and higher technical	Lower professional and higher technical occupations (L4)
LM	Lower managerial and higher supervisory	Lower managerial occupations (L5) Higher supervisory occupations (L6)
I	Intermediate	Intermediate occupations (L7)
SB	Small business owners	Self-employed (L8/L9)
LST	Lower supervisory and lower technical	Lower supervisory occupations (L10) Lower technical occupations (L11)
SR	Semiroutine	Semiroutine occupations (L12)
R	Routine	Routine occupations (L13)

Class positions are heritable through the family. Thus my basic unit of analysis is the family household. A major task of assigning a class position to an individual respondent in a survey is to determine the class position of that person's family. When the ONS conducts surveys using the NS-SEC, it identifies a "household reference person" (formerly a "head of household") who best defines the class position of the household and therefore of all the household's members. Whoever owns the household's domicile or pays the rent is defined as the reference person. In cases of joint householding, the person with the higher income is the reference, and in cases of joint householding and equal income, the older person is chosen. Because of the limitations of the dataset I use in chapters 3 and 4—the General Social Survey (GSS) collected by the National Opinion Research Center at the University of Chicago—I cannot follow the ONS methodology exactly. Therefore I use a slightly different method.

Prior to 2000 the GSS asked each respondent to state his or her relationship to the "head of household" using a completely subjective definition at the discretion of the respondent. Beginning in 2000 the GSS began offering respondents a definition of "head of household" as "the person or one of the persons who own or rents this home." This brought the GSS definition close to that of the NS-SEC. However, because the GSS does not have a method to deal with joint householding, they are not exactly the same. In fact the GSS admits that "for most households there is no meaningful distinction between head and spouse/partner of head." Therefore I use a combination of stated head of household, marital status, and occupational prestige to identify the household reference person. Occupational prestige scores are provided by the GSS for all surveys conducted up to and including 2010. Occupational prestige scores for the 2012 and 2014 GSS are taken from the work of Carl Frederick at the University of Wisconsin.[8] For persons not in employment at the time of the interview (e.g., unemployed, retired, in school, keeping house), the GSS asks them if they have ever worked for as long as one year. If so it codes their occupation as their former job.

For married persons declaring either themselves or their spouse as the head of household, I define the reference person as the spouse with the higher prestige occupation. For married persons declaring a parent as the head of household, the reference person is the one with the highest prestige occupation among respondent, spouse, father, and mother. I define unmarried persons declaring themselves as the head of household to be their own reference person. For unmarried persons declaring a parent as head of household, the reference person is the household member (respondent, father, or mother) with the highest prestige occupation. Data on the respondent's mother's occupation is available only from 1994 onward.

Some respondents have missing data that makes it impossible to determine their class position by this method. This is generally due either to (1) failing to declare a head of household or (2) failing to provide occupational information for the calculated household reference person. Sometimes this is due to a respondent's failure to answer the question, but usually this is because the GSS did not ask the necessary question in the first place. The head of household question was not introduced until 1975 and was not asked of all respondents until 1977. No occupational information has ever been collected on heads of household who are neither a respondent, a spouse, nor a parent. In these cases I impute a household reference person by following the above methodology as closely as possible. For married persons I define the household reference person as the spouse with the higher prestige occupation, the case for 99% of calculated household reference persons. Respondents whose marital status is widowed, divorced, or separated are their own household reference person, the case for 96%, 91%, and 91% of calculated reference persons, respectively. These figures demonstrate that all these imputations are especially well grounded. Never-married respondents are themselves the household reference person if their work status is as follows: employed full-time; temporarily not working due to illness, vacation, or strike; or retired. For such persons the likelihood is high that they are providing their own means of support. For those with calculated household reference persons, 78%, 75%, and 93% of respondents having each respective work status are their own reference person, thus providing a firm empirical foundation for this imputation as well. For never-married persons with any other work status (working part-time, unemployed, in school, keeping house, and other), the imputed household reference person is the person with the higher prestige occupation between self, father, and mother. My assumption is that a large percentage of such persons are likely to be economic dependents of another even if they are living apart from that person. Thus I assign them a parental class status if it is warranted by comparing occupational prestige scores.

The GSS over the years 1972–2014 includes 59,599 individual respondents. At the end of the process of determining a household reference person with occupational data, 50,384 (84.5%) respondents have a calculated value and another 9,132 (15.3%) have an imputed value. Due to missing data, no household reference person with occupational information can be either calculated or imputed for 83 (0.1%) respondents, who were therefore stricken from the dataset.

From this point onward it is a process simple in conception although quite complicated in practice to transform household reference person occupations into respondent class positions. I start with the occupational codes of household reference persons supplied by the GSS. For the years 1972–1987 these are 1970 U.S. Census Bureau occupational codes. For the years 1988–2010 they are 1980 U.S. Census Bureau occupational codes. Finally for the years 2012–2014 they are 2010 U.S. Census Bureau occupational codes. Using a crosswalk supplied by the Minnesota Population Center at the University of Minnesota, I converted 1970 census codes into 1980 census codes. From this point onward the same methodology is applied to data for 1972–2010. Using a crosswalk from the National

Crosswalk Service Center (NCSC), a federally funded organization operated by the State of Iowa, I then transformed 1980 U.S. Census Bureau
codes into 1980 Standard Occupational Classification (SOC) codes from
the U.S. Bureau of Labor Statistics (BLS). Next I transformed the 1980
U.S. SOC codes into those from the International Labour Organization's
1988 International Standard Classification of Occupations (ISCO-88)
using a conversion table created by Torben Iversen at Harvard University,
and then into a European variant of that same schema known as ISCO-
88(COM). The ISCO-88(COM) is nearly identical to the ISCO-88. In the
rare cases when an ISCO-88 code had no translation into ISCO-88(COM),
I invented one based on my analysis of the implicit GSS crosswalk of 1980
U.S. Census codes into ISCO-88 codes. Using a crosswalk supplied by the
United Kingdom Office of National Statistics (ONS), I next translated
ISCO-88(COM) codes into UK SOC 2000 codes. Then these British SOC
codes were sorted into NS-SEC functional operational categories using the
"reduced method" supplied by a derivation table produced by the ONS. I
used information on self-employment and supervisory status collected by
the GSS for sorting respondents into functional operational categories L6
(higher supervisory occupations), L8/L9 (employers in small organizations
and own account workers, which I merge based on a common status as
self-employed), and L10 (lower supervisory occupations). Finally these
twelve functional operational categories are grouped into the nine social
class fractions listed in tables A.2A and 3.1 above.

I used a similar process for the data spanning the years 2012–2014. I
began by transforming the 2010 U.S. Census Bureau occupational codes
into 2010 U.S. SOC codes using a crosswalk supplied by the U.S. Census
Bureau. Next I converted these 2010 U.S. SOC codes into ISCO-08 codes
using a BLS crosswalk, and then into UK SOC 2010 codes with an ONS-
supplied crosswalk. The next step was sorting occupations into NS-SEC
functional operational categories, which I carried out through the "reduced
method" supplied by a derivation table produced by the ONS, and finally
organizing these into the nine social class fractions of table A.2A. I followed the same method for discerning self-employment and supervisor
status as above.

It is rare that an occupational code in one classification schema trans-
lates into a single occupational code in another schema. Therefore choices
must inevitably be made. In transforming occupational codes from system
to system, I followed a few general rules. When faced with multiple choices
for transforming a single code, I chose the most general category if it was

available. If not, I chose the code with the largest number of employees based on the 2000 National Occupational Employment and Wage Estimates produced by the BLS. Before running the final transformations using the statistical software package STATA, I visually inspected every code translation from U.S. Census code to UK SOC code for similarity of occupation, skill level, and social class against the relevant crosswalks discussed above. Two Excel files showing the one-to-one crosswalk between U.S. Census codes and UK SOC codes may be downloaded from my personal website for inspection.

TABLE A.2B. Demographic Profile of the Nine Class Fractions, 2004–2014

Table A.2A Class	Raw total	Raw pct.	Pct. male	Pct. white non-Hispanic	Avg. age
HM	525	3.5%	47.4%	80.5%	48.4
HP	1983	13.0%	51.1%	78.7%	46.8
LP	2877	18.9%	43.3%	75.9%	46.1
LM	1659	10.9%	43.2%	73.2%	44.3
I	2090	13.7%	36.1%	68.3%	46.3
SB	1060	7.0%	48.2%	69.5%	49.1
LST	1595	10.5%	59.1%	65.1%	44.5
SR	1956	12.9%	42.5%	55.3%	46.0
R	1474	9.7%	48.4%	52.8%	44.9
TOTAL	**15,219**	**100.0%**	**45.9%**	**68.6%**	**45.9**

SOURCE: *General Social Survey. All whites without a reported ethnic origin are counted as non-Hispanic whites. Percentages are weighted by year and by the GSS weight variable WTSSALL. The GSS always contains markedly more responses from women than from men. Thus these class fraction figures should be read relative to those of other fractions in the table rather than as indications of the true percentages in American society.*

APPENDIX B

Multiple correspondence analysis (MCA) is not well known or widely used in the United States. This is probably so in part because the method has had to compete with the long-entrenched traditional regression analysis, and in part because MCA has been pioneered and developed in France. It is particularly associated with the work of Pierre Bourdieu, so much so that it is often called "Bourdieu's statistical method."[1] MCA is a form of geometric modeling applied to categorical variables. It allows relationships in a dataset to be plotted in a geometric space.

I used data from the National Survey of Family Growth (NSFG), 2011–2013 to construct the field of the American family discussed in chapter 5. The data were gathered under the auspices of the Centers for Disease Control and Prevention, a U.S. federal government agency. The NSFG 2011–2013 is a nationally representative sample of 10,416 American women and men ages 15–44 interviewed between September 2011 and September 2013. I selected responses to fifteen questions from the interviews relating to sexual behavior and the family to construct the field. I balanced the various questions by combining some responses so that no question had fewer than four nor more than six. In two instances this was because a useful modality had less than 5% of all respondents and thus I merged it with a similar response (such as "strongly disagree" and "disagree").[2] This resulted in seventy-two responses or "modalities" total. I eliminated twelve modalities before conducting the analysis, four to avoid double counting (for example, the modality "respondent has no children" exists for three different questions) and eight to eliminate "junk" modalities that contained no valuable information (that is, responses of "other," "don't know," and "no response"). Thus in the end I used sixty modalities to create the field. All fifteen questions, their NSFG variable names, and the sixty modalities used in the analysis are as follows:

TABLE A.3. NSFG 2011–2013 Survey Questions and Modalities Used to Construct the Field of the American Family

Number of respondent's biological children born out of wedlock [CEBOW]

    Has no children

    Zero children

    One child

    Two children

    Three or more children

Portion of respondent's biological children born out of wedlock [CEBOW / CHILDREN][3]

    All

    Some

Number of cohabitations [TIMESCOH]

    None

    One

    Two

    Three or more

Number of sexual partners (both opposite-sex and same-sex) in lifetime [LIFPRTNR, SAMESEXANY and SAMLIFENUM][4]

    None

    One

    Two to five

    Six to nine

    Ten to nineteen

    Twenty or more

Respondent's age at first live childbirth [AGEBABY1][5]

    Under 18

    18–19

    20–24

    25–29

    30 and over

Respondent's age at first cohabitation [COHAB1][6]

    Under 18

    18–19

    20–24

    25 and over

Respondent's age at first marriage [FMAR1AGE or MARDAT01][7]
      Never married
      Under 20
      20–24
      25–29
      30 and over
Number of same-sex partners in lifetime [SAMESEXANY and SAMLIFENUM][8]
      None
      One
      Two or more
Okay for unmarried woman to have and raise a child [CHSUPPOR]
      Strongly agree
      Agree
      Disagree
      Strongly disagree
Okay for cohabiting couple to have and raise children [CHCOHAB]
      Strongly agree
      Agree
      (Strongly) disagree
All right for unmarried 18-year-olds to have sex if there is strong affection [SXOK18]
      Strongly agree
      Agree
      Disagree
      Strongly disagree
All right for unmarried 16-year-olds to have sex if there is strong affection [SXOK16]
      (Strongly) agree
      Disagree
      Strongly disagree
A young couple should not live together unless married [OKCOHAB]
      Strongly agree
      Agree
      Disagree
      Strongly disagree
Sexual relations between two same-sex adults are all right [SAMESEX]
      Strongly agree
      Agree
      Disagree
      Strongly disagree
Gay adults should have the right to adopt children [GAYADOPT]
      Strongly agree
      Agree
      Disagree
      Strongly disagree

Only data from respondents ages 30–44 were included in the analysis in chapter 5. A handful of respondents were age 44 when first contacted for the interviews but age 45 when the interview was actually conducted. They are included in the analysis. This age restriction reduced the total number of respondents in the dataset from the original 10,416 to 4,597.

I used the statistical software R and the packages FactoMineR® and GDAtools® to conduct a "specific" multiple correspondence analysis. This procedure allowed me to remove the twelve double-counting and junk modalities discussed above from the construction of the field. Data were weighted using the NSFG variable "WGT2011_2013." I used the GDAtools package in R to create the basic graphics found in figures 5.1–5.5, and Adobe Photoshop to make them more reader friendly.

APPENDIX C

In order to account for variations in the patterns of individual responses to the group thermometer questions, raw ratings need to be both relativized and standardized. Consider a respondent who feels "warm" toward everyone and rates each group at 75°. Then consider another respondent who feels "cool" toward all and rates each group at 25°. Without computing relative ratings, we will misinterpret the first person as warm toward group A and the second person as cool toward group A when in fact this is not the case at all. The ratings also need to be standardized to account for different distributions of thermometer ratings. To rate group A 20° cooler than group B means much more for a respondent with a 20° range across all groups than for a respondent with a 100° range.

Therefore I first computed relative thermometer readings for each group against each respondent's mean rating for all relevant groups: twenty-one for the 2008 ANES data used in chapter 4, and thirteen for the 2008 and 2012 data used in chapter 7. Then I standardized these relative ratings by dividing them by the standard deviation of each respondent's twenty-one or thirteen relative thermometer ratings. Means for each educational group's standardized relative thermometer rating were then computed and compared. Survey design was taken into account and responses were weighted when calculating means. In the 2008 ANES survey only face-to-face interviews were conducted. In the 2012 ANES survey both face-to-face interviews and internet interviews were used.

For the comparisons in chapter 7, only 2012 face-to-face interview data were used in order to maintain comparability across the two surveys.

For the principal component analysis performed in chapter 7, missing data first needed to be imputed. The R package missMDA® was used for the imputation. The PCA itself was performed using the R package FactoMineR®.

APPENDIX D

TABLE A.4. 2010 Standard Occupational Classification (SOC) System Codes by Major Group

Occupation	SOC
Management	11
Business and Financial Operations	13
Computer and Mathematical	15
Architecture and Engineering	17
Life, Physical, and Social Science	19
Community and Social Service	21
Legal	23
Education, Training, and Library	25
Arts, Design, Entertainment, Sports, and Media	27
Healthcare Practitioners and Technical	29
Healthcare Support	31
Protective Service	33
Food Preparation and Serving-related	35

TABLE A.4 (cont.)

Building and Grounds Cleaning and Maintenance	37
Personal Care and Service	39
Sales and Related	41
Office and Administrative Support	43
Farming, Fishing, and Forestry	45
Construction and Extraction	47
Installation, Maintenance, and Repair	49
Production	51
Transportation and Material Moving	53

TABLE A.5A. Fertility and Opinion on the Morality of Same-Sex Sexual Relations

Number of Children	Mean Value
0	0.43 (0.28 – 0.58)
1	0.00 (-0.16 – 0.16)
2	-0.16 (-0.30 – -0.03)
3	-0.25 (-0.42 – -0.08)
4	-0.42 (-0.67 – -0.17)
5+	-0.64 (-0.99 – -0.29)
Total	**-0.04 (-0.15 – -0.07)**

TABLE SOURCE: *2011–2013 National Survey of Family Growth. N = 10,401. The question was as follows: "Sexual relations between two adults of the same sex are all right." Mean scores are computed with the following values assigned to the ordinal responses: "strongly agree" = 2; "agree" = 1; "neither agree nor disagree" = 0; "disagree" = -1; "strongly disagree" = -2. Scores are weighted according to the NSFG sample design; 95% confidence intervals are shown in parentheses.*

TABLE A.5B. Fertility and Opinion on the Morality of Same-Sex Sexual Relations, by Sex of Respondent

Number of Children	Female Mean Value	Male Mean Value
0	0.79 (0.58 – 1.00)	0.20 (0.04 – 0.36)
1	0.28 (0.07 – 0.48)	-0.26 (-0.47 – -0.05)
2	-0.04 (-0.21 – 0.13)	-0.31 (-0.52 – -0.11)
3	-0.11 (-0.30 – 0.08)	-0.44 (-0.73 – -0.16)
4+	-0.30 (-0.55 – -0.05)	-0.83 (-1.16 – -0.51)
Total	**0.12** **(-0.01 – 0.25)**	**-0.21** **(-0.33 – -0.10)**

TABLE SOURCE: 2011–2013 National Survey of Family Growth. N = 10,401. The question was as follows: "Sexual relations between two adults of the same sex are all right." Mean scores are computed with the following values assigned to the ordinal responses: "strongly agree" = 2; "agree" = 1; "neither agree nor disagree" = 0; "disagree" = –1; "strongly disagree" = –2. Scores are weighted according to the NSFG sample design; 95% confidence intervals are shown in parentheses.

NOTES

Acknowledgments

1 Pierre Bourdieu, *Distinction: A Social Critique of the Judgement of Taste* (Cambridge, Mass.: Harvard University Press, 1984), xiii.

Chapter 1

1 Lawrence v. Texas, 539 U.S. 558 (2003).
2 Goodridge v. Department of Public Health, 440 Mass. 309, 798 N.E.2d 941 (Mass. 2003).
3 Gay & Lesbian Advocates & Defenders (GLAD) v. Attorney General, 426 Mass. 132 (2002).
4 Göran Therborn, *Between Sex and Power: Family in the World, 1900–2000* (New York: Routledge, 2004), 223.
5 Baehr et al. v. Miike, Circuit Court for the First Circuit, Hawaii No. 91-1394 (1996).
6 104th Congress, H.R. 3396, House roll call 316 & Senate roll call 280.
7 William J. Clinton, "Statement on Same-Gender Marriage," 20 September 1996, in *Public Papers of the Presidents of the United States, William J. Clinton, 1996. Book 2, July 1 to December 31, 1996* (Washington: Government Printing Office, 1998), 1635.
8 "1998 Referendum General Election Results—Hawaii," *Dave Leip's Atlas of U.S. Presidential Elections*, last modified April 23, 2007, http://www.uselectionatlas .org/RESULTS/state.php?fips=15&year=1998&f=0&off=51.

9 Human Rights Campaign, *The State of the Workplace for Lesbian, Gay, Bisexual and Transgender Americans* (Washington, D.C.: Human Rights Campaign Foundation, 2004).

10 Quoted in Marc Gunther, "Queer Inc.: How Corporate America Fell in Love with Gays and Lesbians," *Fortune*, November 30, 2006, 94.

11 *Goodridge v. Department of Public Health*, 50.

12 "Marriage," Gallup, accessed July 17, 2017, http://www.gallup.com/poll/117328/marriage.aspx.

13 Tom W. Smith, "Changes in Family Structure, Family Values, and Politics, 1972–2006," in *Red, Blue and Purple America: The Future of Election Demographics*, ed. Ruy A. Teixeira (Washington, D.C.: Brookings Institution, 2008), 147–93; W. Bradford Wilcox and Jon McEwan, "Marriage, Single Parenthood, and the 2016 Vote," Family Studies, last modified December 7, 2016, https://family-studies.org/marriage-single-parenthood-and-the-2016-vote/.

14 Julissa Cruz, "Marriage: More Than a Century of Change," NCFMR Family Profiles, FFP-13-13, National Center for Family and Marriage Research, Bowling Green State University, 2013, http://www.bgsu.edu/content/dam/BGSU/college-of-arts-and-sciences/NCFMR/documents/FP/FP-13-13.pdf.

15 D'Vera Cohn, Jeffrey S. Passel, Wendy Wang, and Gretchen Livingston, "Barely Half of U.S. Adults Are Married—A Record Low," Pew Research Center: Social and Demographic Trends, last modified December 14, 2011, http://www.pewsocial trends.org/2011/12/14/barely-half-of-u-s-adults-are-married-a-record-low/.

16 Alison Aughinbaugh, Omar Robles, and Hugette Sun, "Marriage and Divorce: Patterns by Gender, Race, and Educational Attainment," Monthly Labor Review, U.S. Bureau of Labor Statistics, October 2013, https://www.bls.gov/opub/mlr/2013/article/marriage-and-divorce-patterns-by-gender-race-and-educational-attainment.htm.

17 Casey E. Copen, Kimberly Daniels, and William D. Mosher, "First Premarital Cohabitation in the United States: 2006–2010 National Survey of Family Growth," *National Health Statistics Reports* 64 (April 4, 2013), a publication of the National Center for Health Statistics, Centers for Disease Control and Prevention, U.S. Department of Health and Human Services.

18 Cruz, "Marriage."

19 Cohn et al., "Barely Half of U.S. Adults Are Married."

20 Aughinbaugh, Robles, and Sun, "Marriage and Divorce."

21 Ralph Richard Banks, *Is Marriage for White People? How the African American Marriage Decline Affects Everyone* (New York: Dutton, 2011).

22 Naomi Cahn and June Carbone, *Red Families v. Blue Families: Legal Polarization and the Creation of Culture* (Oxford: Oxford University Press, 2010).

23 Editorial board, "California's Poisonous Proposal," *New York Times*, March 4, 2000, A14; editorial board, "Marriage and Politics," *New York Times*, October 29, 2004, A24; for Jefford's remarks, see "Federal Marriage Amendment—Motion to Proceed—Resumed," 150 Cong. Rec. S7972, July 13, 2004, https://www.congress

.gov/congressional-record/2004/7/13/senate-section/article/s7962-2; editorial board, "Live Free and Civilly United," *Boston Globe*, April 28, 2007, A10; editorial board, "Setback for Equality: Voters in Three States Approve Bans on Same-Sex Marriage," *Washington Post*, November 8, 2008, A16; editorial board, "Mexico City's Step Forward," *Los Angeles Times*, December 24, 2009, A16; Stephen M. Saland, "Senator Saland's Statement on Marriage Equality," The New York State Senate, June 25, 2011, https://www.nysenate.gov/news-room/press-releases/stephen-m-saland/senator-salands-statement-marriage-equality.

24 Chai Feldblum, "Gay Is Good: The Moral Case for Marriage Equality and More," *Yale Journal of Law and Feminism* 17 (2005): 139–84.

25 Stanley Fish, "The Trouble with Tolerance," *Chronicle of Higher Education*, November 10, 2006, B8.

26 "Tolerance" is used in the following *New York Times* editorials: "California's Poisonous Proposal"; "Canada's Celebration of Marriage," June 19, 2003, 24; "Marriage and Politics," October 29, 2004, A24; and "Six Tests for Equality and Fairness," November 2, 2009, 20. "Fair(ness)" is used in "The Message from Hawaii," December 6, 1996, 38; "Hawaii's Ban on Gay Marriage," December 20, 1999; "Vermont's Momentous Ruling," December 22, 1999, 26; "A Winding Path to Gay Marriage," August 14, 2004; "Where Is the Governor Now?" September 9, 2005, 24; and "Legal Convolutions for Gay Couples," March 24, 2007, 12.

27 See, from the *New York Times* in 2011, "Marriage Equality in New York," February 11; "Marriage Equality in New York," April 26; "Governor Cuomo's List," May 16; "They Need to Be Counted," May 20; "They Need to Stand Up for Equality," June 14; "Politicians Who Fear the Public Light," June 24; "A Milestone for Gay Marriage," June 27.

28 Editorial board, "Victory for Equal Rights," *New York Times*, June 27, 2013, A30.

29 Editorial board, "Marriage Equality in America," *New York Times*, June 27, 2015, A20.

30 *Goodridge* concurring opinion, 12–13.

31 Martha Nussbaum, *From Disgust to Humanity: Sexual Orientation and Constitutional Law* (Oxford: Oxford University Press, 2010).

32 Nussbaum, *From Disgust to Humanity*, 205, xviii.

33 Nussbaum, *From Disgust to Humanity*, 148, 141.

34 Nussbaum, *From Disgust to Humanity*, 205.

35 Nussbaum, *From Disgust to Humanity*, xx. She even tells the story of her own conversion on pages xxii–xxiii.

36 Nussbaum, *From Disgust to Humanity*, 160.

37 Michael J. Klarman, *From the Closet to the Altar: Courts, Backlash, and the Struggle for Same-Sex Marriage* (Oxford: Oxford University Press, 2013).

38 Klarman, *From the Closet to the Altar*, 17.

39 Klarman, *From the Closet to the Altar*, 171.

40 Klarman, *From the Closet to the Altar*, 40, 73, 196–201, 209–10.

41 Gary Mucciaroni, "The Study of LGBT Politics and Its Contributions to Political Science," *PS: Political Science & Politics* 44, no. 1 (2011): 17–21.

42 Andrew Sullivan, "Obama's Cowardice on Marriage," *The Dish*, May 16, 2008, dish.andrewsullivan.com/2008/05/16/gay-marriage-an-3/.

43 Emily Jane Fox, "Gay Marriage's Corporate Boosters," *CNNMoney*, April 1, 2013, http://money.cnn.com/2013/03/29/news/companies/same-sex-marriage -companies/index.html.

Chapter 2

1 Mitchell Baker, "Building a Global, Diverse, Inclusive Mozilla Project: Addressing Controversy," *Lizard Wrangling* (blog), March 26, 2014, accessed June 6, 2014, https://blog.lizardwrangler.com/2014/03/26/building-a-global-diverse -inclusive-mozilla-project-addressing-controversy/.

2 Brendan Eich, "Inclusiveness at Mozilla," *Brendan Eich* (blog), March 26, 2014, accessed June 6, 2014, https://brendaneich.com/2014/03/inclusiveness-at -mozilla/; Baker, "Building." The quotes are from Eich.

3 Gail Sullivan, "Dating Web Site OkCupid Is Breaking Up with Firefox," *Washington Post*, April 1, 2014, http://www.washingtonpost.com/news/morning-mix/ wp/2014/04/01/dating-website-okcupid-is-breaking-up-with-firefox/.

4 Mitchell Baker, "Brendan Eich Steps Down as Mozilla CEO," *The Mozilla Blog*, April 3, 2014, accessed June 6, 2014, https://blog.mozilla.org/blog/2014/04/03/ brendan-eich-steps-down-as-mozilla-ceo/.

5 "Mozilla Supports LGBT Equality," *The Mozilla Blog*, March 29, 2014, accessed June 4, 2014, https://blog.mozilla.org/blog/2014/03/29/mozilla-supports-lgbt -equality/.

6 K. Allan Blume, "'Guilty as Charged,' Cathy Says of Chick-fil-A's Stand on Biblical and Family Values," *Baptist Press*, June 16, 2012, http://www.bpnews .net/38271/guilty-as-charged-cathy-says-of-chickfilas-stand-on-biblical -family-values.

7 Dan Cathy, "6-16 Strong Fathers" (interview), *Ken Coleman Show*, June 18, 2012, https://itunes.apple.com/us/podcast/the-ken-coleman-show/id388714518? mt=2.

8 Quoted in Greg Turner, "Mayor Menino on Chick-fil-A: Stuff It," *Boston Herald*, July 20, 2012. Menino even penned a personal letter to Dan Cathy expressing his views and posted it to the city's Facebook page with the tag. "We are a PROUD city."

9 Quoted in Hal Dardick, "Alderman to Chick-fil-A: No Deal," *Chicago Tribune*, July 25, 2012.

10 Quoted in Ricardo Lopez and Tiffany Hsu, "San Francisco Is the Third City to Tell Chick-fil-A: Keep Out," *Los Angeles Times*, July 26, 2012.

11 Turner, "Mayor Menino on Chick-fil-A."

12 Frank Newport, "Americans' Identification as Middle Class Edges Back Up," Gallup, December 15, 2016, http://www.gallup.com/poll/199727/americans -identification-middle-class-edges-back.aspx.

13 Katie Reilly, "Read Bernie Sanders' Speech Vowing to Continue His Nomina- tion Fight," *Time*, June 8, 2016, http://time.com/4361146/bernie-sanders -democratic-primary-speech-transcript/.

14 Stephan Lesher, *George Wallace: American Populist* (Cambridge, Mass.: Perseus Publishing, 1994), xv.

15 Quoted in Felicia Sonmez, "Santorum: Obama's College Plan Makes Him a 'Snob,'" *Washington Post*, February 26, 2012, A6.

16 Adam Smith, *The Wealth of Nations: Books I–III* (New York: Penguin Classics, 1982), 167–89.

17 Val Burris, "The Discovery of the New Middle Class," *Theory and Society* 15, no. 3 (1986): 317–49. See especially pages 324–31.

18 This typology was originally used in the 1890 census, but those records were extensively damaged by fire in 1921. The 1900 census is thus the first for which we have data.

19 U.S. Census Bureau, 1900 U.S. Census of Population, *Special Report: Occupations*, table 1.

20 U.S. Census Bureau, 1950 U.S. Census of Population, volume 4, *Special Reports Part I, No. 1B: Occupational Characteristics*, table 1.

21 U.S. Census Bureau, 1980 Census of Population, volume 1, *Characteristics of the Population: Chapter C, General Social and Economic Characteristics*, table 89.

22 Defined as SOC 2010 codes 15–29. Source: U.S. Census Bureau, *2006–10 Amer- ican Community Survey 5-Year Estimates*, table C24010.

23 The figure here includes farm managers but excludes farmers. U.S. Census Bureau, 1940 Census of Population, volume 3, *The Labor Force: Part 1, United States Summary*, table 58.

24 U.S. Census Bureau, 1980 Census of Population, volume 1, *Characteristics of the Population: Chapter C, General Social and Economic Characteristics*, table 89.

25 Defined as SOC 2010 codes 11–13. Source: U.S. Census Bureau, *2006–10 Amer- ican Community Survey 5-Year Estimates*, table C24010.

26 The percentage of households with a member in a professional or managerial occupation is necessarily smaller than the percentage of employed persons in a professional or managerial occupation. Increasing the denominator, a large number of households have no employed members at all. For example, in 2015, 27% of U.S. households had no workers in them. Some of these will be retirees whose class status can be derived from their former employment, but many are not. Moreover, fewer currently retired workers were in professional or mana- gerial positions than are current workers, further depressing the percentage of elite households. Decreasing the numerator, the prevalence of class endogamy means that many households have two (or on rare occasion more) members

who are professionals or managers. This also markedly reduces the percentage of elite households.

27 Charles Murray, *Coming Apart: The State of White America, 1960–2010* (New York: Crown Forum, 2012); Richard V. Reeves, *Dream Hoarders: How the American Upper Middle Class Is Leaving Everyone Else in the Dust, Why That Is A Problem, and What to Do about It* (Washington, D.C.: Brookings Institution Press, 2017).

28 Peter Drucker, *Landmarks of Tomorrow* (New York: Harper & Brothers, 1957); Robert B. Reich, *The Work of Nations: Preparing Ourselves for 21st-Century Capitalism* (New York: Knopf, 1991); Richard Florida, *The Rise of the Creative Class: And How It's Transforming Work, Leisure, Community and Everyday Life* (New York: Basic Books, 2002); David Brooks, *Bobos in Paradise: The New Upper Class and How They Got There* (New York: Simon & Schuster, 2000); Reeves, *Dream Hoarders*.

29 Bryan S. Turner, *Medical Power and Social Knowledge* (London: SAGE, 1987).

30 The conservative social critic Mary Eberstadt credits the Catholic Church's clergy abuse scandal of the early 2000s with strengthening what she saw as a waning taboo against "intergenerational sex" between teens and adults. See Eberstadt, "How Pedophilia Lost Its Cool," *First Things*, December 2009.

31 The first edition of the *Diagnostic and Statistical Manual*, issued in 1952, was itself largely a revision of the mental disorders section of the sixth edition of the World Health Organization's *International Statistical Classification of Diseases* (ICD-6), issued in 1949.

32 William N. Eskridge Jr., *Dishonorable Passions: Sodomy Laws in America, 1861–2003* (New York: Viking, 2008).

33 Bryan S. Turner, *The Body and Society: Explorations in Social Theory*, 3rd ed. (Los Angeles: SAGE, 2008); Turner, *Medical Power and Social Knowledge*; Peter Conrad and Joseph Schneider, *Deviance and Medicalization: From Badness to Sickness*, 2nd ed. (Philadelphia: Temple University Press, 1992).

34 American Psychiatric Association, *Diagnostic and Statistical Manual of Mental Disorders*, 2nd ed. (Washington, D.C.: APA, 1968), section 302, 44.

35 See Ronald Bayer, *Homosexuality and American Psychiatry: The Politics of Diagnosis* (New York: Basic Books, 1981), 101–54. This proved to be but a first step toward redefining all sexual disorders away from the practitioner's diagnosis of abnormal desire toward the patient's experience of "a sense of distress" that "must interfere with either satisfactory sexual relations or everyday functioning if the diagnosis is to be made" (American Psychiatric Association, *Diagnostic and Statistical Manual of Mental Disorders*, 4th ed. text revision [DSM-IV-TR] [Washington, D.C.: APA, 2000]). See Andrew C. Hinderliter, "Defining Paraphilia: Excluding Exclusion," *Open Access Journal of Forensic Psychology* 2 (2010): 241–72.

36 J. J. Conger, "Proceedings of the American Psychological Association, Incorporated, for the Year 1974: Minutes of the Annual Meeting of the Council of Representatives," *American Psychologist* 30 (1975): 620–51.

37 Quoted in Tacie L. Vergara, "Meeting the Needs of Sexual Minority Youth: One Program's Response," in *Homosexuality and Social Work*, ed. Robert Schoenberg, Richard S. Goldberg and David A. Shore (New York: Haworth Press, 1984), 37.

38 William Christopher Matthews et al., "Physicians' Attitudes toward Homosexuality: Survey of a California County Medical Society," *Western Journal of Medicine* 144 (1986): 106–10.

39 Cecilia Téllez et al., "Attitudes of Physicians in New Mexico toward Gay Men and Lesbians," *Journal of the Gay and Lesbian Medical Association* 3, no. 3 (1999): 83–89.

40 Jason S. Schneider and Saul Levin, "Uneasy Partners: The Lesbian and Gay Health Care Community and the AMA," *Journal of the American Medical Association* 282, no. 13 (1999): 1287–88; Ronald M. Davis et al., "Health Care Needs of Gay Men and Lesbians in the United States," *Journal of the American Medical Association* 275, no. 17 (1996): 1354–59.

41 Just the Facts Coalition, "Just the Facts about Sexual Orientation and Youth: A Primer for Principals, Educators and School Personnel," 1999, accessed January 17, 2017, http://www.glsenboston.org/JustTheFacts.pdf.

42 American Law Institute, "ALI Overview," http://www.ali.org/index.cfm?fuseaction=about.overview.

43 Daniel R. Pinello, "Homosexuality and the Law," in *The Oxford Companion to American Law*, ed. Kermit L. Hall (New York: Oxford University Press, 2002).

44 Lawrence v. Texas, 18–19.

45 Tony Mauro, "Scalia Lashes 'Law-Profession Culture,'" *Legal Times*, July 7, 2003.

46 The polity of the Presbyterian Church (USA) requires a majority of its regional governing bodies (presbyteries) to ratify doctrinal changes passed by its General Assembly. Following the July 2010 General Assembly vote in favor of allowing ordination of persons in same-sex relationships, this was accomplished in May 2011.

47 "GC2016: How General Conference Works," United Methodist Church, accessed January 17, 2017, www.umc.org/who-we-are/gc2016-how-general-conference-works.

48 Nicole C. Raeburn, *Changing Corporate America from Inside Out: Lesbian and Gay Workplace Rights* (Minneapolis: University of Minnesota Press, 2004).

49 M. V. Lee Badgett, *Money, Myths, and Change: The Economic Lives of Lesbians and Gay Men* (Chicago: University of Chicago Press, 2001), 131.

50 Raeburn, *Changing Corporate America*.

51 Daniel B. Baker, Sean O'Brien Strub, and Bill Henning, *Cracking the Corporate Closet* (New York: HarperBusiness, 1995), 17–19.

52 Badgett, *Money, Myths, and Change*.

53 Nikhar Gaikwad, *From Grassroots to Business Suits: How AIDS Captured the Corporate World*, B.A. honors thesis, Williams College, Williamstown, Mass., 2006, 124–38.

54 Human Rights Campaign, *Corporate Equality Index 2011: Rating American Workplaces on LGBT Equality* (Washington, D.C.: Human Rights Campaign, 2010).

55 This is 2009 data covering only firms that are federal contractors. See M. V. Lee Badgett, "The Impact of Extending Sexual Orientation and Gender Identity Non-Discrimination Requirements to Federal Contractors," The Williams Institute, February 2012, http://williamsinstitute.law.ucla.edu/wp-content/uploads/Badgett-EOImpact-Feb-201211.pdf.

56 "2005 Gay Press Report," Prime Access, Inc. and Rivendell Media Company, Inc., http://rivendellmedia.com/assets/press-reports/GayPressReport2005.pdf.

57 Lauren Joseph, "The Production of Pride: Institutionalization and LGBT Pride Organizations" (Ph.D. diss., Department of Sociology, Stony Brook University, August 2010).

58 "HRC National Dinner: Sponsors," Human Rights Campaign, accessed January 18, 2017, http://hrcnationaldinner.org/sponsors.

59 Human Rights Campaign, *Corporate Equality Index 2017* (Washington, D.C.: Human Rights Campaign, 2017), 7.

60 John Gallagher, "Ikea's Gay Gamble," *The Advocate*, May 3, 1994, 24–27.

61 Katherine Sender, *Business, Not Politics: The Making of the Gay Market* (New York: Columbia University Press, 2004), 95–138; Wan-Hsiu Sunny Tsai, "Assimilating the Queers: Representations of Lesbians, Gay Men, Bisexual, and Transgender People in Mainstream Advertising," *Advertising & Society Review* 11, no. 1 (2010).

62 Michelle Castillo, "Why 2015 Became the Year of LGBT Ads," *CNBC*, December 29, 2015, http://www.cnbc.com/2015/12/29/why-2015-became-the-year-of-lgbt-ads.html; Steven Petrow, "Advertisers Embrace Gay People in an Amazing Year of Firsts for Commercials," *Washington Post*, December 14, 2015.

63 Stuart Elliott, "Commercials with a Gay Emphasis Are Moving to Mainstream Media," *New York Times*, June 25, 2013.

64 Joanne Ostrow, "Ads Move beyond 'Gay Vague' as Marketing Comes Out about Target," *Denver Post*, June 17, 2012, E1.

65 Human Rights Campaign, "Corporate Equality Index Archive," http://www.hrc.org/resources/entry/corporate-equality-index-archives.

66 Human Rights Campaign, "The New Normal: Corporate America Stands with the LGBT Community," November 14, 2012, http://www.hrc.org/press-releases/entry/the-new-normal-corporate-america-stands-with-the-lgbt-community.

67 Daniel Winunwe Rivers, *Radical Relations: Lesbian Mothers, Gay Fathers, and Their Children in the United States Since World War II* (Chapel Hill: University of North Carolina Press, 2013), 67–72.

68 American Psychological Association, *Lesbian and Gay Parenting* (Washington, D.C.: American Psychological Association, 2005), 15.

69 American Law Institute, *Principles of the Law of Family Dissolution: Analysis and Recommendations* (St. Paul, Minn.: American Law Institute Publishers, 2002).

70 Brief of the Massachusetts Psychiatry Society et al., November 8, 2002, http://
www.socialworkers.org/assets/secured/documents/ldf/briefDocuments/
Goodridge%20v.%20Dept.%20of%20Public%20Health.pdf.

71 American Psychiatric Association, "Position Statement on Support of Legal
Recognition of Same-Sex Civil Marriage," July 2005, https://freemarry.3cdn
.net/748b9ed377ee5fedaf_kgm6b5upb.pdf.

72 American Bar Association, Section of Family Law, "Section Recommendation
Adopted by ABA House," *Family Law eNewsletter*, February 2004, http://www
.americanbar.org/content/newsletter/publications/family_law_enewsletter
_home/2004_february.html.

73 American Bar Association, "ABA Recommendation 111," adopted by the
ABA House of Delegates August 12, 2010, http://www.abajournal.com/files/
RResolution_111.pdf.

74 Joan Biskupic, "U.S. Law Firms Flock to Gay-Marriage Proponents, Shun Other
Side," *Reuters*, June 10, 2014, http://www.reuters.com/article/2014/06/10/
us-usa-court-gaymarriage-insight-idUSKBN0EL10820140610.

75 Human Rights Campaign, *Corporate Equality Index 2015: Rating American Workplaces on Lesbian, Gay, Bisexual and Transgender Equality* (Washington, D.C.:
Human Rights Campaign, 2014).

76 "The Right Reverend Mary Douglas Glasspool," Episcopal Diocese of Los
Angeles, 2014, accessed January 19, 2017, http://www.ladiocese.org/bishop/
suffraganglasspool.html.

77 Eleventh General Synod of the United Church of Christ, "Recommendations in
Regard to the Human Sexuality Study," July 1–5, 1977, accessed February 8, 2017,
http://ucccoalition.org/wp-content/uploads/2013/09/1977-RECOMMENDA
TIONS-IN-REGARD-TO-THE-HUMAN-SEXUALITY-STUDY.pdf.

78 Twenty-First General Synod of the United Church of Christ, "Fidelity and Integrity in All Covenanted Relationships," July 3–8, 1997, accessed February 8,
2017, http://www.ucc.org/assets/pdfs/1997-FIDELITY-AND-INTEGRITY-IN
-ALL-COVENANTED-RELATIONSHIPS.pdf.

79 Twenty-Fifth General Synod of the United Church of Christ, "In Support of
Equal Marriage Rights for All," July 4, 2005, accessed February 8, 2017, http://
www.ucc.org/assets/pdfs/in-support-of-equal-marriage-rights-for-all-with
-background.pdf.

80 Human Rights Campaign, *The State of the Workplace for Lesbian, Gay, Bisexual,
and Transgendered Americans* (Washington, D.C.: Human Rights Campaign,
1999, 2004, 2007–2008).

81 Kaiser Family Foundation and Health Research and Educational Trust, *Annual
Employer Health Benefits Survey*, 1999, 2004, and 2015 editions, http://kff.org/
health-costs/report/employer-health-benefits-annual-survey-archives/.

82 The Human Rights Campaign reports that 67% of Fortune 500 firms in 2015
"offer equivalent medical benefits between spouses and partners." See Human
Rights Campaign, *The State of the Workplace for Lesbian, Gay, Bisexual, and*

Transgendered Americans (Washington, D.C.: Human Rights Campaign, 1999, 2004); Human Rights Campaign, *Corporate Equality Index 2016* (Washington, D.C.: Human Rights Campaign, 2016).

83 Kaiser Family Foundation and Health Research and Educational Trust, *Annual Employer Health Benefits Survey*, 1999, 2004, and 2015 editions.

84 Brief of 278 employers and organizations representing employers as amici curiae in support of respondent Edith Schlain Windsor (merits brief), United States v. Windsor, 570 U.S. __ (2013).

85 Larry Gross, *Up From Invisibility: Lesbians, Gay Men, and the Media in America* (New York: Columbia University Press, 2001).

86 James M. Donovan, "Same-Sex Union Announcements: Whether Newspapers Must Publish Them, and Why We Should Care," *Brooklyn Law Review* 68, no. 3 (2003): 721–807.

87 Demian, "Announcing Your Commitment: Newspapers That Publish Same-Sex Couples' Nuptial Notices," Partners Task Force for Gay & Lesbian Couples, December 2, 2015, accessed February 9, 2017, http://www.buddybuddy.com/n-papers.html.

88 Daniel Okrent, "Is the *New York Times* a Liberal Newspaper?" *New York Times*, July 25, 2004.

89 Patrick P. Pexton, "Is the Post 'Pro-Gay'?" *Washington Post*, February 24, 2013, A17.

90 Pew Research Center, *News Coverage Conveys Strong Momentum for Same-Sex Marriage*, June 17, 2013, http://www.journalism.org/2013/06/17/news-coverage-conveys-strong-momentum/.

91 Blake Ellis, "Veto Follows Business Backlash over Arizona Anti-Gay Bill," *CNN Money*, February 26, 2014, http://money.cnn.com/2014/02/25/news/economy/arizona-anti-gay-bill/.

92 Delta Air Lines, "Delta Issues Statement on Proposed Legislation," *Delta: News Archive*, February 25, 2014, accessed July 17, 2017, http://news.delta.com/delta-issues-statement-proposed-legislation.

93 The first quote is from HRC President Chad Griffin. The second is from the director of the HRC's Workplace Equality Program, Deena Fidas. See Griffin, "Corporate America Becomes a Beacon of Progress for Gay Rights," *MSNBC*, February 27, 2014, accessed June 25, 2014, http://www.msnbc.com/msnbc/corporations--gay-rights-arizona; Jena McGregor, "Corporate America's Gay-Rights Evolution," *On Leadership* (blog), *Washington Post*, February 27, 2014, accessed June 25, 2014, http://www.washingtonpost.com/blogs/on-leadership/wp/2014/02/27/corporate-americas-gay-rights-evolution/.

94 In response to the veto, White House Press Secretary Jay Carney stated, "It was gratifying to see Americans from all walks of life, including business leaders, faith leaders, regardless of party, speak out against this measure. . . . It's time to get on the right side of history." See Chris Johnson, "Carney: Brewer 'Did the Right Thing' by Vetoing Anti-Gay Bill," *Washington Blade*, February 28, 2014,

accessed June 25, 2014, http://www.washingtonblade.com/2014/02/28/carne
y-brewer-right-thing-vetoing-anti-gay-bill/.

Chapter 3

1 "Transcript: Robin Roberts ABC News Interview with President Obama." *ABC News*, May 9, 2012, http://abcnews.go.com/Politics/transcript-robin-roberts-abc
-news-interview-president-obama/story?id=16316043.

2 Brian Montopoli, "Obama on Gay Marriage: 'Attitudes Evolve, Including Mine,'"
CBS News, October 28, 2010, http://www.cbsnews.com/news/obama-on
-gay-marriage-attitudes-evolve-including-mine/; Montopoli, "Obama Stands By Opposition to Same-Sex Marriage—But Feelings 'Evolving,'" *CBS News*, December 22, 2010, http://www.cbsnews.com/news/obama-stands-by-opposition
-to-same-sex-marriage-but-feelings-evolving/.

3 Bourke v. Beshear, 3:13-CV-750-H (W.D.Ky.), February 12, 2014.

4 Obergefell v. Hodges, 576 U.S. __ (2015).

5 Andrew E. Smith, "*Boston Globe* Poll—May 2005—US Opinions on Gay Marriage." The Survey Center: University of New Hampshire, 2005, 11.

6 Pew Forum on Religion and Public Life and Pew Research Center for the People & the Press, *More Americans Question Religion's Role in Politics*, Durham, NC, August 21, 2008, http://www.people-press.org/2008/08/21/
more-americans-question-religions-role-in-politics/.

7 Richard K. Ormrod and David B. Cole, "Tolerance and Rejection: The Vote on Colorado's Amendment Two," *Professional Geographer* 48 (1996): 14–27; Kathleen O'Reilly and Gerald R. Webster, "A Sociodemographic and Partisan Analysis of Voting in Three Anti-Gay Rights Referenda in Oregon," *Professional Geographer* 50, no. 4 (1998): 498–515; Raymond Christopher Burnett and William M. Salka, "Determinants of Electoral Support for Anti-Gay Marriage: An Examination of 2006 Votes on Ballot Measures in the State," *Journal of Homosexuality* 56 (2009): 1071–82; William M. Salka and Raymond Christopher Burnett, "Determinants of Electoral Support for Anti-Gay Marriage Constitutional Amendments: An Examination of Ballot Issues in California and Florida," *Sexuality and Culture* 16 (2012): 59–75.

8 Steven H. Haeberle, "Gay Men and Lesbians at City Hall," *Social Science Quarterly* 77 (1996), 190–97.

9 The SOC actually includes a twenty-third major group, "military specific occupations," which I leave out of the analysis.

10 The General Social Survey began in 1972 and has been carried out thirty-one times through 2016. The number of annual respondents ranges from around 1,500 to roughly 3,000. The number of questions is tremendous, with each interview running approximately ninety minutes. The GSS stands as the largest, most comprehensive general long-running survey in the United States.

11 Because of limitations in sample design for the earliest years of the GSS, the data analyzed here begin with the 1976 survey. The 2016 survey results had not been released as of the time of writing.

12 It is reasonable to conclude that persons reporting a "sometimes wrong" opinion embrace a pronormalization viewpoint. The response "sometimes wrong" most likely represents a belief that same-sex sexual relations are subject to the same or similar moral standards as opposite-sex sexual relations that can also be "sometimes wrong," e.g., rape, adultery, incest, prostitution, etc.

13 On December 20, 2013, the U.S. District Court for the District of Utah ruled that Utah's marriage law that "recognize[d] as marriage only the legal union of a man and a woman" violated the U.S. Constitution. This was the second time a federal court overturned a state marriage law defining marriage as a strictly opposite-sex institution but the first of a large and rapid wave of federal court decisions overturning state marriage laws across the country following the Supreme Court's June 2013 decisions in *Windsor v. United States* and *Hollingsworth v. Perry*. See Kitchen v. Herbert, 961 F.Supp.2d 1181 (D. Utah 2013). The first such federal court ruling was *Perry v. Schwarzenegger* by the U.S. District Court for the Northern District of California in 2010 that overturned California's referendum-approved marriage law.

14 The pattern described here is substantially identical to that of earlier years.

15 The correlation with median owner-occupied housing values is less accurate than the correlation with the percentage of residents with a bachelor's degree or more, due to a limitation of the U.S. Census Bureau data. The highest median home value recorded by the Census Bureau is $1 million. The median home value for 384 California census tracts is simply reported as "$1,000,000+." These were converted to $1,000,000 to achieve a correlation figure. In light of California's extremely high house values, a great amount of data is lost due to this cutoff and the accuracy of the correlation is diminished.

16 U.S. Census Bureau, *2005–2009 American Community Survey*, tables S1501 and B25077. The Greater San Francisco Bay Area is defined as the eleven counties of the San Jose-San Francisco-Oakland Combined Statistical Area. San Joaquin County was added as a twelfth county after the 2010 census.

17 Defined by the U.S. Census Bureau as the San Francisco-Oakland-Fremont Metropolitan Statistical Area (MSA), including the counties of Alameda, Contra Costa, Marin, San Francisco, and San Mateo. Since 2013 it has been officially known as the San Francisco-Oakland-Hayward MSA.

18 These are the 5.1% of California census tracts with "yes" vote means more than two standard deviations below the statewide mean.

19 High education is defined as those census tracts with percent of population holding bachelor's degrees more than one standard deviation above the statewide mean (i.e., greater than 49.05%).

20 Greater Los Angeles is defined as the Los Angeles-Long Beach Combined Statistical Area, encompassing five California counties: Los Angeles, Orange, Riverside, San Bernardino, and Ventura.

Chapter 4

1 Quoted in Deepa Bharath, "Schuller Sr. Speaks Out against Crystal Cathedral Anti-Gay Covenant," *Orange County Register*, March 16, 2011.

2 Theodor W. Adorno et al., *The Authoritarian Personality* (New York: Harper, 1950).

3 For an overview of this argument, see Lawrence Bobo and Frederick C. Licari, "Education and Political Tolerance: Testing the Effects of Cognitive Sophistication and Target Group Affect," *Public Opinion Quarterly* 53 (1989): 285–308.

4 Summarized in Christopher Lasch, *The True and Only Heaven: Progress and Its Critics* (New York: W. W. Norton, 1991), 476–532. A contemporary example is Chris Mooney, *The Republican Brain: The Science of Why They Deny Science—and Reality* (Hoboken, N.J.: John Wiley & Sons, 2012).

5 Seymour Martin Lipset, "Democracy and Working-Class Authoritarianism," *American Sociological Review* 24 (1959): 482–502; Mayhill Fowler, "Obama: No Surprise That Hard-Pressed Pennsylvanians Turn Bitter," *Huffington Post*, April 11, 2008; Katie Reilly, "Read Hillary Clinton's 'Basket of Deplorables' Remarks about Donald Trump Supporters," *Time*, September 10, 2016, http://time.com/4486502/hillary-clinton-basket-of-deplorables-transcript/.

6 Robert Altemeyer, *The Authoritarian Specter* (Cambridge, Mass.: Harvard University Press, 1996); Bernard E. Whitley Jr. and Sarah E. Lee, "The Relationship of Authoritarianism and Related Constructs to Attitudes toward Homosexuality," *Journal of Applied Social Psychology* 30, no. 1 (2000): 144–70; W. W. Wilkinson, "Religiosity, Authoritarianism, and Homophobia: A Multidimensional Approach," *International Journal for the Psychology of Religion* 14 (2004): 55–67; Nussbaum, *From Disgust to Humanity*.

7 Eric G. Lambert, Lois A. Ventura, Daniel E. Hall, and Terry Cluse-Tolar, "College Students' Views on Gay and Lesbian Issues: Does Education Make a Difference?" *Journal of Homosexuality* 50, no. 4 (2006): 1–20.

8 "Victory for Equal Rights," June 27, 2013, A30.

9 "Marriage Equality in America," June 27, 2015, A20.

10 "Scouting's Move toward Equality," May 24, 2013, A24.

11 "The Threat to Gay Americans," June 15, 2016, A24.

12 Fish, "The Trouble with Tolerance," B8.

13 See, for example, Joseph Raz, "Autonomy, Toleration, and the Harm Principle," in *Justifying Toleration: Conceptual and Historical Perspectives*, ed. Susan Mendus (Cambridge: Cambridge University Press, 1988), 155–76; Michael Sandel, "Moral Argument and Liberal Toleration: Abortion and Homosexuality," *California Law Review* 77, no. 3 (1989): 521–38; Anna Elisabetta Galeotti, *Toleration as Recognition* (Cambridge: Cambridge University Press, 2002).

14 Preston King, *Toleration* (New York: St. Martin's, 1976), 44–54.

15 Rainer Forst, *Toleration in Conflict: Past and Present*, trans. Ciaran Cronin (Cambridge: Cambridge University Press, 2013), 18–23.

16 A response of "don't know" to the question about the morality of same-sex sexual relations may be evidence of a respondent's moral relativism or skepticism, which some insist should count as toleration and thus an instance of objection rather than indifference. Therefore "don't know" is counted here as objection. Possible answers to the same-sex marriage question include "neither agree nor disagree" and "can't choose." There seems no clear theoretical way of sorting such answers into acceptance or rejection of same-sex marriage. They may reflect support for domestic partnerships or civil unions, for example (which persons responding "disagree" could also support). They may also indicate a lack of reflection on the question, which would disqualify responses as cases of toleration. For these reasons, such responses to the same-sex marriage question were removed from the sample.

17 *Perry v. Schwarzenegger*, 67.

18 *United States v. Windsor*, 18.

19 The speech and teaching results are not statistically different from one another at a 95% confidence interval.

20 The differences between the middle and working classes are not statistically significant at the 95% confidence interval on any of the three questions when measuring only those with "objection" views of homosexuality.

21 The single exception statistically speaking is routine workers on the library question, where the tolerant and the rejectionists are not distinguishable at the 95% confidence interval level.

22 See in particular *United States v. Windsor*, 20–26.

23 Eskridge, *Dishonorable Passions*, 357.

24 This is a very popular account among leading social science and legal scholars. Take political scientist Gary Mucciaroni, who asserts that personal appeals that "create empathy and counter negative stereotypes" are politically successful in advancing the cause of gay rights. The greater the personal knowledge of LGBT persons, the greater the support for normalization and same-sex marriage. See Gary Mucciaroni, *Same Sex, Different Politics: Success and Failure in the Struggles over Gay Rights* (Chicago: University of Chicago Press, 2008), 272–75. Mucciaroni is so bold as to sum up "the story of sexual politics" in the contemporary United States as "a narrative about a heterosexist majority that has used religion and ideology to maintain its cultural and legal privileges and a story of social learning in which disproportionately younger, more educated citizens have come to know openly gay people and have responded with greater tolerance and support for LGBT equality." See Mucciaroni, "Study of LGBT Politics," 17–21. Although focused on the role of the courts, political scientist Jason Pierceson agrees with Mucciaroni's overall argument. Through same-sex marriage litigation, courts force the general public to listen to the voices of LGBT persons framed, thanks to judges, by the "richer" or "better liberalism" of equality and inclusion. Playing upon preexisting "liberal tenets of sympathy with outsiders and a belief in legally enforceable rights," courts stimulate both rational and imaginative

powers within the majority that "chip away at this [heterosexual] arrogance and force an understanding" of sexual minorities. See Jason Pierceson, *Same-Sex Marriage in the United States: The Road to the Supreme Court* (Lanham, Md.: Rowman & Littlefield, 2013), 194, 36. Harvard Law School Professor Michael Klarman places special importance on "'coming out' as a political act" to explain the progression of LGBT persons "from the closet to the altar" in his book by that name. Klarman in *From the Closet to the Altar* appeals repeatedly to the "power of the coming-out phenomenon" to imaginatively and emotionally engage heterosexuals, elicit their sympathy, and transform them personally (40, 73, 196–201, 209–10). Yale Law School professor William Eskridge Jr. presents his own version of the theory integrating the political analysis of Pierceson with the moral self-congratulation of Martha Nussbaum. By taking on same-sex marriage cases, courts force the heterosexual majority both to recognize the identities and lives of LGBT persons and to engage their political demands. Being "out of the closet and openly engaged in a same-sex union, partnership, or marriage" makes "LGBT persons and families . . . better known to a larger portion of the population." "Homophobia" can then be countered by personal knowledge and experience. While a backlash "politics of disgust" does sometimes occur, such a response fades over time. As the arguments of normalization's opponents are proven to be "scandalously contrary to both fact and reason," space opens up for the interpersonal work of individual transformation. See William N. Eskridge Jr., "Backlash Politics: How Constitutional Litigation Has Advanced Marriage Equality in the United States," *Boston University Law Review* 93 (2013): 275–323. The quotes appear on pp. 295–96.

25 George Chauncey, *Why Marriage? The History Shaping Today's Debate Over Gay Equality* (New York: Basic Books, 2004), 34–35.

26 Chauncey, *Why Marriage?*, xx.

27 "Gay Soldiers and Teachers," April 2, 2004, A18.

28 See the references in Mucciaroni, *Same Sex*, 32, 272; and Eskridge, "Backlash Politics," 314.

29 Sue Ann Skipworth, Andrew Garner, and Bryan J. Dettrey, "Limitations of the Contact Hypothesis: Heterogeneity in the Contact Effect on Attitudes toward Gay Rights," *Politics & Policy* 38 (2010): 887–906; Gregory B. Lewis, "The Friends and Family Plan: Contact with Gays and Support for Gay Rights," *Policy Studies Journal* 39 (2011): 217–38; Brittany H. Bramlett, "The Cross-Pressures of Religion and Contact with Gays and Lesbians, and Their Impact on Same-Sex Marriage Opinion," *Politics & Policy* 40 (2012): 13–42; Stephen M. Merino, "Contact with Gays and Lesbians and Same-Sex Marriage Support: The Moderating Role of Social Context," *Social Science Research* 42 (2013): 1156–66; Joshua J. Dyck and Shanna Pearson-Merkowitz, "To Know You Is Not Necessarily to Love You: The Partisan Mediators of Intergroup Contact," *Political Behavior* (online only), July 2013.

30 Lewis, "Friends and Family Plan," 236.

31 Nussbaum, *From Disgust to Humanity*, xvii.

32 Nussbaum, *From Disgust to Humanity*, xviii.

33 "Significant" in this context means statistically significant at p ≤ 0.05.

34 Alasdair MacIntyre, *After Virtue*, 3rd ed. (Notre Dame, Ind.: University of Notre Dame Press, 2007 [1981]), 111–13.

35 Quoted in John T. Faris, *The Paradise of the Pacific* (New York: Doubleday, 1929), 299.

36 "Deprive the taboo rules of their original context and they at once are apt to appear as a set of arbitrary prohibitions, as indeed they characteristically do appear when the initial context is lost, when those background beliefs in the light of which the taboo rules had originally been understood have not only been abandoned but forgotten" (MacIntyre, *After Virtue*, 112).

37 Casey E. Copen, Kimberly Daniels, Jonathan Vespa, and William D. Mosher, "First Marriages in the United States: Data from the 2006–2010 National Survey of Family Growth," *National Health Statistics Reports* 49 (March 22, 2012).

38 Cruz, "Marriage."

39 Joyce A. Martin et al., "Births: Final Data for 2015," *National Vital Statistics Report* 66, no. 1 (January 5, 2017), 8.

40 Cruz, "Marriage."

41 Copen, Daniels, and Mosher, "First Premarital Cohabitation in the United States."

42 Rachel M. Shattuck and Rose M. Kreider, "Social and Economic Characteristics of Currently Unmarried Women with a Recent Birth: 2011," *American Community Survey Reports* ACS-21 (May 2013), table 2.

43 This liberal-romantic vision of marriage was proposed and pioneered by the nineteenth-century philosopher John Stuart Mill. Political scientist Scott Yenor observes in Mill's theory of the family "a forgetting of children." Yenor observes, "As children are outside the purpose of marriage, the institution is not defined for them. Mill ignores the kids in order to propound an alluring promise of spousal friendship—the idea that husbands and wives will share the same experiences and the hope that they will be soul mates. . . . The legal and cultural institutions of the older family must be jettisoned to encourage a new, safer kind of love based on a revocable commitment to personal regeneration and growth. Leaving children outside of the purpose of marriage marks a decisive shift from a family that constitutes a unity where children are an outward, concrete, living expression of ethical love to a marriage defined by sympathetic equality for adults." Scott Yenor, *Family Politics: The Idea of Marriage in Modern Political Thought* (Waco, Tex.: Baylor University Press, 2011), 134–35.

44 *Perry v. Schwarzenegger*, 113.

45 The *Goodridge* majority vigorously asserted, "Nothing in our opinion today should be construed as relaxing or abrogating the consanguinity or polygamous prohibitions of our marriage laws. . . . Rather, the statutory provisions concerning consanguinity or polygamous marriages shall be construed in a gender

neutral manner" (60). The same court ruled in 2012 that the state of Massachusetts must recognize all marriages and civil unions contracted in other jurisdictions "even if such marriages would be prohibited here, unless the marriage violates Massachusetts public policy, including polygamy, consanguinity and affinity." Elia-Warnken v. Elia, 463 Mass. 29 (2012). See also the former domestic partner legislation in Maryland and New Jersey.

46 C. E. Tygart, "Genetic Causation Attribution and Public Support of Gay Rights," *International Journal of Public Opinion Research* 12 (2000): 259–75; Donald P. Haider-Markel and Mark R. Joslyn, "Beliefs about the Origins of Homosexuality and Support for Gay Rights: An Empirical Test of Attribution Theory," *Public Opinion Quarterly* 72 (2008): 291–310; Elizabeth Suhay and Toby Epstein Jayaratne, "Does Biology Justify Ideology? The Politics of Genetic Attribution," *Public Opinion Quarterly* 77 (2013): 497–521.

47 "Gay and Lesbian Rights," Gallup, updated May 2016, http://www.gallup.com/poll/1651/gay-lesbian-rights.aspx.

48 For example, Eve Kosofsky Sedgwick, *Epistemology of the Closet* (Berkeley: University of California Press, 1990); Judith Butler, *Gender Trouble: Feminism and the Subversion of Identity* (New York: Routledge, 1990); David M. Halperin, *One Hundred Years of Homosexuality and Other Essays on Greek Love* (New York: Routledge, 1990); Michael Warner, *The Trouble with Normal* (Cambridge, Mass.: Harvard University Press, 2000); Judith Butler, *Undoing Gender* (New York: Routledge, 2004).

49 Lisa M. Diamond, *Sexual Fluidity: Understanding Women's Love and Desire* (Cambridge, Mass.: Harvard University Press, 2008); Kelly K. Kinnish, Donald S. Strassberg, and Charles W. Turner, "Sex Differences in the Flexibility of Sexual Orientation: A Multidimensional Retrospective Assessment," *Archives of Sexual Behavior* 34 (2005): 173–83; Steven E. Mock and Richard P. Eibach, "Stability and Change in Sexual Orientation Identity over a 10-Year Period in Adulthood," *Archives of Sexual Behavior* 41 (2012): 641–48.

50 Benoit Denizet-Lewis, "The Scientific Quest to Prove—Once and for All—That Someone Can Truly Be Attracted to Both a Man and a Woman," *New York Times Magazine*, March 20, 2014, MM20.

51 Michael C. Seto, "Is Pedophilia a Sexual Orientation?" *Archives of Sexual Behavior* 41 (2012), 231–36; Laura Kane, "Is Pedophilia a Sexual Orientation?" *Toronto Star*, December 22, 2013, https://www.thestar.com/news/insight/2013/12/22/is_pedophilia_a_sexual_orientation.html.

52 Ilan Dar-Nimrod and Steven J. Heine, "Genetic Essentialism: On the Deceptive Determinism of DNA," *Psychological Bulletin* 137, no. 5 (2011): 800–818.

Chapter 5

1 American Psychological Association, *Lesbian and Gay Parenting*, 15.

2 Tara Parker-Pope, "Gay Unions Shed Light on Gender in Marriage," *New York Times*, June 10, 2008.

3 Tara Parker-Pope, "Gay Marriage: Same but Different," *New York Times*, July 1, 2013.

4 Lisa Belkin, "What's Good for the Kids," *New York Times Magazine*, November 5, 2009.

5 Stephanie Pappas, "Gay Parents Better Than Straight Parents? What Research Says," *Huffington Post*, January 16, 2012, http://www.huffingtonpost.com/2012/01/16/gay-parents-better-than-straights_n_1208659.html.

6 Liza Mundy, "The Gay Guide to Wedded Bliss," *Atlantic*, June 2013.

7 Simon R. Crouch et al., "Parent-Reported Measures of Child Health and Wellbeing in Same-Sex Parent Families: A Cross-Sectional Survey," *BMC Public Health* 14 (2014): 635.

8 According to the Thomson Reuters ISI impact factor, in 2010 the journal *BMC Public Health* ranked #44 in the "public health, environmental and occupational health" category. In 2013 it ranked #59 in the same category according to the Scimago SJR indicator.

9 Crouch et al., "Parent-Reported Measures."

10 German Lopez, "Largest-Ever Study of Same-Sex Couples' Kids Finds They're Better Off Than Other Children," *Vox*, July 7, 2014, http://www.vox.com/2014/7/7/5873781/largest-ever-study-of-same-sex-couples-kids-finds-theyre-better-off.

11 Mark Regnerus, "How Different Are the Adult Children of Parents Who Have Same-Sex Relationships? Findings from the New Family Structures Study," *Social Science Research* 41 (2012): 752–70.

12 Darren E. Sherkat, "The Editorial Process and Politicized Scholarship: Monday Morning Editorial Quarterbacking and a Call for Scientific Vigilance," *Social Science Review* 41 (2012): 1346–49; Tom Bartlett, "Controversial Gay-Parenting Study Is Severely Flawed, Journal's Audit Finds," *Percolator* (blog), *Chronicle of Higher Education*, July 26, 2012, http://chronicle.com/blogs/percolator/controversial-gay-parenting-study-is-severely-flawed-journals-audit-finds/30255.

13 James D. Wright, "Introductory Remarks," *Social Science Review* 41 (2012): 1339–45.

14 Human Rights Campaign, *The Regnerus Fallout*, 2013, http://www.regnerusfallout.org/. The site was discontinued by the Human Rights Campaign sometime between October 2016 and March 2017. As late as June 2016 a Google search of "Regnerus" returned the website as its first result.

15 Andrew Ferguson, "Revenge of the Sociologists," *Weekly Standard* 17, no. 43 (July 30, 2012). Regnerus got to relive the episode in 2014 as part of his posttenure review at the University of Texas. See *Daily Texan* Editorial Board, "Liberal Arts Dean Diehl Shouldn't Give Regnerus a Pass," *Daily Texan*, March 31, 2015.

16 Gary J. Gates et al., "Letter to the Editors and Advisory Editors at *Social Science Research*," *Social Science Research* 41 (2012): 1350–51.

17 Mark Regnerus, "Is Same-Sex Parenting Better for Kids? The New Australian Study Can't Tell Us," *Public Discourse* (online), July 9, 2014, http://www.the publicdiscourse.com/2014/07/13451/.

18 Douglas S. Massey, "Comment," *Social Science Research* 41 (2012): 1378; Douglas W. Allen, "The Regnerus Debate," *National Review Online*, June 14, 2012, http://www.nationalreview.com/article/302749/regnerus-debate-douglas-w-allen.

19 A worthwhile summary of the literature to date can be found in the National Marriage Project and Institute for American Values, *The State of Our Unions: Marriage in America 2012* (Charlottesville, VA, 2012). http://www.stateofour unions.org/2012/SOOU2012.pdf.

20 John Tosh, "New Men? The Bourgeois Cult of Home," *History Today*, December 1996, 9–15.

21 Therborn, *Between Sex and Power*, 24; Andrew Cherlin, *Labor's Love Lost: The Rise and Fall of the Working-Class Family in America* (New York: Russell Sage Foundation Publications, 2014).

22 Allan Carlson, *The "American Way": Family and Community in the Shaping of the American Identity* (Wilmington, Del.: ISI Books, 2003), 55–77.

23 Christopher Lasch, *Haven in a Heartless World* (New York: Basic Books, 1977).

24 Cahn and Carbone, *Red Families v. Blue Families.*

25 Therborn would consider the red and blue family ideals to be minor variations on the "European" family system, one of five major world models of the family that "derive from a specific value system, of religious/philosophical origin, and [are] shaped by the history of the area." This European system is dominant in the United States today, characterized by adult autonomy from parents, equal family rights between fathers and mothers, a significant minority (10%–20%) of never-married persons, high levels of female education, the rise of informal cohabitation displacing marriage, divorce, rising nonmarital births, low fertility, ubiquitous birth control, and abortion. See Therborn, *Between Sex and Power*, 10–12, 34–37.

26 Kathryn Edin and Maria Kefalas, *Promises I Can Keep: Why Poor Women Put Motherhood before Marriage* (Berkeley: University of California Press, 2005); Kathryn Edin and Timothy J. Nelson, *Doing the Best I Can: Fatherhood in the Inner City* (Berkeley: University of California Press, 2013).

27 The age of a household is defined here as the age of the male householder. The childlessness figure for cohabiting couples refers only to the biological children of an opposite-sex couple. U.S. Census Bureau, *America's Families and Living Arrangements: 2016*, https://www.census.gov/data/tables/2016/demo/families/cps-2016.html.

28 See appendix B for details on the methodology used to create the field.

29 Pierre Bourdieu, *The State Nobility* (Stanford, Calif.: Stanford University Press, 1996), 2.

30 Brigitte Le Roux and Henry Rouanet, *Multiple Correspondence Analysis* (Los Angeles: SAGE, 2010), 69–71.

31 One can see the same relationships in less dramatic form by projecting concentration ellipses for level of education onto dimensions 1 and 3. There is a distinct shift of center points toward the lower left of the graph as level of education increases. This is precisely toward the blue family model identified in figure 5.3.

32 June Carbone and Naomi R. Cahn, "Class, Politics, Gender and the Marriage Divide in the United States," *Families, Relationships and Societies* 4 (2015): 163–69.

33 W. Bradford Wilcox, *Soft Patriarchs, New Men: How Christianity Shapes Fathers and Husbands* (Chicago: University of Chicago Press, 2004). See also John P. Bartkowski, *Remaking the Godly Marriage: Gender Negotiation in Evangelical Families* (New Brunswick, N.J.: Rutgers University Press, 2001).

34 V. Gene Robinson, *In the Eye of the Storm: Swept to the Center by God* (New York: Seabury Books, 2008), 40, 98–99.

35 Therborn, *Between Sex and Power*, 13.

36 Gretchen E. Gooding and Rose M. Kreider, "Women's Marital Naming Choices in a Nationally Representative Sample," *Journal of Family Issues* 31 (2010): 681–701.

37 Miriam Liss and Mindy J. Erchull, "Differences in Beliefs and Behaviors between Feminist Actual and Anticipated Mothers," *Psychology of Women Quarterly* 37 (2012): 381–91.

38 Laura Hamilton, Claudia Geist, and Brian Powell, "Marital Name Change as a Window into Gender Attitudes," *Gender & Society* 25 (2011): 145–75.

39 Nancy Folbre, "Of the Patriarchy Born: The Political Economy of Fertility Decisions," *Feminist Studies* 9 (1983): 261–84; Nancy Folbre, "The Future of the Elephant-Bird," *Population and Development Review* 23 (1997): 647–54; Ron Lesthaeghe, "The Second Demographic Transition in Western Countries: An Interpretation," in *Gender and Family Change in Industrialized Countries*, ed. Karen Oppenheim Mason and An-Magritt Jensen (Oxford: Clarendon, 1995).

40 Beginning in the 1960s a "second demographic transition" began sweeping over all Western countries, including the United States. Between 1960 and 1976 the fertility rate of American women of childbearing age fell from 118 births per 1,000 to just 65, and it has remained in the 60s almost ever since. (In 1990 the fertility rate did reach 70.9 per 1,000 women, but it fell into the 60s again the next year.) See Martin et al., "Births: Final Data for 2015." Alongside a much lower fertility rate has been a rising rate of childlessness. The percentage of women who bore no children by the end of their fertility roughly doubled, from 8.5% of women born in 1935 to 16.3% of women born in 1960. See Centers for Disease Control and Prevention, "Data Brief 68: Childbearing Differences among Three Generations of U.S. Women," August 2011, https://www.cdc.gov/nchs/products/databriefs/db68.htm. Among those women bearing children, first births increasingly come later and later. Throughout the 1960s the mean age of American women at first birth was under 22 years old. Since the early

1970s it has risen steadily and significantly so that by 2015 it reached 26.4 years old, an all-time national record high. See National Center for Health Statistics, *Vital Statistics of the United States: 1980–2003*, table 1-6, https://www.cdc.gov/nchs/products/vsus/vsus_1980_2003.htm. All these trends have been most acute among the most highly educated. Their fertility rates are the lowest, and their rates of childlessness and their mean age at first birth are the highest. See Lindsay M. Monte and Renee R. Ellis, *Fertility of Women in the United States: 2012*, U.S. Census Bureau, July 2014, http://www.census.gov/content/dam/Census/library/publications/2014/demo/p20-575.pdf.

41 A good brief overview of the literature on this topic is Ushma D. Upadhyay et al., "Women's Empowerment and Fertility: A Review of the Literature," *Social Science and Medicine* 115 (2014): 111–20.

42 Weighted data from the 2011–2013 NSFG. Thus the data only refer to persons ages 15–44. Support for normalization is defined as responding "strongly agree" or "agree" to the statement. "Sexual relations between two adults of the same sex are all right." Percentages exclude responses of "refused" and "don't know." "The young" are defined as men and women ages 15–29. "The irreligious" are those whose religious affiliation is "none." "Highly educated women" are women with an advanced degree. "The voluntarily childless" are women who both have borne no biological children and expect to have none in their lifetimes, whether they are physically able to bear children or are surgically sterile for contraceptive reasons.

43 Philip Longman, "The Return of Patriarchy," *Foreign Policy*, March/April 2006, 56–65.

44 Between 55% and 65% of all same-sex marriages in the United States are of female couples despite the fact that a gay identity is more common among men than women. The low-end estimate of female-female married couples as a percentage of all same-sex married couples comes from Robin Fisher, Geof Gee, and Adam Looney, "Joint Filing by Same-Sex Couples after *Windsor*: Characteristics of Married Tax Filers in 2013 and 2014," Office of Tax Analysis, Department of the Treasury, Working Paper 108, August 2016. The high-end estimate comes from M. V. Lee Badgett and Jody L. Herman, "Patterns of Relationship Recognition by Same-Sex Couples in the United States," The Williams Institute, November 2011, https://williamsinstitute.law.ucla.edu/wp-content/uploads/Marriage-Dissolution-FINAL.pdf. The National Center for Health Statistics estimates that, in 2013, 1.8% of American men identified as gay while 1.5% of American women identified as lesbian. UCLA demographer Gary Gates estimated in 2011 that 2.2% of U.S. men identified as gay while just 1.1% of women identified as lesbian. See Brian W. Ward et al., "Sexual Orientation and Health among U.S. Adults: National Health Interview Survey, 2013," *National Health Statistics Reports* 77 (July 15, 2014); Gary J. Gates, "How Many People Are Lesbian, Gay, Bisexual and Transgender?" The Williams Institute, April 2011,

http://williamsinstitute.law.ucla.edu/wp-content/uploads/Gates-How-Many-People-LGBT-Apr-2011.pdf.

45 The most prominent work documenting nonmonogamy among gay male couples is the Gay Couples Study from San Francisco State University. See Colleen C. Hoff et al., "Serostatus Differences and Agreements about Sex with Outside Partners among Gay Male Couples," *AIDS Education and Prevention* 21 (2009): 25–38; and Colleen C. Hoff et al., "Relationship Characteristics and Motivations behind Agreements among Gay Male Couples: Differences by Agreement Type and Couple Serostatus," *AIDS Care* 22 (2010): 827–35. Separate work confirms these figures. See, for example, Jeffrey T. Parsons, Tyrel J. Starks, Kristi E. Gamarel, and Christian Grov, "Non-Monogamy and Sexual Relationship Quality among Same-Sex Male Couples," *Journal of Family Psychology* 25 (2012): 669–77; Jeffrey T. Parsons et al., "Alternatives to Monogamy among Gay Male Couples in a Community Survey: Implications for Mental Health and Sexual Risk," *Archives of Sexual Behavior* 42 (2013): 303–12; and Jason W. Mitchell, "Characteristics and Allowed Behaviors of Gay Male Couples' Sexual Agreements," *Journal of Sex Research* 51 (2014): 316–28.

46 Jocelyn Kiley, "It's Father's Day for Many American Men, including 23% of Those Who Are LGBT," *Factank* (online), Pew Research Center, June 16, 2013, http://www.pewresearch.org/fact-tank/2013/06/16/its-fathers-day-for-many-american-men-including-23-of-those-who-are-lgbt/.

47 Krista K. Payne, "Demographic Profile of Same-Sex Couple Households with Minor Children, 2012," NCFMR Family Profiles FP-14-03, National Center for Family and Marriage Research, Bowling Green State University, 2014; Jonathan Vespa, Jamie M. Lewis, and Rose M. Kreider, *America's Families and Living Arrangements: 2012*, U.S. Census Bureau, August 2013, https://www.census.gov/library/publications/2013/demo/p20-570.html.

48 For wealthy countries with exceptionally low infant mortality, the replacement total fertility rate is generally considered to be 2.1. The only other advanced country above that level in 2007 was New Zealand at 2.18. See the Organisation for Economic Cooperation and Development (OECD) data on Statistics/Demography/Fertility rates (indicator), doi: 10.1787/8272fb01-en, accessed March 5, 2017, http://www.oecd-ilibrary.org/content/indicator/8272fb01-en.

49 Martin et al., "Births: Final Data for 2015."

Chapter 6

1 Quoted in Sal Paolantonio, "Who Wants to Become an Eagles Exec?" *Philadelphia Inquirer*, January 9, 1994, E9.

2 Office of the Press Secretary, The White House, "Weekly Address: President Obama Vows to Continue Standing Up to the Special Interests on Behalf of the American People," January 23, 2010, https://obamawhitehouse.archives.gov/the-press-office/weekly-address-president-obama-vows-continue-standing-special-interests-behalf-amer.

3 Olson by his own testimony was "present at the founding" of the Federalist Society in 1982 while serving in the Reagan administration. See David Boies and Theodore B. Olson, *Redeeming the Dream: The Case for Marriage Equality* (New York: Viking, 2014), 65. The quote "hard core of the extreme right" is from Peter J. Rubin, founder and former president of the Federalist Society's liberal alter ego, the American Constitution Society. Quoted in Michael A. Fletcher, "What the Federalist Society Stands for," *Washington Post*, July 29, 2005, A21.

4 Quoted in Biskupic, "U.S. Law Firms Flock to Gay-Marriage Proponents."

5 This section relies strongly on the work of Lauren B. Edelman, Sally Riggs Fuller, and Iona Mara-Drita, "Diversity Rhetoric and the Managerialization of Law," *American Journal of Sociology* 106 (2001): 1589–1641; Frank Dobbin, *Inventing Equal Opportunity* (Princeton, N.J.: Princeton University Press, 2009); and Ellen Berrey, *The Enigma of Diversity: The Language of Race and the Limits of Racial Justice* (Chicago: University of Chicago Press, 2015).

6 Office of the Press Secretary, The White House, "Remarks of President Barack Obama—State of the Union Address as Delivered," January 13, 2016, https://obamawhitehouse.archives.gov/the-press-office/2016/01/12/remarks-president-barack-obama---prepared-delivery-state-union-address.

7 Berrey, *Enigma*, 26.

8 Dobbin, *Inventing Equal Opportunity*, 87.

9 Dobbin, *Inventing Equal Opportunity*, 138.

10 In the brief liberally quoted by Justice Powell, Harvard College's diversity-based admissions policy did not mention sex at all, likely because Harvard refused admission to women until 1977. See "Appendix to Opinion of Powell, J., Harvard College Admissions Program," Regents of the University of California v. Bakke, 458 U.S. 265 (1978), 321–24.

11 Dobbin, *Inventing Equal Opportunity*, 133–60.

12 Quoted in Berrey, *Enigma*, 71–72, 74–75.

13 James Duderstadt, *The Michigan Mandate: A Strategic Linking of Academic Excellence and Social Diversity* (Ann Arbor: University of Michigan, 1990).

14 Daniel N. Lipson, "Where's the Justice? Affirmative Action's Severed Civil Rights Roots in the Age of Diversity," *Perspectives on Politics* 6 (2008): 691–706.

15 Daniel N. Lipson, "Embracing Diversity: The Institutionalization of Affirmative Action as Diversity Management at UC-Berkeley, UT-Austin, and UW-Madison," *Law & Social Inquiry* 32 (2007): 985–1026.

16 Korn Ferry, "Executive Attitudes on Diversity Positive, but Actions Lagging, Korn/Ferry Institute Survey Finds," *Korn Ferry*, November 4, 2013, http://www.kornferry.com/press/15143/.

17 "Brief of Fortune-100 and Other Leading American Businesses as Amici Curiae in Support of Respondents," Fisher v. University of Texas, 579 U.S. ___ (2015).

18 For a broad overview of the literature and its conflicting results, see George Gotsis and Zoe Kortezi, "Workplace Diversity: A Resource or a Source of Conflict?" in Gotsis and Kortezi, *Critical Studies in Diversity Management Literature:*

A Review and Synthesis (Dordrecht, The Netherlands: Springer, 2015), 1–12. For scholarship supporting the business case for diversity, see Cedric Herring, "Does Diversity Pay? Race, Gender, and the Business Case for Diversity," *American Sociological Review* 74 (2009): 208–24; Alison Cook and Christy Glass, "Do Minority Leaders Affect Corporate Practice? Analyzing the Effect of Leadership Composition on Governance and Product Development," *Strategic Organization* 13 (2015): 117–40; Sangeeta Badal and James K. Harter, "Gender Diversity, Business-Unit Engagement, and Performance," *Journal of Leadership & Organizational Studies* 21 (2014): 354–65; and Sheen S. Levine et al., "Ethnic Diversity Deflates Price Bubbles," *Proceedings of the National Academy of Sciences of the United States of America* 111, no. 52 (2014): 18524–29. Research rejecting the business case for diversity includes Renee B. Adams and Daniel Ferreira, "Women in the Boardroom and Their Impact on Governance and Performance," *Journal of Financial Economics* 94 (2009): 291–309; Deborah Rhode and Amanda K. Packel, "Diversity on Corporate Boards: How Much Difference Does Difference Make?" *Delaware Journal of Corporate Law* 39 (2014): 377–426; Tessa L. Dover et al., "Members of High-Status Groups Are Threatened by Pro-Diversity Organizational Messages," *Journal of Experimental Psychology* 62 (2016): 58–67; Makan Amini et al., "Does Gender Diversity Promote Nonconformity?" *Management Science*, published online, March 25, 2016, http://pubsonline.informs.org/ doi/abs/10.1287/mnsc.2015.2382; and Dragana Stojmenovska, Thijs Bol, and Thomas Leopold, "Does Diversity Pay? A Replication of Herring (2009)," *American Sociological Review*, published online, July 7, 2017, http://journals.sagepub .com/doi/abs/10.1177/0003122417714422.

19 Alexandra Kalev et al., "Best Practices or Best Guesses? Assessing the Efficacy of Corporate Affirmative Action and Diversity Policies," *American Sociological Review* 71 (2006): 589–617.

20 See the literature review and meta-analysis in Nicholas A. Bowman, "College Diversity Experiences and Cognitive Development: A Meta-Analysis," *Review of Educational Research* 80 (2010): 4–33.

21 Peter Arcidiacono and Michael Lovenheim, "Affirmative Action and the Quality-Fit Trade-Off," *Journal of Economic Literature* 54 (2016): 3–51.

22 Berrey, *Enigma*.

23 Dobbin, *Inventing Equal Opportunity*, 50–51.

24 According to *Forbes* magazine, 71% of U.S. human resources managers were women in 2011. See Jenna Goudreau, "Top 10 Best-Paying Jobs for Women in 2011," *Forbes*, April 20, 2011, https://www.forbes.com/2011/04/20/best-paying -jobs-for-women_slide_2.html. The argument that white women are the primary beneficiaries of diversity comes from Kalev et al., "Best Practices?"

25 See Harold Perkin, *The Rise of Professional Society: England Since 1880* (London: Routledge, 1989); Christopher Pollitt, *Managerialism and the Public Services: The Anglo-American Experience* (Cambridge, Mass.: Basil Blackwell, 1990); Willard F.

Enteman, *Managerialism: The Emergence of a New Ideology* (Madison: University of Wisconsin Press, 1993).

26 Edelman, Fuller, and Mara-Drita, "Diversity Rhetoric," 1610; Angela T. Ragusa, "Social Change and the Corporate Construction of Gay Markets in the *New York Times'* Advertising Business News," *Media, Culture & Society* 27 (2005): 653–76.

27 "Gay Branding: Refining Rainbows," *Design Week*, July 9, 2009, 17. In 1995 the rainbow flag's designer and creator, Gilbert Baker, expressed pleasure that the rainbow flag was "displacing" the pink triangle as American gays' and lesbians' preferred symbol. See Deb Price, "Symbol for a 'Rainbow' of People," *San Francisco Examiner*, April 11, 1995, B7. By 1997 the pink triangle was clearly "on the decline." See Thomas Brady, "How Some Gays Choose to Show the Colors," *Philadelphia Inquirer*, November 19, 1997, D1.

28 "World Peace Flag," http://www.flagguys.com/peace.html.

29 To ensure none missed the symbolic meaning of the rainbow, the novel's author made the Soviet commander's slogan "Conquer and Breed." Floyd Gibbons, *The Red Napoleon* (Carbondale: Southern Illinois University Press, 1976 [1929]), 9, 276.

30 Gilbert Baker, "The Prideful Story of Our Rainbow Flag" (interview), *IGLA Bulletin* 10 (1994): 4–5; Clive Moore, *Sunshine and Rainbows: The Development of Gay and Lesbian Culture in Queensland* (St. Lucia, Queensland: University of Queensland Press, 2001), 22–23; "Gay Pride Flag Creator Proud but Humble," *CBS Chicago*, June 24, 2012, http://chicago.cbslocal.com/2012/06/24/gay-pride-flag-creator-proud-but-humble/; Paola Antonelli and Michelle Millar Fisher, "MoMA Acquires the Rainbow Flag," *Inside/Out*, June 17, 2015, http://www.moma.org/explore/inside_out/2015/06/17/moma-acquires-the-rainbow-flag; Ana Swanson, "How the Rainbow Became the Symbol of Gay Pride," Wonkblog, *Washington Post*, June 29, 2015, https://www.washingtonpost.com/news/wonk/wp/2015/06/29/how-the-rainbow-became-the-symbol-of-gay-pride/?utm_term=.57687274b090.

31 Steven Seidman and Chet Meeks, "The Politics of Authenticity: Civic Individualism and the Cultural Roots of Gay Normalization," *Cultural Sociology* 5 (2011): 519–36.

32 Sender, *Business, Not Politics*, 108.

33 While such an image is hardly a normal American LGBT experience, statistics are quite beside the point. See Badgett, *Money, Myths, and Change*.

34 Anna Kirkland and Ben B. Hansen, "'How Do I Bring Diversity?' Race and Class in the College Admissions Essay," *Law & Society Review* 45 (2011): 103–38. The quote appears on page 111.

35 Daniel Nussbaum, "Doritos Goes Gay, and Other Foods That Have Shown Support for the LGBT Cause," *Breitbart*, September 17, 2015, http://www.breitbart.com/big-hollywood/2015/09/17/doritos-goes-gay-foods-shown-support-lgbt-cause/.

36 Renée Frojo, "Gap Goes Gay for 'True Outfitters' Campaign," *San Francisco Business Times*, February 21, 2014, http://www.bizjournals.com/sanfrancisco/blog/2014/02/banana-republic-same-sex-couple-campaign.html.

37 "Target's Same-Sex Registry Ad Praised by LGBT Advocacy Bloggers," *Huffington Post*, July 26, 2012, http://www.huffingtonpost.com/2012/07/26/target-same-sex-registry-ad-gay-marriage_n_1706599.html.

38 Curtis M. Wong, "Tylenol's 'For What Matters Most' Re-Imagines Norman Rockwell Painting with Lesbian Moms," *Huffington Post*, February 2, 2016, http://www.huffingtonpost.com/2014/12/22/tylenol-lesbian-commercial-_n_6367800.html.

39 *The Advocate*, Tumblr, http://theadvocatemag.tumblr.com/post/21874992166/italian-sunglasses-manufacturer-ray-ban-released.

40 Bruce Horovitz, "Burger King Sells Gay Pride Whopper," *USA Today*, July 1, 2014, http://www.usatoday.com/story/money/business/2014/07/01/burger-king-gay-pride-burger-parade-fast-food-gay-rights/11903861/.

41 Kacey Culliney, "Lucky Charms Rainbow Pride Campaign Targeted Diverse Millennials, Says General Mills," *BakeryandSnacks.com*, July 3, 2013, http://www.bakeryandsnacks.com/Manufacturers/Lucky-Charms-rainbow-Pride-campaign-targeted-diverse-millennials-says-General-Mills.

42 Lisa Tomassen, "Lucky Charms Asks What Makes You Lucky?" *Taste of General Mills* (blog), June 3, 2014, http://www.blog.generalmills.com/2014/06/luckytobe/.

43 Kevin Hunt, "Show Us Why You Are #LuckyToBe," *Taste of General Mills* (blog), June 4, 2015, http://blog.generalmills.com/2015/06/show-us-why-you-are-luckytobe/.

44 Yasmin Aslam, "#LoveWins on the Internet," *MSNBC.com*, June 27, 2015, http://www.msnbc.com/msnbc/love-wins-the-internet; Justin Lafferty, "#LoveWins: How the Same-Sex Marriage Decision Spread through Social," *SocialTimes*, June 30, 2015, http://www.adweek.com/socialtimes/lovewins-how-the-same-sex-marriage-decision-spread-through-social/622661; Kerry Flynn, "How #LoveWins on Twitter Became the Most Viral Hashtag of the Same-Sex Marriage Ruling," *International Business Times*, June 26, 2015; Gemma Craven, "The Lasting Impact of #LoveWins on Social Brand Marketing," *Spredfast*, July 1, 2015, https://www.spredfast.com/social-marketing-blog/lasting-impact-lovewins-social-brand-marketing.

45 Berrey, *Enigma*, 122.

46 Berrey, *Enigma*, 205.

47 Florida, *Rise of the Creative Class*; *Cities and the Creative Class* (New York: Routledge, 2005); *The Flight of the Creative Class* (New York: HarperCollins, 2005); and *The Rise of the Creative Class, Revisited* (New York: Basic Books, 2012).

48 Florida, *Rise of the Creative Class, Revisited*, 186.

49 Florida, *Rise of the Creative Class*, 79.

50 Florida's definition of the "creative class" is for the most part the U.S. Standard Occupational Classification (SOC) definition of managers (SOC 11–13) and

professionals (SOC 15–29) (see table A.4 in appendix D). Florida adds "high-end" sales occupations (SOC 41) without any stated methodology for identifying which sales jobs are "high-end" versus "low-end." This sentiment does reflect, however, the NS-SEC schema that I use in my precise definition of elites (see appendix A). The primary difference between my definition and Florida's is his exclusion of "community and social services occupations" (SOC 21) such as counselors, therapists, social workers, and the clergy. See Florida, *Rise of the Creative Class*, 328.

51 Florida, *Cities and the Creative Class*, 130.

52 The correlation value was 0.1 and not statistically significant. Florida, *Rise of the Creative Class*, 254–55; *Cities and the Creative Class*, 40. Subsequent research by other scholars found similarly small, although statistically significant, correlations of around 0.2. Stephen Rausch and Cynthia Negrey, "Does the Creative Engine Run? A Consideration of the Effect of Creative Class on Economic Strength and Growth," *Journal of Urban Affairs* 28 (2006): 473–89; Mary Donegan et al., "Which Indicators Explain Metropolitan Economic Performance Best? Traditional or Creative Class," *Journal of the American Planning Association* 74 (2008): 180–95; Michele Hoyman and Christopher Faricy, "It Takes a Village: A Test of the Creative Class, Social Capital, and Human Capital Theories," *Urban Affairs Review* 44 (2009): 311–33.

53 Florida, *Rise of the Creative Class*, 262–63.

54 Hoyman and Faricy, "It Takes a Village."

55 Richard Florida and Charlotta Mellander, *Segregated City: The Geography of Economic Segregation in America's Metros* (Toronto: Martin Prosperity Institute, Rotman School of Management, University of Toronto, 2015), 70–72.

56 Bradley Bereitschaft and Rex Cammack, "Neighborhood Diversity and the Creative Class in Chicago," *Applied Geography* 63 (2015): 166–83.

57 Florida, *Rise of the Creative Class*, 256–58; *Cities and the Creative Class*, 131.

58 Rausch and Negrey, "Does the Creative Engine Run?"; Donegan et al., "Which Indicators?"; Hoyman and Faricy, "It Takes a Village."

59 Florida and Mellander, *Segregated City*, 39.

60 The correlations are 0.17 and 0.18, respectively. Bereitschaft and Cammack, "Neighborhood Diversity."

61 Florida, *Cities and the Creative Class*, 131.

62 Florida, *Rise of the Creative Class*, 227, 256. See also Richard Florida, Charlotta Mellander, and Kevin Stolarick, "Inside the Black Box of Regional Development—Human Capital, the Creative Class and Tolerance," *Journal of Economic Geography* 8 (2008): 615–49.

63 Quoted in Todd Babiak, "Creative Class Warfare," *Edmonton Journal*, July 7, 2003, C5.

64 Edward O. Laumann et al., eds., *The Social Organization of Sexuality: Sexual Practices in the United States* (Chicago: University of Chicago Press, 1994); Andrew M. Francis, "Family and Sexual Orientation: The Family-Demographic Correlates of

Homosexuality in Men and Women," *Journal of Sex Research* 45 (2008): 371–77; Dan A. Black, Hoda R. Makar, Seth G. Sanders, and Lowell J. Taylor, "The Earnings Effects of Sexual Orientation," *Industrial and Labor Relations Review* 56 (2003): 449–69; Anjani Chandra et al., "Sexual Behavior, Sexual Attraction, and Sexual Identity in the United States: Data from the 2006–2008 National Survey of Family Growth," *National Health and Statistics Reports* 36 (2011); Prudential Financial, *The LGBT Financial Experience: 2012–2013 Prudential Research Study*, November 2012, http://www.prudential.com/media/managed/Prudential _LGBT_Financial_Experience.pdf; U.S. Census Bureau, "Table 2. Educational Attainment of the Population 25 Years and Over, by Selected Characteristics: 2012," *Annual Social and Economic Supplement of the Current Population Survey* (2012), https://www.census.gov/topics/education/educational-attainment/ data/tables.2012.html.

65 Amanda K. Baumle, D'Lane Compton, and Dudley L. Poston Jr., *Same-Sex Partners: The Social Demography of Sexual Orientation* (Albany: State University of New York Press, 2009), 156–69; Nasser Daneshvary, C. Jeffrey Waddoups, and Bradley S. Wimmer, "Previous Marriage and the Lesbian Wage Premium," *Industrial Relations* 48, no. 3 (2009): 432–53; Marieka Klawitter, "Meta-Analysis of the Effects of Sexual Orientation on Earnings," *Industrial Relations* 54 (2015): 4–32.

66 Aldous Huxley, *Brave New World* (New York: Harper Perennial Modern Classics, 2006 [1932]), 238.

Chapter 7

1 Bethany Moreton, *To Serve God and Wal-Mart: The Making of Christian Free Enterprise* (Cambridge, Mass.: Harvard University Press, 2009). The Ralph Reed quote originally appeared in Dan McGraw, "The Christian Capitalists," *U.S. News and World Report* 118, no. 10, March 13, 1995, 52.

2 "Our statement on Arkansas #HB1228," Walmart Newsroom, *Twitter*, March 31, 2015, https://twitter.com/WalmartNewsroom/status/583032659787448320/ photo/1.

3 1 United States Code § 1: "the words 'person' and 'whoever' include corporations, companies, associations, firms, partnerships, societies, and joint stock companies, as well as individuals."

4 Human Rights Campaign, "HRC Calls on AZ Gov. Jan Brewer to Veto License to Discriminate Law," press release, February 21, 2014, http://www.hrc.org/press/ hrc-calls-on-az-gov.-jan-brewer-to-veto-license-to-discriminate-law.

5 Stephen Peters, "Déjà Vu All Over Again: Indiana Sees Extreme Anti-LGBT 'Super-RFRA' Advance in Legislature," *Human Rights Campaign*, January 25, 2015, http://www.hrc.org/blog/deja-vu-all-over-again-indiana-sees-extreme -anti-lgbt-super-rfra-advance-in.

6 Louise Melling, "ACLU: Why We Can No Longer Support the Federal 'Religious Freedom' Law," *Washington Post*, June 25, 2015.

7 Chai Feldblum, "Moral Conflict and Liberty: Gay Rights and Religion," *Brooklyn Law Review* 72 (2006): 61–123.

8 Pew Research Center, *"Nones" on the Rise: One-in-Five Adults Have No Religious Affiliation*, October 9, 2012, http://www.pewforum.org/2012/10/09/nones-on-the-rise/.

9 Louis Bolce and Gerald de Maio, "Our Secularist Democratic Party," *National Affairs* 149 (2002): 3–20.

10 Ryan T. Anderson, quoted in Valerie Richardson, "Arkansas, Indiana Religious Freedom Bill Revisions Spark More Debates," *Washington Times*, April 2, 2015.

11 A ProQuest newspaper search shows the phrase "so-called religious freedom" appeared 256 times in 2015. Over the years 1993–2014 it appeared 196 times.

12 Paul Horwitz, "The Hobby Lobby Moment," 128 *Harvard Law Review* 154, November 10, 2014.

13 While this argument can be found in many places, its classic expression is political writer Thomas Frank's 2004 book *What's the Matter with Kansas?* In struggling to understand how so many members of the country's white middle and working classes have come to support conservative Republicans over liberal Democrats, Frank offers up a withering psychological diagnosis. Downscale whites are practitioners of "the politics of self-delusion." These "suicidal" voters suffer from "derangement." Since they are captivated by a "fury which passeth all understanding," they cannot recognize "any set of facts that are merely material, merely true." Thomas Frank, *What's the Matter with Kansas? How Conservatives Won the Heart of America* (New York: Metropolitan Books, 2004).

14 Pierre Bourdieu, "The Social Space and the Genesis of Groups," *Theory and Society* 14 (1985): 723–44. The quote is from p. 729.

15 Bourdieu, *Distinction*, 478.

16 Bourdieu, "Social Space," 730.

17 Joseph R. Gusfield, *Symbolic Crusade: Status Politics and the American Temperance Movement*, 2nd ed. (Champaign: University of Illinois Press, 1986); Christian Smith, "Introduction: Rethinking the Secularization of American Public Life," in *The Secular Revolution: Power, Interests, and Conflict in the Secularization of American Public Life*, ed. Christian Smith (Berkeley: University of California Press, 2003), 1–96.

18 Robert P. Jones, *The End of White Christian America* (New York: Simon & Schuster, 2016).

19 Ryan L. Claassen, *Godless Democrats and Pious Republicans? Party Activists, Party Capture, and the "God Gap"* (Cambridge: Cambridge University Press, 2015), 50.

20 Editorial board, "Respect for Privacy," *New York Times*, January 24, 1973, 40.

21 D. Michael Lindsay, *Faith in the Halls of Power: How Evangelicals Joined the American Elite* (Oxford: Oxford University Press, 2007).

22 Matthew Connelly, *Fatal Misconception: The Struggle to Control World Population* (Cambridge, Mass.: Belknap Press, 2008).

23 N. J. Demerath III, "Cultural Victory and Organizational Defeat in the Paradox-ical Decline of Liberal Protestantism," *Journal for the Scientific Study of Religion* 34 (1995): 458–69; Christian Smith and Patricia Snell, *Souls in Transition: The Religious and Spiritual Lives of Emerging Adults* (Oxford: Oxford University Press, 2009), 287–89; David A. Hollinger, "After Cloven Tongues of Fire: Ecumenical Protestantism and the Modern American Encounter with Diversity," *The Journal of American History* 98 (2011): 21–48.

24 Joseph Bottum, *An Anxious Age* (New York: Image, 2014).

25 The literature on the second demographic transition is vast. For a brief overview, see Ron Lesthaeghe, "The Second Demographic Transition: A Concise Overview of Its Development," *Proceedings of the National Academy of Sciences of the United States of America* 111, no. 51 (2014): 18112–15. A longer introduction is Ron Lesthaeghe, "The Unfolding Story of the Second Demographic Transition," *Population and Development Review* 36 (2010): 211–51.

26 Ronald Inglehart, *Culture Shift in Advanced Industrial Society* (Princeton, N.J.: Princeton University Press, 1990); Ronald Inglehart and Pippa Norris, *Rising Tide: Gender Equality and Cultural Change around the World* (Cambridge: Cambridge University Press, 2003); Johan Surkyn and Ron Lesthaeghe, "Value Orientations and the Second Demographic Transition (SDT) in Northern, Western and Southern Europe: An Update," *Demographic Research*, Special Collection 3 (2004); Ron J. Lesthaeghe and Lisa Neidert, "The Second Demographic Transition in the United States: Exception or Textbook Example?" *Population and Demographic Review* 32 (2006): 669–98.

27 Louis Bolce and Gerald de Maio, "Religious Outlook, Culture War Politics, and Antipathy toward Christian Fundamentalists," *Public Opinion Quarterly* 63 (1999): 29–61; Louis Bolce and Gerald de Maio, "The Anti-Christian Fundamentalist Factor in Contemporary Politics," *Public Opinion Quarterly* 63 (1999): 508–42; Bolce and de Maio, "Our Secularist Democratic Party"; Louis Bolce and Gerald de Maio, "A Prejudice for the Thinking Classes: Media Exposure, Political Sophistication, and the Anti-Christian Fundamentalist," *American Politics Research* 36 (2008): 155–85; George Yancey, "Who Has Religious Prejudice? Differing Sources of Anti-Religious Animosity in the United States," *Review of Religious Research* 52 (2010): 159–71; George Yancey and David A. Williamson, *So Many Christians, So Few Lions: Is There Christianophobia in the United States?* (Lanham, Md.: Rowman & Littlefield, 2015).

28 Yancey and Williamson define "relative animosity" toward a group as a feelings thermometer reading at least one standard deviation lower than the average given to all other racial and religious groups. See Yancey, "Who Has Religious Prejudice?"; Yancey and Williamson, *So Many Christians*, 33.

29 In 2007, 26% of Evangelical Protestants agreed with the statement "homosexuality should be accepted by society" while 27% of Muslims said the same. Fifty percent of all Americans agreed at that time. See p. 106 of Pew Research Center, *U.S. Public Becoming Less Religious*, November 3, 2015, http://www.pewforum

.org/2015/11/03/u-s-public-becoming-less-religious/; and p. 59 of Pew Research Center, *Muslim Americans: No Signs of Growth in Alienation or Support for Extremism*, August 30, 2011, http://www.people-press.org/2011/08/30/muslim -americans-no-signs-of-growth-in-alienation-or-support-for-extremism/.

30 A descriptive statistical method called "principal component analysis" (PCA)— part of a family of methods including multiple correspondence analysis used in chapter 5—enables a more sophisticated view beyond simple pair-wise correlations. PCA rearranges a larger number of correlated original variables into a smaller number of uncorrelated new variables called the "principal components." These new variables reveal the underlying structure of the original data and explain the variance in it. Just like multiple correspondence analysis, the first component explains the largest percentage of the variance, the second the second-most, and so on down the list. A PCA of the 2008 feeling thermometer readings reveals a complex structure in the data: thirteen components in total with five required to explain most (i.e., over 50%) of the variance. Despite this complexity, we can still detect the strong negative relationship between views of fundamentalists and views of gay men and lesbians. Among the five retained components, these two variables load only on the first, that is, the one that explains the most variance in the data. By "loading only on the first" component I mean that both are statistically significant and the absolute value of their correlation is greater than 0.35 only on the first component. In addition, they not only have opposite signs but each has the highest correlation value among the thirteen groups. The first dimension captures the familiar red vs. blue cultural divide in the United States, with gays and lesbians on the one hand and fundamentalists on the other respectively playing key and opposite symbolic roles for both camps.

The structure of the 2012 data is a bit different. Views toward fundamentalists and views toward gays and lesbians still load strongly on the first component and have opposite signs, but the correlations are not as high. We still see the red vs. blue cultural divide explaining the largest portion of the variance. However, attitudes toward minority racial groups have displaced attitudes toward LGBT persons as most definitive of blue views. Fundamentalists continue to load only on the first dimension. Gay men and lesbians, however, load on both the first and the second. The second dimension seems to represent the class divide within blue America. Conservative groups don't load at all while all the variance is between views of racial groups (including whites) and of blue cultural groups (liberals, gays and lesbians, feminists, Muslims, and atheists). Interestingly, gays and lesbians load more strongly on the second dimension than the first. While difficult to interpret, this evidence may indicate that between 2008 and 2012 positive views of LGBT persons were displaced from the symbolic center of the blue tribe in general but remained a key referent group for its most culturally liberal members.

31 Measured as mean relative standardized thermometer reading at the 10th percentile.

32 In 2008 feelings toward Christians loaded only on the first dimension and had the second highest negative correlation behind only views toward fundamentalists, while in 2012 feelings toward Christians again loaded only on the first dimension and had the highest negative correlation of all. This means that relatively positive feelings toward Christians were strongly indicative of membership in the red tribe, while relatively negative feelings toward Christians were strongly indicative of membership in the blue tribe.

33 The heading for this section is from Philip Rieff, *My Life among the Deathworks: Illustrations of the Aesthetics of Authority, Volume 1: Sacred Order / Social Order* (Charlottesville: University of Virginia Press, 2006), 1–2.

34 "The field of power is the locus of struggles that have as one of their stakes the hierarchy of the principles of ethical evaluation. . . . Celebratory discourses—eulogies, reception speeches, etc.—in which various groups sing their own praises in singing the praises of their members . . . are essential moments in the work of expression, systematization, and universalization through which a group tends to convert its ethos into an ethic, transmuting the objectively systematic principles of a shared habitus, nearly universalized within the confines of a group, into an intentionally coherent system of explicit norms with claims to universality." Bourdieu, *State Nobility*, 44.

35 James Davison Hunter, *Culture Wars: The Struggle to Define America* (New York: Basic Books, 1991), 52.

36 Farr A. Curlin et al., "The Relationship between Psychiatry and Religion among U.S. Physicians," *Psychiatric Services* 58 (2007): 1193–98.

37 Neil Gross and Solon Simmons, "The Religiosity of American College and University Professors," *Sociology of Religion* 70 (2009): 101–29; Pew Research Center, *U.S. Religious Landscape Survey: Religious Affiliation, Diverse and Dynamic*, February 1, 2008, http://www.pewforum.org/files/2013/05/report-religious-landscape-study-full.pdf.

38 Stephanie Valutis and Deborah Rubin, "Value Conflicts in Social Work: Categories and Correlates," *Journal of Social Work Values and Ethics* 13 (2016): 11–24.

39 Christina R. Miller et al., "An Online Survey of Social Workers' Family Values," *Journal of Social Work Values and Ethics* 13 (2016): 59–72.

40 As of July 2017, the nine states are: California, Connecticut, Illinois, Nevada, New Jersey, New Mexico, Oregon, Rhode Island, and Vermont. New York's ban thus far is not a law but an executive order of the governor banning coverage of conversion therapy by insurers and conversion therapy practices in state-run facilities.

41 See, for example: California SB-1172 Sexual orientation change efforts (2011–2012), bill text, http://leginfo.legislature.ca.gov/faces/billNavClient .xhtml?bill_id=201120120SB1172#; New Jersey A3371 Protects minors by prohibiting attempts to change sexual orientation (2012–2013), bill text, http://

legiscan.com/NJ/text/A3371/2012; Rhode Island H5277 Substitute A An act relating to health and safety (2017), bill text, http://webserver.rilin.state.ri.us/BillText17/HouseText17/H5277A.pdf.

42 Council on Social Work Education, "2015 Educational Policy and Accreditation Standards," https://www.cswe.org/getattachment/Accreditation/Accreditation-Process/2015-EPAS/2015EPAS_Web_FINAL.pdf.aspx.

43 See Ward v. Polite, U.S. Court of Appeals for the Sixth Circuit (2012); Keeton v. Anderson-Wiley, U.S. District Court for the Southern District of Georgia, Augusta Division (2012).

44 In the first case, four professors were disciplined for their actions while the student was offered a graduate scholarship at the university. See Brooker v. The Governors of Missouri State University, U.S. District Court for the Western District of Missouri, Southern Division (2006). In the second case, the university settled out of court and agreed to pay the student's tuition to complete his degree at a different university.

45 David R. Hodge, "Does Social Work Oppress Evangelical Christians? A 'New Class' Analysis of Society and Social Work," *Social Work* 47 (2002): 401–14. The quote appears on page 405. See also Lawrence E. Ressler and David R. Hodge, "Religious Discrimination in Social Work: Preliminary Evidence," *Journal of Religion and Spirituality in Social Work: Social Thought* 24 (2006): 55–74; Bruce A. Thyer and Laura L. Myers, "Religious Discrimination in Social Work Academic Programs: Whither Social Justice?" *Journal of Religion and Spirituality in Social Work: Social Thought* 28 (2009): 144–60.

46 Sarah Todd and Diana Coholic, "Christian Fundamentalism and Anti-Oppressive Social Work Pedagogy," *Journal of Teaching in Social Work* 27, nos. 3/4 (2007): 5–25.

47 Kristin A. Hancock, "Student Beliefs, Multiculturalism, and Client Welfare," *Psychology of Sexual Orientation and Gender Diversity* 1 (2014): 1–9.

48 Gregory F. Zoeller, "Duty to Defend and the Rule of Law," *Indiana Law Journal* 90, no. 2 (2015): 513–57.

49 Biskupic, "U.S. Law Firms Flock to Gay-Marriage Proponents." The only recourse for major law firm attorneys interested in defending opposite-sex-only marriage laws was to quit. The two most prominent resignations were of former U.S. Solicitor General Paul Clement from King & Spalding (#27 on the Am Law 200 rankings in 2015) and veteran Supreme Court litigator Gene Schaerr from Winston & Strawn (#39 in 2015).

50 American Bar Association, "Model Rule of Professional Conduct 8.4," https://www.americanbar.org/groups/professional_responsibility/committees_commissions/ethicsandprofessionalresponsibility/modruleprofconduct8_4.html.

51 Walter Olson, "Eugene Volokh vs. Deborah Rhode on Hostile Environment and ABA 8.4(g)," *Overlawyered*, December 8, 2016, https://www.overlawyered.com/2016/12/eugene-volokh-vs-deborah-rhode-hostile-environment-aba-8-4g/. The quote is from Stanford University law professor Deborah Rhode.

52 Neil Gross and Solon Simmons, "The Social and Political Views of American College and University Professors," in *Professors and Their Politics*, ed. Neil Gross and Solon Simmons (Baltimore: Johns Hopkins University Press, 2014), 19–52.

53 Bruce L. R. Smith, Jeremy D. Mayer, and A. Lee Fritschler, *Closed Minds? Politics and Ideology in American Universities* (Washington, D.C.: Brookings Institution Press, 2008), 189.

54 The number of conservatives of any kind in higher education is quite small. A 1999 survey found that 12% of American college and university faculty self-identified as conservative. A 2006 survey found that figure had dropped to a mere 9%. In fact, self-identified left radicals are more common on campus than self-identified conservatives. Ideological conservatives are strongly underrepresented at the most elite institutions, independent of their academic achievement in the areas of research and publishing. They are likewise most prevalent at low-prestige community colleges and universities that do not grant Ph.D. degrees. We can be confident that their numbers in elite research universities and elite liberal arts colleges fall far below even 9%. In the social science fields that dominate academic research, legal testimony, and public discourse on homosexuality, conservatives make up only 5% of professors across all institutions. The number is surely vanishingly small at elite levels. Stanley Rothman, S. Robert Lichter, and Neil Nevitte, "Politics and Professional Advancement among College Faculty," *The Forum* 3, no. 1 (2005); Stanley Rothman and S. Robert Lichter, "The Vanishing Conservative—Is There a Glass Ceiling?" in *The Politically Correct University: Problems, Scope, and Reforms*, ed. Robert Maranto, Richard E. Redding, and Frederick M. Hess (Washington, D.C.: AEI Press, 2009), 60–76; Gross and Simmons, "Social and Political Views."

55 Jon A. Shields and Joshua M. Dunn Sr., *Passing on the Right: Conservative Professors in the Progressive University* (Oxford: Oxford University Press, 2016).

56 Rothman, Lichter, and Nevitte, "Politics and Professional Advancement."

57 Gary A. Tobin and Aryeh K. Weinberg, *Profiles of the American University, Volume II: Religious Beliefs and Behavior of College Faculty* (San Francisco: Institute for Jewish and Community Research, 2007).

58 George Yancey, *Compromising Scholarship: Religious and Political Bias in American Higher Education* (Waco, Tex.: Baylor University Press, 2011).

59 Ross Douthat, "The Terms of Our Surrender," *New York Times*, March 1, 2014.

60 Both Connecticut and Rhode Island do have state RFRAs, passed in 1993. Neither recognizes any possible legal exemption from antidiscrimination laws on the basis of religious freedom.

61 In June 2017 a federal appeals court struck down the initial injunction on Mississippi's RFRA on the grounds that the original plaintiffs in the case lacked standing. In that the law had never gone into effect, they could not claim any harm had been done to them. The case will certainly continue to wend its way through the federal courts.

62 Sarah Jones, "The Loud Rise and Quiet Fall of Roy Moore," *New Republic*, September 30, 2016, https://newrepublic.com/article/137358/loud-rise-quiet-fall-roy-moore.

Conclusion

1 Douglas Laycock and Thomas C. Berg, "Brief of Douglas Laycock, Thomas C. Berg, David Blankenhorn, Marie A. Failinger, and Edward McGlynn Gaffney, as Amici Curiae in Support of Petitioners," in the case of *Obergefell v. Hodges*, March 6, 2015.

2 Douglas Laycock, "Religious Liberty and the Culture Wars," *University of Illinois Law Review* (2014): 839–80.

3 Declared by no less an authority than the *New York Times* about six weeks afterward in an editorial. See "The Next Civil Rights Frontier," August 1, 2013, A20.

4 The Human Rights Campaign does not provide figures for the Fortune 500 on official gender transition guidelines. The tally here refers to the total number from the category "major employers," which is defined as all firms listed in the Fortune 1000; all firms listed in the AmLaw 200; and an unspecified number of others with at least 500 employees.

5 "Non-Discrimination Ordinance: Public Accommodation FAQs," City of Charlotte, N.C., http://charlottenc.gov/NonDiscrimination/Pages/default.aspx; viewed January 5, 2017. Notably the city council's explanation of the implications of the new ordinance included statements insisting that discrimination on the basis of sex in restrooms, locker rooms, changing facilities, and the like was still perfectly legal. A business could still require "non-transgender person[s]" to segregate on the basis of sex and fully comply with the law; only "transgender persons" could not be so required. The city council defended this different treatment on the basis of the protected status of gender expression and gender identity. It failed to recognize the obvious point that sex is also a protected category in the ordinance.

6 Mark Berman, "North Carolina Lawmakers Will Meet Wednesday to Consider Repealing Bathroom Bill," *Washington Post*, December 19, 2016.

7 Corrine Jurney, "North Carolina's Bathroom Bill Flushes Away $630 Million in Lost Business," *Forbes*, November 3, 2016, http://www.forbes.com/sites/corinnejurney/2016/11/03/north-carolinas-bathroom-bill-flushes-away-750-million-in-lost-business/.

8 U.S. Department of Justice, Office of Public Affairs, "Attorney General Loretta E. Lynch Delivers Remarks at Press Conference Announcing Complaint against the State of North Carolina to Stop Discrimination against Transgender Individuals," May 9, 2016, https://www.justice.gov/opa/speech/attorney-general-loretta-e-lynch-delivers-remarks-press-conference-announcing-complaint.

9 U.S. Department of Justice, Office of Public Affairs, "Head of the Civil Rights Division Vanita Gupta Delivers Remarks at Press Conference Announcing Complaint against the State of North Carolina to Stop Discrimination against Transgender Individuals," May 9, 2016, https://www.justice.gov/opa/speech/

head-civil-rights-division-vanita-gupta-delivers-remarks-press-conference
-announcing-0.

10 Ironically, probusiness Republicans proved unable to undo what they had done. The McCrory-Cooper governor's race was so close that a recount followed the original ballot tally. It took nearly four weeks for McCrory to finally concede the race. Cooper then spent much of the next two weeks negotiating with Republican leaders in the legislature for a special session to repeal HB2. The very morning the governor-elect announced he had reached a deal, the Charlotte City Council without warning repealed its gender identity ordinance so as to pave the way for action by the legislature. It proved insufficient. Social conservatives in the North Carolina House demanded a clause in the HB2 repeal bill that prevented any county or municipal government from passing a similar transgender ordinance for six months. This proved a deal-breaker for Democrats—essentially because the Charlotte City Council intended simply to pass the same ordinance again in 2017. ("The City of Charlotte is deeply dedicated to protecting the rights of all people from discrimination and, with House Bill 2 repealed, will be able to pursue that priority for our community.") When the Republican-sponsored HB2 repeal bill with the "cooling off period" came up for a vote in the state Senate, only sixteen of forty-eight senators voted "yes"— and all sixteen were Republicans. Every Democratic senator voted "no" as well as the other sixteen Republican senators who actually supported HB2 and opposed any version of the repeal. Under pressure of an NCAA-imposed deadline, Cooper and probusiness Republicans resurrected the bill three months later. This time Democrats conceded a three-year ban on municipal ordinances and HB2 was repealed by a 32-16 vote in the state Senate and a 70-48 vote in the state House. Of the sixteen socially conservative Republicans who held out in support of HB2 in December 2016, only eight could bring themselves to stick with the law in March 2017. The Gill quote comes from Andy Kroll, "Meet the Megadonor behind the LGBTQ Rights Movement," *Rolling Stone*, June 23, 2017, http://www.rollingstone.com/politics/features/meet-tim-gill-megadonor -behind-lgbtq-rights-movement-wins-w489213.

11 Planned Parenthood of Southeastern Pennsylvania v. Casey, 505 U.S. 833 (1992), 851.

12 Sheila Jeffreys, *Gender Hurts: A Feminist Analysis of the Politics of Transgenderism* (New York: Routledge, 2014).

13 National Center for Transgender Equality, *The Report of the 2015 U.S. Transgender Survey* (Washington, D.C.: National Center for Transgender Equality, 2017), http://www.ustranssurvey.org/report.

14 The long-standing feminist play *The Vagina Monologues* has suffered a wave of cancellations across American college campuses starting in 2014 due to its failure to include women without vaginas. Thomas Beatie has been celebrated throughout American popular culture as the "pregnant man." The transgender

activist Danielle Muscato regularly wears a man's suit and tie in public while presenting a balding head and full beard, all while identifying as a woman.

15 On the matter of medical authority, see especially the case of the psychologist Kenneth Zucker and the Child Youth and Family Gender Identity Clinic in Toronto discussed in Jesse Singal, "How the Fight Over Transgender Kids Got a Leading Sex Researcher Fired," New York Magazine, February 7, 2016, http://nymag.com/scienceofus/2016/02/fight-over-trans-kids-got-a-researcher-fired.html. On the matter of parental authority, see the case of Annmarie Calgaro in Minnesota, discussed in Stephen Montemayor, "Gender Transition Lawsuit Dismissed," StarTribune (Minneapolis), May 24, 2017, B1.

16 Paul McHugh, "Transgender Surgery Isn't the Solution," Wall Street Journal, June 13, 2014, A14, republished online May 13, 2016. The newspaper has called McHugh's op-ed "one of the most widely read pieces we have published." See editorial board, "Obama's Transgender 'Guidance,'" Wall Street Journal, May 17, 2016, A18.

17 Gallup, "Confidence in Institutions," updated July 10, 2017, http://www.gallup.com/poll/1597/confidence-institutions.aspx.

18 Joseph de Maistre, Considerations on France (Montreal: McGill-Queen's University Press, 1974 [1796]), 30.

19 Office of the Press Secretary, The White House, "Remarks by the President at a Hillary For America Rally—Jacksonville, Florida," November 3, 2016, https://obamawhitehouse.archives.gov/the-press-office/2016/11/03/remarks-president-hillary-america-rally-jacksonville-florida.

Appendix A

1 For discussions of Bourdieu in these fields, see David L. Swartz, "Pierre Bourdieu and North American Political Sociology: Why He Doesn't Fit In but Should," French Politics 4 (2006): 84–99; Didier Bigo and Mikael R. Madsen, "Special Issue: Bourdieu and the International," International Political Sociology 5, no. 3 (2011); Rebecca Adler-Nissen, ed., Bourdieu in International Relations: Rethinking Key Concepts in IR (New York: Routledge, 2013).

2 This brief critical overview of Bourdieu's approach relies strongly on the summary work of the sociologist David L. Swartz. See Swartz, Culture and Power: The Sociology of Pierre Bourdieu (Chicago: University of Chicago Press, 1997); and Swartz, Symbolic Power, Politics, and Intellectuals: The Political Sociology of Pierre Bourdieu (Berkeley: University of California Press, 2013).

3 Bourdieu offers a fourth form, symbolic capital, which manifests in honor, prestige, and legitimacy. Swartz notes, however, that symbolic capital is unlike the others in that it is not a separate form that applies to particular objects. Instead it becomes an aspect of other forms of capital, in Swartz's words, "a kind of metacapital." See Swartz, Symbolic Power, 111–15.

4 Bourdieu, Distinction, 479.

5 Yves Simon, A General Theory of Authority (Notre Dame, Ind.: University of Notre Dame Press, 1980).

6 Bourdieu, *Distinction*, 379–80.

7 David Rose and David J. Pevalin, *The National Statistics Socio-economic Classification: Origins, Development and Use*, Institute for Social and Economic Research, University of Essex (Basingstoke, U.K.: Palgrave Macmillan, 2005), 14–19.

8 Carl Frederick, "A Crosswalk for Using Pre-2000 Occupational Status and Prestige Codes with Post-2000 Occupation Codes," CDE Working Paper No. 2010-03, Center for Demography and Ecology, University of Wisconsin-Madison, April 6, 2010. I use the values of the variable "H&W 1997 Total SEI."

Appendix B

1 Le Roux and Rouanet, *Multiple Correspondence Analysis*, 4.

2 Le Roux and Rouanet, *Multiple Correspondence Analysis*, 61–62.

3 If CHILDREN ≠ 0.

4 For all, value equals LIFPRTNR plus SAMELIFNUM if SAMESEXANY equals "yes." If SAMESEXANY equals "refused" or "don't know," value equals LIFPRTNR + 1.

5 For females, the value equals int(AGEBABY1/100). For males, the value is AGEBABY1.

6 For all, the value equals int((COHAB1-CMBIRTH)/12).

7 For females, the value equals FMAR1AGE. For males, the value equals int((MARDAT01- CMBIRTH)/12).

8 For all, the value equals 0 if SAMESEXANY equals "no." If SAMESEXANY equals "yes" then the value equals SAMLIFENUM. All others are missing values.

BIBLIOGRAPHY

Court Cases

Baehr et al. v. Miike, Circuit Court for the First Circuit, Hawaii No. 91-1394 (1996)

Bourke v. Beshear, 3:13-CV-750-H (W.D.Ky.) (2014)

Brooker v. The Governors of Missouri State University, U.S. District Court for the Western District of Missouri, Southern Division (2006)

Elia-Warnken v. Elia, 463 Mass. 29 (2012)

Fisher v. University of Texas, 570 U.S. ___ (2013)

Fisher v. University of Texas, 579 U.S. ___ (2015)

Gay & Lesbian Advocates & Defenders (GLAD) v. Attorney General, 426 Mass. 132 (2002)

Goodridge v. Department of Public Health, 440 Mass. 309, 798 N.E.2d 941 (Mass. 2003)

Hollingsworth v. Perry, 570 U.S. ___, 133 S.Ct. 2652 (2013)

Keeton v. Anderson-Wiley, U.S. District Court for the Southern District of Georgia, Augusta Division (2012)

Kitchen v. Herbert, 961 F.Supp.2d 1181 (D. Utah 2013)

Lawrence v. Texas, 539 U.S. 558 (2003)

Obergefell v. Hodges, 576 U.S. ___, 135 S.Ct. 2584 (2015)

Perry v. Schwarzenegger, 704 F. Supp. 2d. 921, 1003 (N.D. Cal. 2010)

Planned Parenthood of Southeastern Pennsylvania v. Casey, 505 U.S. 833 (1992)

Regents of the University of California v. Bakke, 458 U.S. 265 (1978)

United States v. Windsor, 570 U.S. ___, 133 S.Ct. 2675 (2013)
Ward v. Polite, U.S. Court of Appeals for the Sixth Circuit (2012)

New York Times Editorials

"Respect for Privacy." January 24, 1973, 40.
"The Message from Hawaii." December 6, 1996, 38.
"Hawaii's Ban on Gay Marriage." December 20, 1999.
"Vermont's Momentous Ruling." December 22, 1999, 26.
"California's Poisonous Proposal." March 4, 2000, A14.
"Canada's Celebration of Marriage." June 19, 2003, 24.
"Gay Soldiers and Teachers." April 2, 2004, A18.
"A Winding Path to Gay Marriage." August 14, 2004.
"Marriage and Politics." October 29, 2004, A24.
"Where Is the Governator Now?" September 9, 2005, 24.
"Legal Convolutions for Gay Couples." March 24, 2007, 12.
"Six Tests for Equality and Fairness." November 2, 2009, 20.
"Marriage Equality in New York." February 11, 2011.
"Marriage Equality in New York." April 26, 2011.
"Governor Cuomo's List." May 16, 2011.
"They Need To Be Counted." May 20, 2011.
"They Need to Stand Up for Equality." June 14, 2011.
"Politicians Who Fear the Public Light." June 24, 2011.
"A Milestone for Gay Marriage." June 27, 2011.
"Scouting's Move toward Equality." May 24, 2013, A24.
"Victory for Equal Rights." June 27, 2013, A30.
"The Next Civil Rights Frontier." August 1, 2013, A20.
"Marriage Equality in America." June 27, 2015, A20.
"The Threat to Gay Americans." June 15, 2016, A24.

Other Editorials

Boston Globe Editorial Board. "Live Free and Civilly United." Boston Globe,
    April 28, 2007, A10.
Daily Texan Editorial Board. "Liberal Arts Dean Diehl Shouldn't Give Regnerus
    a Pass." Daily Texan, March 31, 2015.
Los Angeles Times Editorial Board. "Mexico City's Step Forward." Los Angeles
    Times, December 24, 2009, A16.
Wall Street Journal Editorial Board. "Obama's Transgender 'Guidance.'" Wall
    Street Journal, May 17, 2016, A18.

Washington Post Editorial Board. "Setback for Equality: Voters in Three States Approve Bans on Same-Sex Marriage." *Washington Post*, November 8, 2008, A16.

Primary Sources

"1998 Referendum General Election Results—Hawaii." *Dave Leip's Atlas of U.S. Presidential Elections*, last modified April 23, 2007, http://www.uselection atlas.org/RESULTS/state.php?fips=15&year=1998&f=0&off=51.

"2005 Gay Press Report." Prime Access, Inc. and Rivendell Media Company, Inc., http://rivendellmedia.com/assets/press-reports/GayPressReport2005.pdf.

Adams, Renee B., and Daniel Ferreira. "Women in the Boardroom and Their Impact on Governance and Performance." *Journal of Financial Economics* 94 (2009): 291–309.

Adler-Nissen, Rebecca, ed. *Bourdieu in International Relations: Rethinking Key Concepts in IR*. New York: Routledge, 2013.

Adorno, Theodor W., et al. *The Authoritarian Personality*. New York: Harper, 1950.

Allen, Douglas W. "The Regnerus Debate." *National Review Online*, June 14, 2012, http://www.nationalreview.com/article/302749/regnerus-debate -douglas-w-allen.

Altemeyer, Robert. *The Authoritarian Specter*. Cambridge, Mass.: Harvard University Press, 1996.

American Bar Association. "ABA Recommendation 111." Adopted by the ABA House of Delegates August 12, 2010, http://www.abajournal.com/files/ RResolution_111.pdf.

————. Section of Family Law. "Section Recommendation Adopted by ABA House." *Family Law eNewsletter*, February 2004, http://www.americanbar .org/content/newsletter/publications/family_law_enewsletter_home/2004 _february.html.

American Law Institute. *Principles of the Law of Family Dissolution: Analysis and Recommendations*. St. Paul, Minn.: American Law Institute Publishers, 2002.

American Psychiatric Association. *Diagnostic and Statistical Manual of Mental Disorders*. 2nd ed. Washington, D.C.: APA, 1968.

————. *Diagnostic and Statistical Manual of Mental Disorders*. 4th ed. text revision (DSM-IV-TR). Washington, D.C.: APA, 2000.

————. "Position Statement on Support of Legal Recognition of Same-Sex Civil Marriage." July 2005, https://freemarry.3cdn.net/748b9ed377ee5fedaf _kgm6b5upb.pdf.

American Psychological Association. *Lesbian and Gay Parenting*. Washington, D.C.: American Psychological Association, 2005.

Amini, Makan, et al. "Does Gender Diversity Promote Nonconformity?" *Management Science*, published online, March 25, 2016, http://pubsonline.informs .org/doi/abs/10.1287/mnsc.2015.2382.

Antonelli, Paola, and Michelle Millar Fisher. "MoMA Acquires the Rainbow Flag." *Inside/Out*, June 17, 2015, http://www.moma.org/explore/ inside_out/2015/06/17/moma-acquires-the-rainbow-flag.

Arcidiacono, Peter, and Michael Lovenheim. "Affirmative Action and the Quality-Fit Trade-Off." *Journal of Economic Literature* 54 (2016): 3–51.

Aslam, Yasmin. "#LoveWins on the Internet." *MSNBC.com*, June 27, 2015, http:// www.msnbc.com/msnbc/love-wins-the-internet.

Aughinbaugh, Alison, Omar Robles, and Hugette Sun. "Marriage and Divorce: Patterns by Gender, Race, and Educational Attainment." Monthly Labor Review, U.S. Bureau of Labor Statistics, October 2013, https://www.bls.gov/ opub/mlr/2013/article/marriage-and-divorce-patterns-by-gender-race-and -educational-attainment.htm.

Babiak, Todd. "Creative Class Warfare." *Edmonton Journal*, July 7, 2003, C5.

Badal, Sangeeta, and James K. Harter. "Gender Diversity, Business-Unit Engagement, and Performance." *Journal of Leadership & Organizational Studies* 21 (2014): 354–65.

Badgett, M. V. Lee. *Money, Myths, and Change: The Economic Lives of Lesbians and Gay Men*. Chicago: University of Chicago Press, 2001.

———. "The Impact of Extending Sexual Orientation and Gender Identity Non-Discrimination Requirements to Federal Contractors." The Williams Institute, February 2012, http://williamsinstitute.law.ucla.edu/wp-content/ uploads/Badgett-EOImpact-Feb-201211.pdf.

Badgett, M. V. Lee, and Jody L. Herman. "Patterns of Relationship Recognition by Same-Sex Couples in the United States." The Williams Institute, November 2011, https://williamsinstitute.law.ucla.edu/wp-content/uploads/ Marriage-Dissolution-FINAL.pdf.

Badinter, Elisabeth. *Man/Woman: The One Is the Other*. London: Collins Harvill, 1989.

Baker, Daniel B., Sean O'Brien Strub, and Bill Henning. *Cracking the Corporate Closet*. New York: HarperBusiness, 1995.

Baker, Gilbert. "The Prideful Story of Our Rainbow Flag" (interview). *IGLA Bulletin* 10 (1994): 4–5.

Baker, Mitchell. "Building a Global, Diverse, Inclusive Mozilla Project: Addressing Controversy." *Lizard Wrangling* (blog), March 26, 2014, accessed June 6, 2014, https://blog.lizardwrangler.com/2014/03/26/building-a-global-diverse -inclusive-mozilla-project-addressing-controversy/.

———. "Brendan Eich Steps Down as Mozilla CEO." *The Mozilla Blog*, April 3, 2014, accessed June 6, 2014, https://blog.mozilla.org/blog/2014/04/03/ brendan-eich-steps-down-as-mozilla-ceo/.

Banks, Ralph Richard. *Is Marriage for White People? How the African American Marriage Decline Affects Everyone*. New York: Dutton, 2011.

Bartkowski, John P. *Remaking the Godly Marriage: Gender Negotiation in Evangelical Families*. New Brunswick, N.J.: Rutgers University Press, 2001.

Bartlett, Tom. "Controversial Gay-Parenting Study Is Severely Flawed, Journal's Audit Finds." *Percolator* (blog), *Chronicle of Higher Education*, July 26, 2012, http://chronicle.com/blogs/percolator/controversial-gay-parenting-study-is-severely-flawed-journals-audit-finds/30255.

Baumle, Amanda K., D'Lane Compton, and Dudley L. Poston Jr. *Same-Sex Partners: The Social Demography of Sexual Orientation*. Albany: State University of New York Press, 2009.

Bayer, Ronald. *Homosexuality and American Psychiatry: The Politics of Diagnosis*. New York: Basic Books, 1981.

Belkin, Lisa. "What's Good for the Kids." *New York Times Magazine*, November 5, 2009.

Bereitschaft, Bradley, and Rex Cammack. "Neighborhood Diversity and the Creative Class in Chicago." *Applied Geography* 63 (2015): 166–83.

Berger, Peter, Grace Davie, and Effie Fokas. *Religious America, Secular Europe? A Theme and Variations*. Burlington, Vt.: Ashgate, 2008.

Berman, Mark. "North Carolina Lawmakers Will Meet Wednesday to Consider Repealing Bathroom Bill." *Washington Post*, December 19, 2016.

Berrey, Ellen. *The Enigma of Diversity: The Language of Race and the Limits of Racial Justice*. Chicago: University of Chicago Press, 2015.

Bharath, Deepa. "Schuller Sr. Speaks Out against Crystal Cathedral Anti-Gay Covenant." *Orange County Register*, March 16, 2011.

Bigo, Didier, and Mikael R. Madsen. "Special Issue: Bourdieu and the International." *International Political Sociology* 5, no. 3 (2011).

Biskupic, Joan. "U.S. Law Firms Flock to Gay-Marriage Proponents, Shun Other Side." *Reuters*, June 10, 2014, http://www.reuters.com/article/2014/06/10/us-usa-court-gaymarriage-insight-idUSKBN0EL10820140610.

Black, Dan A., Hoda R. Makar, Seth G. Sanders, and Lowell J. Taylor. "The Earnings Effects of Sexual Orientation." *Industrial and Labor Relations Review* 56 (2003): 449–69.

Blume, K. Allan. "'Guilty as Charged,' Cathy Says of Chick-fil-A's Stand on Biblical and Family Values." *Baptist Press*, June 16, 2012, http://www.bpnews.net/38271/guilty-as-charged-cathy-says-of-chickfilas-stand-on-biblical-family-values.

Bobo, Lawrence, and Frederick C. Licari. "Education and Political Tolerance: Testing the Effects of Cognitive Sophistication and Target Group Affect." *Public Opinion Quarterly* 53 (1989): 285–308.

Boies, David, and Theodore B. Olson. *Redeeming the Dream: The Case for Marriage Equality*. New York: Viking, 2014.

Bolce, Louis, and Gerald de Maio. "The Anti-Christian Fundamentalist Factor in Contemporary Politics." *Public Opinion Quarterly* 63 (1999): 508–42.

———. "Religious Outlook, Culture War Politics, and Antipathy toward Christian Fundamentalists." *Public Opinion Quarterly* 63 (1999): 29–61.

———. "Our Secularist Democratic Party." *National Affairs* 149 (2002): 3–20.

———. "A Prejudice for the Thinking Classes: Media Exposure, Political Sophistication, and the Anti-Christian Fundamentalist." *American Politics Research* 36 (2008): 155–85.

Bottum, Joseph. *An Anxious Age*. New York: Image, 2014.

Bourdieu, Pierre. *Distinction: A Social Critique of the Judgement of Taste*. Cambridge, Mass.: Harvard University Press, 1984.

———. "The Social Space and the Genesis of Groups." *Theory and Society* 14 (1985): 723–44.

———. *The State Nobility*. Stanford, Calif.: Stanford University Press, 1996.

Bowman, Nicholas A. "College Diversity Experiences and Cognitive Development: A Meta-Analysis." *Review of Educational Research* 80 (2010): 4–33.

Brady, Thomas. "How Some Gays Choose to Show the Colors." *Philadelphia Inquirer*, November 19, 1997, D1.

Bramlett, Brittany H. "The Cross-Pressures of Religion and Contact with Gays and Lesbians, and Their Impact on Same-Sex Marriage Opinion." *Politics & Policy* 40 (2012): 13–42.

Brooks, David. *Bobos in Paradise: The New Upper Class and How They Got There*. New York: Simon & Schuster, 2000.

Burnett, Raymond Christopher, and William M. Salka. "Determinants of Electoral Support for Anti-Gay Marriage: An Examination of 2006 Votes on Ballot Measures in the State." *Journal of Homosexuality* 56 (2009): 1071–82.

Burris, Val. "The Discovery of the New Middle Class." *Theory and Society* 15, no. 3 (1986): 317–49.

———. *Gender Trouble: Feminism and the Subversion of Identity*. New York: Routledge, 1990.

Butler, Judith. *Undoing Gender*. New York: Routledge, 2004.

Cahn, Naomi, and June Carbone. *Red Families v. Blue Families: Legal Polarization and the Creation of Culture*. Oxford: Oxford University Press, 2010.

Carbone, June, and Naomi R. Cahn. "Class, Politics, Gender and the Marriage Divide in the United States." *Families, Relationships and Societies* 4 (2015): 163–69.

Carlson, Allan. *The "American Way": Family and Community in the Shaping of the American Identity*. Wilmington, Del.: ISI Books, 2003.

Castillo, Michelle. "Why 2015 Became the Year of LGBT Ads." *CNBC*, December 29, 2015, http://www.cnbc.com/2015/12/29/why-2015-became-the-year-of-lgbt-ads.html.

Cathy, Dan. "6-16 Strong Fathers" (interview). *Ken Coleman Show*, June 18, 2012, https://itunes.apple.com/us/podcast/the-ken-coleman-show/id388714518?mt=2.

Centers for Disease Control and Prevention. "Data Brief 68: Childbearing Differences among Three Generations of U.S. Women." August 2011, https://www.cdc.gov/nchs/products/databriefs/db68.htm.

Chandra, Anjani, et al. "Sexual Behavior, Sexual Attraction, and Sexual Identity in the United States: Data from the 2006–2008 National Survey of Family Growth." *National Health and Statistics Reports* 36 (2011).

Chauncey, George. *Why Marriage? The History Shaping Today's Debate Over Gay Equality.* New York: Basic Books, 2004.

Cherlin, Andrew. *Labor's Love Lost: The Rise and Fall of the Working-Class Family in America.* New York: Russell Sage Foundation Publications, 2014.

Claassen, Ryan L. *Godless Democrats and Pious Republicans? Party Activists, Party Capture, and the "God Gap."* Cambridge: Cambridge University Press, 2015.

Clinton, William J. "Statement on Same-Gender Marriage." In *Public Papers of the Presidents of the United States, William J. Clinton, 1996. Book 2, July 1 to December 31, 1996*, 1635. Washington: Government Printing Office, 1998.

Cohn, D'Vera, Jeffrey S. Passel, Wendy Wang, and Gretchen Livingston. "Barely Half of U.S. Adults Are Married—A Record Low." Pew Research Center: Social and Demographic Trends, last modified December 14, 2011, http://www.pewsocialtrends.org/2011/12/14/barely-half-of-u-s-adults-are-married-a-record-low/.

Conger, J. J. "Proceedings of the American Psychological Association, Incorporated, for the Year 1974: Minutes of the Annual Meeting of the Council of Representatives." *American Psychologist* 30 (1975): 620–51.

Connelly, Matthew. *Fatal Misconception: The Struggle to Control World Population.* Cambridge, Mass.: Belknap Press, 2008.

Conrad, Peter, and Joseph Schneider. *Deviance and Medicalization: From Badness to Sickness.* 2nd ed. Philadelphia: Temple University Press, 1992.

Cook, Alison, and Christy Glass. "Do Minority Leaders Affect Corporate Practice? Analyzing the Effect of Leadership Composition on Governance and Product Development." *Strategic Organization* 13 (2015): 117–40.

Copen, Casey E., Kimberly Daniels, and William D. Mosher. "First Premarital Cohabitation in the United States: 2006–2010 National Survey of Family Growth." *National Health Statistics Reports* 64 (April 4, 2013).

Copen, Casey E., Kimberly Daniels, Jonathan Vespa, and William D. Mosher. "First Marriages in the United States: Data from the 2006–2010 National Survey of Family Growth." *National Health Statistics Reports* 49 (March 22, 2012).

Craven, Gemma. "The Lasting Impact of #LoveWins on Social Brand Marketing." *Spredfast*, July 1, 2015, https://www.spredfast.com/social-marketing-blog/lasting-impact-lovewins-social-brand-marketing.

Crouch, Simon R., et al. "Parent-Reported Measures of Child Health and Well-being in Same-Sex Parent Families: A Cross-Sectional Survey." *BMC Public Health* 14 (2014): 635.

Cruz, Julissa. "Marriage: More Than a Century of Change." NCFMR Family Profiles, FFP-13-13. National Center for Family and Marriage Research, Bowling Green State University, 2013, http://www.bgsu.edu/content/dam/BGSU/college-of-arts-and-sciences/NCFMR/documents/FP/FP-13-13.pdf.

Culliney, Kacey. "Lucky Charms Rainbow Pride Campaign Targeted Diverse Millennials, Says General Mills." *BakeryandSnacks.com*, July 3, 2013, http://www.bakeryandsnacks.com/Manufacturers/Lucky-Charms-rainbow-Pride-campaign-targeted-diverse-millennials-says-General-Mills.

Curlin, Farr A., et al. "The Relationship between Psychiatry and Religion among U.S. Physicians." *Psychiatric Services* 58 (2007): 1193–98.

Daneshvary, Nasser, C. Jeffrey Waddoups, and Bradley S. Wimmer. "Previous Marriage and the Lesbian Wage Premium." *Industrial Relations* 48, no. 3 (2009): 432–53.

Dar-Nimrod, Ilan, and Steven J. Heine. "Genetic Essentialism: On the Deceptive Determinism of DNA." *Psychological Bulletin* 137, no. 5 (2011): 800–818.

Dardick, Hal. "Alderman to Chick-fil-A: No Deal." *Chicago Tribune*, July 25, 2012.

Davis, Ronald M., et al. "Health Care Needs of Gay Men and Lesbians in the United States." *Journal of the American Medical Association* 275, no. 17 (1996): 1354–59.

de Maistre, Joseph. *Considerations on France*. Montreal: McGill-Queen's University Press, 1974 [1796].

Demerath, N. J., III. "Cultural Victory and Organizational Defeat in the Paradoxical Decline of Liberal Protestantism." *Journal for the Scientific Study of Religion* 34 (1995): 458–69.

Demian. "Announcing Your Commitment: Newspapers That Publish Same-Sex Couples' Nuptial Notices." Partners Task Force for Gay & Lesbian Couples. December 2, 2015, accessed February 9, 2017, http://www.buddybuddy.com/n-papers.html.

Denizet-Lewis, Benoit. "The Scientific Quest to Prove—Once and for All—That Someone Can Truly Be Attracted to Both a Man and a Woman." *New York Times Magazine*, March 20, 2014, MM20.

Diamond, Lisa M. *Sexual Fluidity: Understanding Women's Love and Desire*. Cambridge, Mass.: Harvard University Press, 2008.

Dobbin, Frank. *Inventing Equal Opportunity*. Princeton, N.J.: Princeton University Press, 2009.

Donegan, Mary, et al. "Which Indicators Explain Metropolitan Economic Performance Best? Traditional or Creative Class." *Journal of the American Planning Association* 74 (2008): 180–95.

Donovan, James M. "Same-Sex Union Announcements: Whether Newspapers Must Publish Them, and Why We Should Care." *Brooklyn Law Review* 68, no. 3 (2003): 721–807.

Douthat, Ross. "The Terms of Our Surrender." *New York Times*, March 1, 2014.

Dover, Tessa L., et al. "Members of High-Status Groups Are Threatened by Pro-Diversity Organizational Messages." *Journal of Experimental Psychology* 62 (2016): 58–67.

Drucker, Peter. *Landmarks of Tomorrow*. New York: Harper and Brothers, 1957.

Duderstadt, James. *The Michigan Mandate: A Strategic Linking of Academic Excellence and Social Diversity*. Ann Arbor: University of Michigan, 1990.

Dyck, Joshua J., and Shanna Pearson-Merkowitz, "To Know You Is Not Necessarily to Love You: The Partisan Mediators of Intergroup Contact." *Political Behavior* (online only), July 2013.

Eberstadt, Mary. "How Pedophilia Lost Its Cool." *First Things*, December 2009.

Edelman, Lauren B., Sally Riggs Fuller, and Iona Mara-Drita. "Diversity Rhetoric and the Managerialization of Law." *American Journal of Sociology* 106 (2001): 1589–1641.

Edin, Kathryn, and Maria Kefalas. *Promises I Can Keep: Why Poor Women Put Motherhood before Marriage*. Berkeley: University of California Press, 2005.

Edin, Kathryn, and Timothy J. Nelson. *Doing the Best I Can: Fatherhood in the Inner City*. Berkeley: University of California Press, 2013.

Eich, Brendan. "Inclusiveness at Mozilla." *Brendan Eich* (blog), March 26, 2014, accessed June 6, 2014, https://brendaneich.com/2014/03/inclusiveness-at-mozilla/.

Elliott, Stuart. "Commercials with a Gay Emphasis Are Moving to Mainstream Media." *New York Times*, June 25, 2013.

Ellis, Blake. "Veto Follows Business Backlash over Arizona Anti-Gay Bill." *CNN Money*, February 26, 2014, http://money.cnn.com/2014/02/25/news/economy/arizona-anti-gay-bill/.

Enteman, Willard F. *Managerialism: The Emergence of a New Ideology*. Madison: University of Wisconsin Press, 1993.

Eskridge, William N., Jr. *Dishonorable Passions: Sodomy Laws in America, 1861–2003*. New York: Viking, 2008.

———. "Backlash Politics: How Constitutional Litigation Has Advanced Marriage Equality in the United States." *Boston University Law Review* 93 (2013): 275–323.

Faris, John T. *The Paradise of the Pacific*. New York: Doubleday, 1929.

Feldblum, Chai. "Gay Is Good: The Moral Case for Marriage Equality and More." *Yale Journal of Law and Feminism* 17 (2005): 139–84.

———. "Moral Conflict and Liberty: Gay Rights and Religion." *Brooklyn Law Review* 72 (2006): 61–123.

Ferguson, Andrew. "Revenge of the Sociologists." *Weekly Standard* 17, no. 43 (July 30, 2012).

Fish, Stanley. "The Trouble with Tolerance." *Chronicle of Higher Education*, November 10, 2006, B8.

Fisher, Robin, Geof Gee, and Adam Looney. "Joint Filing by Same-Sex Couples after *Windsor*: Characteristics of Married Tax Filers in 2013 and 2014." Office of Tax Analysis, Department of the Treasury, Working Paper 108, August 2016.

Fletcher, Michael A. "What the Federalist Society Stands for." *Washington Post*, July 29, 2005, A21.

Florida, Richard. *The Rise of the Creative Class: And How It's Transforming Work, Leisure, Community and Everyday Life*. New York: Basic Books, 2002.

———. *Cities and the Creative Class*. New York: Routledge, 2005.

———. *The Flight of the Creative Class*. New York: HarperCollins, 2005.

———. *The Rise of the Creative Class, Revisited*. New York: Basic Books, 2012.

Florida, Richard, and Charlotta Mellander. *Segregated City: The Geography of Economic Segregation in America's Metros*. Toronto: Martin Prosperity Institute, Rotman School of Management, University of Toronto, 2015.

Florida, Richard, Charlotta Mellander, and Kevin Stolarick. "Inside the Black Box of Regional Development—Human Capital, the Creative Class and Tolerance." *Journal of Economic Geography* 8 (2008): 615–49.

Flynn, Kerry. "How #LoveWins on Twitter Became the Most Viral Hashtag of the Same-Sex Marriage Ruling." *International Business Times*, June 26, 2015.

Folbre, Nancy. "Of the Patriarchy Born: The Political Economy of Fertility Decisions." *Feminist Studies* 9 (1983): 261–84.

———. "The Future of the Elephant-Bird." *Population and Development Review* 23 (1997): 647–54.

Forst, Rainer. *Toleration in Conflict: Past and Present*. Translated by Ciaran Cronin. Cambridge: Cambridge University Press, 2013.

Fowler, Mayhill. "Obama: No Surprise That Hard-Pressed Pennsylvanians Turn Bitter." *Huffington Post*, April 11, 2008.

Fox, Emily Jane. "Gay Marriage's Corporate Boosters." *CNNMoney*, April 1, 2013, http://money.cnn.com/2013/03/29/news/companies/same-sex -marriage-companies/index.html.

Francis, Andrew M. "Family and Sexual Orientation: The Family-Demographic Correlates of Homosexuality in Men and Women." *Journal of Sex Research* 45 (2008): 371–77.

Frank, Thomas. *What's the Matter with Kansas? How Conservatives Won the Heart of America*. New York: Metropolitan Books, 2004.

Frederick, Carl. "A Crosswalk for Using Pre-2000 Occupational Status and Prestige Codes with Post-2000 Occupation Codes." CDE Working Paper No. 2010-03, Center for Demography and Ecology, University of Wisconsin-Madison, April 6, 2010.

Frojo, Renée. "Gap Goes Gay for 'True Outfitters' Campaign." *San Francisco Business Times*, February 21, 2014, http://www.bizjournals.com/sanfrancisco/blog/2014/02/banana-republic-same-sex-couple-campaign.html.

Gaikwad, Nikhar. *From Grassroots to Business Suits: How AIDS Captured the Corporate World*. B.A. honors thesis, Williams College, Williamstown, Mass., 2006.

Galeotti, Anna Elisabetta. *Toleration as Recognition*. Cambridge: Cambridge University Press, 2002.

Gallagher, John. "Ikea's Gay Gamble." *The Advocate*, May 3, 1994, 24–27.

Gallup. "Gay and Lesbian Rights." Updated May 2016, http://www.gallup.com/poll/1651/gay-lesbian-rights.aspx.

———. "Marriage." Accessed July 17, 2017, http://www.gallup.com/poll/117328/marriage.aspx.

Gates, Gary J. "How Many People Are Lesbian, Gay, Bisexual and Transgender?" The Williams Institute, April 2011, http://williamsinstitute.law.ucla.edu/wp-content/uploads/Gates-How-Many-People-LGBT-Apr-2011.pdf.

Gates, Gary J., et al. "Letter to the Editors and Advisory Editors at *Social Science Research*." *Social Science Research* 41 (2012): 1350–51.

"Gay Branding: Refining Rainbows." *Design Week*, July 9, 2009, 17.

"Gay Pride Flag Creator Proud but Humble." *CBS Chicago*, June 24, 2012, http://chicago.cbslocal.com/2012/06/24/gay-pride-flag-creator-proud-but-humble/.

Gibbons, Floyd. *The Red Napoleon*. Carbondale: Southern Illinois University Press, 1976 [1929].

Gooding, Gretchen E., and Rose M. Kreider. "Women's Marital Naming Choices in a Nationally Representative Sample." *Journal of Family Issues* 31 (2010): 681–701.

Gotsis, George, and Zoe Kortezi. "Workplace Diversity: A Resource or a Source of Conflict?" In *Critical Studies in Diversity Management Literature: A Review and Synthesis*, by George Gotsis and Zoe Kortezi, 1–12. Dordrecht, The Netherlands: Springer, 2015.

Goudreau, Jenna. "Top 10 Best-Paying Jobs for Women in 2011." *Forbes*, April 20, 2011, https://www.forbes.com/2011/04/20/best-paying-jobs-for-women_slide_2.html.

Griffin, Chad. "Corporate America Becomes a Beacon of Progress for Gay Rights." *MSNBC*, February 27, 2014, accessed June 25, 2014, http://www.msnbc.com/msnbc/corporations—gay-rights-arizona.

Gross, Larry. *Up From Invisibility: Lesbians, Gay Men, and the Media in America*. New York: Columbia University Press, 2001.

Gross, Neil, and Solon Simmons. "The Religiosity of American College and University Professors." *Sociology of Religion* 70 (2009): 101–29.

———. "The Social and Political Views of American College and University Professors." In *Professors and Their Politics*, edited by Neil Gross and Solon Simmons, 19–52. Baltimore: Johns Hopkins University Press, 2014.

Gunther, Marc. "Queer Inc.: How Corporate America Fell in Love with Gays and Lesbians." *Fortune*, November 30, 2006, 94.

Gusfield, Joseph R. *Symbolic Crusade: Status Politics and the American Temperance Movement.* 2nd ed. Champaign: University of Illinois Press, 1986.

Haeberle, Steven H. "Gay Men and Lesbians at City Hall." *Social Science Quarterly* 77 (1996): 190–97.

Haider-Markel, Donald P., and Mark R. Joslyn. "Beliefs about the Origins of Homosexuality and Support for Gay Rights: An Empirical Test of Attribution Theory." *Public Opinion Quarterly* 72 (2008): 291–310.

Halperin, David M. *One Hundred Years of Homosexuality and Other Essays on Greek Love.* New York: Routledge, 1990.

Hamilton, Laura, Claudia Geist, and Brian Powell. "Marital Name Change as a Window into Gender Attitudes." *Gender & Society* 25 (2011): 145–75.

Hancock, Kristin A. "Student Beliefs, Multiculturalism, and Client Welfare." *Psychology of Sexual Orientation and Gender Diversity* 1 (2014): 1–9.

Herring, Cedric. "Does Diversity Pay? Race, Gender, and the Business Case for Diversity." *American Sociological Review* 74 (2009): 208–24.

Hinderliter, Andrew C. "Defining Paraphilia: Excluding Exclusion." *Open Access Journal of Forensic Psychology* 2 (2010): 241–72.

Hodge, David R. "Does Social Work Oppress Evangelical Christians? A 'New Class' Analysis of Society and Social Work." *Social Work* 47 (2002): 401–14.

Hoff, Colleen C., et al. "Relationship Characteristics and Motivations behind Agreements among Gay Male Couples: Differences by Agreement Type and Couple Serostatus." *AIDS Care* 22 (2010): 827–35.

———. "Serostatus Differences and Agreements about Sex with Outside Partners among Gay Male Couples." *AIDS Education and Prevention* 21 (2009): 25–38.

Hollinger, David A. "After Cloven Tongues of Fire: Ecumenical Protestantism and the Modern American Encounter with Diversity." *The Journal of American History* 98 (2011): 21–48.

Horovitz, Bruce. "Burger King Sells Gay Pride Whopper." *USA Today*, July 1, 2014, http://www.usatoday.com/story/money/business/2014/07/01/burger-king -gay-pride-burger-parade-fast-food-gay-rights/11903861/.

Horwitz, Paul. "The Hobby Lobby Moment." 128 *Harvard Law Review* 154, November 10, 2014.

Hoyman, Michele, and Christopher Faricy. "It Takes a Village: A Test of the Creative Class, Social Capital, and Human Capital Theories." *Urban Affairs Review* 44 (2009): 311–33.

Human Rights Campaign. *The State of the Workplace for Lesbian, Gay, Bisexual and Transgender Americans*. Washington, D.C.: Human Rights Campaign Foundation, 1999–2008.

———. *Corporate Equality Index: Rating American Workplaces on LGBT Equality*. Washington, D.C.: Human Rights Campaign, 2010–2017.

Hunt, Kevin. "Show Us Why You Are #LuckyToBe." *Taste of General Mills* (blog), June 4, 2015, http://blog.generalmills.com/2015/06/show-us-why -you-are-luckytobe/.

Hunter, James Davison. *Culture Wars: The Struggle to Define America*. New York: Basic Books, 1991.

Huxley, Aldous. *Brave New World*. New York: Harper Perennial Modern Classics, 2006 [1932].

Inglehart, Ronald. *Culture Shift in Advanced Industrial Society*. Princeton, N.J.: Princeton University Press, 1990.

Inglehart, Ronald, and Pippa Norris. *Rising Tide: Gender Equality and Cultural Change around the World*. Cambridge: Cambridge University Press, 2003.

Jeffreys, Sheila. *Gender Hurts: A Feminist Analysis of the Politics of Transgenderism*. New York: Routledge, 2014.

Johnson, Chris. "Carney: Brewer 'Did the Right Thing' by Vetoing Anti-Gay Bill." *Washington Blade*, February 28, 2014, accessed June 25, 2014, http://www.washingtonblade.com/2014/02/28/carney-brewer-right -thing-vetoing-anti-gay-bill/.

Jones, Robert P. *The End of White Christian America*. New York: Simon & Schuster, 2016.

Jones, Sarah. "The Loud Rise and Quiet Fall of Roy Moore." *New Republic*, September 30, 2016, https://newrepublic.com/article/137358/loud-rise -quiet-fall-roy-moore.

Joseph, Lauren. "The Production of Pride: Institutionalization and LGBT Pride Organizations." Ph.D. diss., Department of Sociology, Stony Brook University, August 2010.

Jurney, Corrine. "North Carolina's Bathroom Bill Flushes Away $630 Million in Lost Business." *Forbes*, November 3, 2016, http://www.forbes .com/sites/corinnejurney/2016/11/03/north-carolinas-bathroom -bill-flushes-away-750-million-in-lost-business/.

Just the Facts Coalition. "Just the Facts about Sexual Orientation and Youth: A Primer for Principals, Educators and School Personnel." 1999, http://www .glsenboston.org/JustTheFacts.pdf.

Kaiser Family Foundation and Health Research and Educational Trust. *Annual Employer Health Benefits Survey.* 1999, 2004, and 2015 editions, http://kff .org/health-costs/report/employer-health-benefits-annual-survey-archives/.

Kalev, Alexandra, et al. "Best Practices or Best Guesses? Assessing the Efficacy of Corporate Affirmative Action and Diversity Policies." *American Sociological Review* 71 (2006): 589–617.

Kane, Laura. "Is Pedophilia a Sexual Orientation?" *Toronto Star*, December 22, 2013.

Kiley, Jocelyn. "It's Father's Day for Many American Men, including 23% of Those Who Are LGBT." *Factank* (online), Pew Research Center, June 16, 2013, http://www.pewresearch.org/fact-tank/2013/06/16/its-fathers-day-for -many-american-men-including-23-of-those-who-are-lgbt/.

King, Preston. *Toleration.* New York: St. Martin's, 1976.

Kinnish, Kelly K., Donald S. Strassberg, and Charles W. Turner. "Sex Differences in the Flexibility of Sexual Orientation: A Multidimensional Retrospective Assessment." *Archives of Sexual Behavior* 34 (2005): 173–83.

Kirkland, Anna, and Ben B. Hansen. "'How Do I Bring Diversity?' Race and Class in the College Admissions Essay." *Law & Society Review* 45 (2011): 103–38.

Klarman, Michael J. *From the Closet to the Altar: Courts, Backlash, and the Struggle for Same-Sex Marriage.* Oxford: Oxford University Press, 2013.

Klawitter, Marieka. "Meta-Analysis of the Effects of Sexual Orientation on Earnings." *Industrial Relations* 54 (2015): 4–32.

Kroll, Andy. "Meet the Megadonor behind the LGBTQ Rights Movement." *Rolling Stone*, June 23, 2017, http://www.rollingstone.com/politics/features/meet-ti m-gill-megadonor-behind-lgbtq-rights-movement-wins-w489213.

Lafferty, Justin. "#LoveWins: How the Same-Sex Marriage Decision Spread through Social." *SocialTimes*, June 30, 2015, http://www.adweek.com/ socialtimes/lovewins-how-the-same-sex-marriage-decision-spread-through -social/622661.

Lambert, Eric G., Lois A. Ventura, Daniel E. Hall, and Terry Cluse-Tolar. "College Students' Views on Gay and Lesbian Issues: Does Education Make a Difference?" *Journal of Homosexuality* 50, no. 4 (2006): 1–20.

Lasch, Christopher. *Haven in a Heartless World.* New York: Basic Books, 1977.

———. *The True and Only Heaven: Progress and Its Critics.* New York: W. W. Norton, 1991.

Laumann, Edward O., et al., eds. *The Social Organization of Sexuality: Sexual Practices in the United States.* Chicago: University of Chicago Press, 1994.

Laycock, Douglas. "Religious Liberty and the Culture Wars." *University of Illinois Law Review* (2014): 839–80.

Le Roux, Brigitte, and Henry Rouanet. *Multiple Correspondence Analysis.* Los Angeles: SAGE, 2010.

Lesher, Stephan. *George Wallace: American Populist*. Cambridge, Mass.: Perseus Publishing, 1994.

Lesthaeghe, Ron. "The Second Demographic Transition in Western Countries: An Interpretation." In *Gender and Family Change in Industrialized Countries*, edited by Karen Oppenheim Mason and An-Magritt Jensen. Oxford: Clarendon, 1995.

———. "The Unfolding Story of the Second Demographic Transition." *Population and Development Review* 36 (2010): 211–51.

———. "The Second Demographic Transition: A Concise Overview of Its Development." *Proceedings of the National Academy of Sciences of the United States of America* 111, no. 51 (2014): 18112–15.

Lesthaeghe, Ron J., and Lisa Neidert. "The Second Demographic Transition in the United States: Exception or Textbook Example?" *Population and Demographic Review* 32 (2006): 669–98.

Levine, Sheen S., et al. "Ethnic Diversity Deflates Price Bubbles." *Proceedings of the National Academy of Sciences of the United States of America* 111, no. 52 (2014): 18524–29.

Lewis, Gregory B. "The Friends and Family Plan: Contact with Gays and Support for Gay Rights." *Policy Studies Journal* 39 (2011): 217–38.

Lindsay, D. Michael. *Faith in the Halls of Power: How Evangelicals Joined the American Elite*. Oxford: Oxford University Press, 2007.

Lipset, Seymour Martin. "Democracy and Working-Class Authoritarianism." *American Sociological Review* 24 (1959): 482–502.

Lipson, Daniel N. "Embracing Diversity: The Institutionalization of Affirmative Action as Diversity Management at UC-Berkeley, UT-Austin, and UW-Madison." *Law & Social Inquiry* 32 (2007): 985–1026.

———. "Where's the Justice? Affirmative Action's Severed Civil Rights Roots in the Age of Diversity." *Perspectives on Politics* 6 (2008): 691–706.

Liss, Miriam, and Mindy J. Erchull. "Differences in Beliefs and Behaviors between Feminist Actual and Anticipated Mothers." *Psychology of Women Quarterly* 37 (2012): 381–91.

Longman, Philip. "The Return of Patriarchy." *Foreign Policy*, March/April 2006, 56–65.

Lopez, German. "Largest-Ever Study of Same-Sex Couples' Kids Finds They're Better Off Than Other Children." *Vox*, July 7, 2014, http://www.vox.com/2014/7/7/5873781/largest-ever-study-of-same-sex-couples-kids-finds-theyre-better-off.

Lopez, Ricardo, and Tiffany Hsu. "San Francisco Is the Third City to Tell Chick-fil-A: Keep Out." *Los Angeles Times*, July 26, 2012.

MacIntyre, Alasdair. *After Virtue*. 3rd ed. Notre Dame, Ind.: University of Notre Dame Press, 2007 [1981].

Martin, Joyce A., et al. "Births: Final Data for 2015." *National Vital Statistics Report* 66, no. 1 (January 5, 2017).

Massey, Douglas S. "Comment." *Social Science Research* 41 (2012): 1378.

Matthews, William Christopher, et al. "Physicians' Attitudes toward Homosexuality: Survey of a California County Medical Society." *Western Journal of Medicine* 144 (1986): 106–10.

Mauro, Tony. "Scalia Lashes 'Law-Profession Culture.'" *Legal Times*, July 7, 2003.

McGraw, Dan. "The Christian Capitalists." *U.S. News and World Report* 118, no. 10, March 13, 1995, 52.

McGregor, Jena. "Corporate America's Gay-Rights Evolution." *On Leadership* (blog), *Washington Post*, February 27, 2014, accessed June 25, 2014, http://www.washingtonpost.com/blogs/on-leadership/wp/2014/02/27/corporate-americas-gay-rights-evolution/.

McHugh, Paul. "Transgender Surgery Isn't the Solution." *Wall Street Journal*, June 13, 2014, A14. Republished online May 13, 2016.

Melling, Louise. "ACLU: Why We Can No Longer Support the Federal 'Religious Freedom' Law." *Washington Post*, June 25, 2015.

Merino, Stephen M. "Contact with Gays and Lesbians and Same-Sex Marriage Support: The Moderating Role of Social Context." *Social Science Research* 42 (2013): 1156–66.

Miller, Christina R., et al. "An Online Survey of Social Workers' Family Values." *Journal of Social Work Values and Ethics* 13 (2016): 59–72.

Mitchell, Jason W. "Characteristics and Allowed Behaviors of Gay Male Couples' Sexual Agreements." *Journal of Sex Research* 51 (2014): 316–28.

Mock, Steven E., and Richard P. Eibach. "Stability and Change in Sexual Orientation Identity over a 10-Year Period in Adulthood." *Archives of Sexual Behavior* 41 (2012): 641–48.

Montemayor, Stephen. "Gender Transition Lawsuit Dismissed." *StarTribune* (Minneapolis), May 24, 2017, B1.

Montopoli, Brian. "Obama on Gay Marriage: 'Attitudes Evolve, Including Mine.'" *CBS News*, October 28, 2010, http://www.cbsnews.com/news/obama-on-gay-marriage-attitudes-evolve-including-mine/.

———. "Obama Stands By Opposition to Same-Sex Marriage—But Feelings 'Evolving.'" *CBS News*, December 22, 2010, http://www.cbsnews.com/news/obama-stands-by-opposition-to-same-sex-marriage-but-feelings-evolving/.

Mooney, Chris. *The Republican Brain: The Science of Why They Deny Science—and Reality*. Hoboken, N.J.: John Wiley & Sons, 2012.

Moore, Clive. *Sunshine and Rainbows: The Development of Gay and Lesbian Culture in Queensland*. St. Lucia, Queensland: University of Queensland Press, 2001.

Moreton, Bethany. *To Serve God and Wal-Mart: The Making of Christian Free Enterprise*. Cambridge, Mass.: Harvard University Press, 2009.

"Mozilla Supports LGBT Equality." *The Mozilla Blog*, March 29, 2014, accessed June 4, 2014, https://blog.mozilla.org/blog/2014/03/29/mozilla-supports-lgbt-equality/.

Mucciaroni, Gary. *Same Sex, Different Politics: Success and Failure in the Struggles over Gay Rights*. Chicago: University of Chicago Press, 2008.

———. "The Study of LGBT Politics and Its Contributions to Political Science." *PS: Political Science & Politics* 44, no. 1 (2011): 17–21.

Mundy, Liza. "The Gay Guide to Wedded Bliss." *Atlantic*, June 2013.

Murray, Charles. *Coming Apart: The State of White America, 1960–2010*. New York: Crown Forum, 2012.

National Center for Health Statistics. *Vital Statistics of the United States: 1980–2003*. https://www.cdc.gov/nchs/products/vsus/vsus_1980_2003.htm.

National Center for Transgender Equality. *The Report of the 2015 U.S. Transgender Survey*. Washington, D.C.: National Center for Transgender Equality, 2017, http://www.ustranssurvey.org/report.

National Marriage Project and Institute for American Values. *The State of Our Unions: Marriage in America 2012*. 2012.

Newport, Frank. "Americans' Identification as Middle Class Edges Back Up." Gallup, December 15, 2016, http://www.gallup.com/poll/199727/americans-identification-middle-class-edges-back.aspx.

Nussbaum, Daniel. "Doritos Goes Gay, and Other Foods That Have Shown Support for the LGBT Cause." *Breitbart*, September 17, 2015, http://www.breitbart.com/big-hollywood/2015/09/17/doritos-goes-gay-foods-shown-support-lgbt-cause/.

Nussbaum, Martha. *From Disgust to Humanity: Sexual Orientation and Constitutional Law*. Oxford: Oxford University Press, 2010.

Office of the Press Secretary, The White House. "Remarks by the President at a Hillary For America Rally—Jacksonville, Florida." November 3, 2016, https://obamawhitehouse.archives.gov/the-press-office/2016/11/03/remarks-president-hillary-america-rally-jacksonville-florida.

———. "Remarks of President Barack Obama—State of the Union Address as Delivered." January 13, 2016, https://obamawhitehouse.archives.gov/the-press-office/2016/01/12/remarks-president-barack-obama---prepared-delivery-state-union-address.

———. "Weekly Address: President Obama Vows to Continue Standing Up to the Special Interests on Behalf of the American People." January 23, 2010, https://obamawhitehouse.archives.gov/the-press-office/weekly-address-president-obama-vows-continue-standing-special-interests-behalf-amer.

Okrent, Daniel. "Is the *New York Times* a Liberal Newspaper?" *New York Times*, July 25, 2004.

Olson, Walter. "Eugene Volokh vs. Deborah Rhode on Hostile Environment and ABA 8.4(g)." *Overlawyered*, December 8, 2016, https://www

.overlawyered.com/2016/12/eugene-volokh-vs-deborah-rhode-hostile
-environment-aba-8-4g/.

O'Reilly, Kathleen, and Gerald R. Webster. "A Sociodemographic and Partisan Analysis of Voting in Three Anti-Gay Rights Referenda in Oregon." *Professional Geographer* 50, no. 4 (1998): 498–515.

Organisation for Economic Cooperation and Development. Statistics/Demography/Fertility rates (indicator), doi: 10.1787/8272fb01-en, accessed March 5, 2017, http://www.oecd-ilibrary.org/content/indicator/8272fb01-en.

Ormrod, Richard K., and David B. Cole. "Tolerance and Rejection: The Vote on Colorado's Amendment Two." *Professional Geographer* 48 (1996): 14–27.

Ostrow, Joanne. "Ads Move beyond 'Gay Vague' as Marketing Comes Out about Target." *Denver Post*, June 17, 2012, E1.

Paolantonio, Sal. "Who Wants to Become an Eagles Exec?" *Philadelphia Inquirer*, January 9, 1994, E9.

Pappas, Stephanie. "Gay Parents Better Than Straight Parents? What Research Says." *Huffington Post*, January 16, 2012, http://www.huffingtonpost.com/2012/01/16/gay-parents-better-than-straights_n_1208659.html.

Parker-Pope, Tara. "Gay Unions Shed Light on Gender in Marriage." *New York Times*, June 10, 2008.

———. "Gay Marriage: Same but Different." *New York Times*, July 1, 2013.

Parsons, Jeffrey T., Tyrel J. Starks, Kristi E. Gamarel, and Christian Grov. "Non-Monogamy and Sexual Relationship Quality among Same-Sex Male Couples." *Journal of Family Psychology* 25 (2012): 669–77.

Parsons, Jeffrey T., Tyrel J. Starks, Steve DuBois, Christian Grov, and Sarit A. Golub. "Alternatives to Monogamy among Gay Male Couples in a Community Survey: Implications for Mental Health and Sexual Risk." *Archives of Sexual Behavior* 42 (2013): 303–12.

Payne, Krista K. "Demographic Profile of Same-Sex Couple Households with Minor Children, 2012." NCFMR Family Profiles FP-14-03, National Center for Family and Marriage Research, Bowling Green State University, 2014.

Perkin, Harold. *The Rise of Professional Society: England Since 1880*. London: Routledge, 1989.

Petrow, Steven. "Advertisers Embrace Gay People in an Amazing Year of Firsts for Commercials." *Washington Post*, December 14, 2015.

Pew Forum on Religion and Public Life, and Pew Research Center for the People & the Press. *More Americans Question Religion's Role in Politics*, Durham, NC. August 21, 2008, http://www.people-press.org/2008/08/21/more-americans-question-religions-role-in-politics/.

Pew Research Center. *America's Changing Religious Landscape*. May 12, 2015, http://www.pewforum.org/2015/05/12/americas-changing-religious-landscape/.

———. *Muslim Americans: No Signs of Growth in Alienation or Support for Extremism.* August 30, 2011, http://www.people-press.org/2011/08/30/muslim-americans-no-signs-of-growth-in-alienation-or-support-for-extremism/.

———. *"Nones" on the Rise: One-in-Five Adults Have No Religious Affiliation.* October 9, 2012, http://www.pewforum.org/2012/10/09/nones-on-the-rise/.

———. *News Coverage Conveys Strong Momentum for Same-Sex Marriage.* June 17, 2013, http://www.journalism.org/2013/06/17/news-coverage-conveys-strong-momentum/.

———. *A Portrait of American Orthodox Jews.* August 26, 2015, http://www.pewforum.org/2015/08/26/a-portrait-of-american-orthodox-jews/.

———. *A Portrait of Jewish Americans.* October 1, 2013, http://www.pewforum.org/2013/10/01/jewish-american-beliefs-attitudes-culture-survey/.

———. *U.S. Public Becoming Less Religious.* November 3, 2015, http://www.pewforum.org/2015/11/03/u-s-public-becoming-less-religious/.

———. *U.S. Religious Landscape Survey: Religious Affiliation, Diverse and Dynamic.* February 1, 2008, http://www.pewforum.org/files/2013/05/report-religious-landscape-study-full.pdf.

Pexton, Patrick P. "Is the Post 'Pro-Gay'?" *Washington Post,* February 24, 2013, A17.

Pierceson, Jason. *Same-Sex Marriage in the United States: The Road to the Supreme Court.* Rowman & Littlefield, 2013.

Pinello, Daniel R. "Homosexuality and the Law." In *The Oxford Companion to American Law,* edited by Kermit L. Hall. New York: Oxford University Press, 2002.

Pollitt, Christopher. *Managerialism and the Public Services: The Anglo-American Experience.* Cambridge, Mass.: Basil Blackwell, 1990.

Price, Deb. "Symbol for a 'Rainbow' of People." *San Francisco Examiner,* April 11, 1995, B7.

Prudential Financial. *The LGBT Financial Experience: 2012–2013 Prudential Research Study.* November 2012, http://www.prudential.com/media/managed/Prudential_LGBT_Financial_Experience.pdf.

Raeburn, Nicole C. *Changing Corporate America from Inside Out: Lesbian and Gay Workplace Rights.* Minneapolis: University of Minnesota Press, 2004.

Ragusa, Angela T. "Social Change and the Corporate Construction of Gay Markets in the *New York Times*' Advertising Business News." *Media, Culture & Society* 27 (2005): 653–76.

Rausch, Stephen, and Cynthia Negrey. "Does the Creative Engine Run? A Consideration of the Effect of Creative Class on Economic Strength and Growth." *Journal of Urban Affairs* 28 (2006): 473–89.

Raz, Joseph. "Autonomy, Toleration, and the Harm Principle." In *Justifying Toleration: Conceptual and Historical Perspectives,* edited by Susan Mendus, 155–76. Cambridge: Cambridge University Press, 1988.

Reeves, Richard V. *Dream Hoarders: How the American Upper Middle Class Is Leaving Everyone Else in the Dust, Why That Is A Problem, and What to Do about It.* Washington, D.C.: Brookings Institution Press, 2017.

Regnerus, Mark. "How Different Are the Adult Children of Parents Who Have Same-Sex Relationships? Findings from the New Family Structures Study." *Social Science Research* 41 (2012): 752–70.

———. "Is Same-Sex Parenting Better for Kids? The New Australian Study Can't Tell Us." *Public Discourse* (online), July 9, 2014, http://www.thepublic discourse.com/2014/07/13451/.

Reich, Robert B. *The Work of Nations: Preparing Ourselves for 21st-Century Capitalism.* New York: Knopf, 1991.

Reilly, Katie. "Read Bernie Sanders' Speech Vowing to Continue His Nomination Fight." *Time*, June 8, 2016, http://time.com/4361146/bernie -sanders-democratic-primary-speech-transcript/.

———. "Read Hillary Clinton's 'Basket of Deplorables' Remarks about Donald Trump Supporters." *Time*, September 10, 2016, http://time.com/4486502/ hillary-clinton-basket-of-deplorables-transcript/.

Ressler, Lawrence E., and David R. Hodge. "Religious Discrimination in Social Work: Preliminary Evidence." *Journal of Religion and Spirituality in Social Work: Social Thought* 24 (2006): 55–74.

Rhode, Deborah, and Amanda K. Packel. "Diversity on Corporate Boards: How Much Difference Does Difference Make?" *Delaware Journal of Corporate Law* 39 (2014): 377–426.

Richardson, Valerie. "Arkansas, Indiana Religious Freedom Bill Revisions Spark More Debates." *Washington Times*, April 2, 2015.

Rieff, Philip. *My Life among the Deathworks: Illustrations of the Aesthetics of Authority, Volume 1: Sacred Order / Social Order.* Charlottesville: University of Virginia Press, 2006.

Rivers, Daniel Winunwe. *Radical Relations: Lesbian Mothers, Gay Fathers, and Their Children in the United States Since World War II.* Chapel Hill: University of North Carolina Press, 2013.

Robinson, V. Gene. *In the Eye of the Storm: Swept to the Center by God.* New York: Seabury Books, 2008.

Rose, David, and David J. Pevalin. *The National Statistics Socio-economic Classification: Origins, Development and Use.* Institute for Social and Economic Research, University of Essex. Basingstoke, U.K.: Palgrave Macmillan, 2005.

Rothman, Stanley, and S. Robert Lichter. "The Vanishing Conservative—Is There a Glass Ceiling?" In *The Politically Correct University: Problems, Scope, and Reforms*, edited by Robert Maranto, Richard E. Redding, and Frederick M. Hess, 60–76. Washington, D.C.: AEI Press, 2009.

Rothman, Stanley, S. Robert Lichter, and Neil Nevitte. "Politics and Professional Advancement among College Faculty." *The Forum* 3, no. 1 (2005).

Saland, Stephen M. "Senator Saland's Statement on Marriage Equality." New York State Senate, June 25, 2011, https://www.nysenate.gov/news room/press-releases/stephen-m-saland/senator-salands-statement -marriage-equality.

Salka, William M., and Raymond Christopher Burnett. "Determinants of Electoral Support for Anti-Gay Marriage Constitutional Amendments: An Examination of Ballot Issues in California and Florida." *Sexuality and Culture* 16 (2012): 59–75.

Sandel, Michael. "Moral Argument and Liberal Toleration: Abortion and Homosexuality." *California Law Review* 77, no. 3 (1989): 521–38.

Schneider, Jason S., and Saul Levin. "Uneasy Partners: The Lesbian and Gay Health Care Community and the AMA." *Journal of the American Medical Association* 282, no. 13 (1999): 1287–88.

Sedgwick, Eve Kosofsky. *Epistemology of the Closet*. Berkeley: University of California Press, 1990.

Seidman, Steven, and Chet Meeks. "The Politics of Authenticity: Civic Individualism and the Cultural Roots of Gay Normalization." *Cultural Sociology* 5 (2011): 519–36.

Sender, Katherine. *Business, Not Politics: The Making of the Gay Market*. New York: Columbia University Press, 2004.

Seto, Michael C. "Is Pedophilia a Sexual Orientation?" *Archives of Sexual Behavior* 41 (2012): 231–36.

Shattuck, Rachel M., and Rose M. Kreider. "Social and Economic Characteristics of Currently Unmarried Women with a Recent Birth: 2011." *American Community Survey Reports* ACS-21 (May 2013).

Sherkat, Darren E. "The Editorial Process and Politicized Scholarship: Monday Morning Editorial Quarterbacking and a Call for Scientific Vigilance." *Social Science Review* 41 (2012): 1346–49.

Shields, Jon A., and Joshua M. Dunn Sr. *Passing on the Right: Conservative Professors in the Progressive University*. Oxford: Oxford University Press, 2016.

Simon, Yves. *A General Theory of Authority*. Notre Dame, Ind.: University of Notre Dame Press, 1980.

Singal, Jesse. "How the Fight Over Transgender Kids Got a Leading Sex Researcher Fired." *New York Magazine*, February 7, 2016, http://nymag.com/science ofus/2016/02/fight-over-trans-kids-got-a-researcher-fired.html.

Skipworth, Sue Ann, Andrew Garner, and Bryan J. Dettrey. "Limitations of the Contact Hypothesis: Heterogeneity in the Contact Effect on Attitudes toward Gay Rights." *Politics & Policy* 38 (2010): 887–906.

Smith, Adam. *The Wealth of Nations: Books I–III*. New York: Penguin Classics, 1982.

Smith, Andrew E. "*Boston Globe* Poll—May 2005—US Opinions on Gay Marriage." The Survey Center: University of New Hampshire, 2005.

Smith, Bruce L. R., Jeremy D. Mayer, and A. Lee Fritschler. *Closed Minds? Politics and Ideology in American Universities*. Washington, D.C.: Brookings Institution Press, 2008.

Smith, Christian. "Introduction: Rethinking the Secularization of American Public Life." In *The Secular Revolution: Power, Interests, and Conflict in the Secularization of American Public Life*, edited by Christian Smith, 1–96. Berkeley: University of California Press, 2003.

Smith, Christian, and Patricia Snell. *Souls in Transition: The Religious and Spiritual Lives of Emerging Adults*. Oxford: Oxford University Press, 2009.

Smith, Tom W. "Changes in Family Structure, Family Values, and Politics, 1972–2006." In *Red, Blue and Purple America: The Future of Election Demographics*, edited by Ruy A. Teixeira, 147–93. Washington, D.C.: Brookings Institution, 2008.

Sonmez, Felicia. "Santorum: Obama's College Plan Makes Him a 'Snob.'" *Washington Post*, February 26, 2012, A6.

Stojmenovska, Dragana, Thijs Bol, and Thomas Leopold. "Does Diversity Pay? A Replication of Herring (2009)." *American Sociological Review*, published online. July 7, 2017, http://journals.sagepub.com/doi/abs/10.1177/0003122417714422.

Suhay, Elizabeth, and Toby Epstein Jayaratne. "Does Biology Justify Ideology? The Politics of Genetic Attribution." *Public Opinion Quarterly* 77 (2013): 497–521.

Sullivan, Andrew. "Obama's Cowardice on Marriage." *The Dish*, May 16, 2008, dish.andrewsullivan.com/2008/05/16/gay-marriage-an-3/.

Sullivan, Gail. "Dating Web Site OkCupid Is Breaking Up with Firefox." *Washington Post*, April 1, 2014, http://www.washingtonpost.com/news/morning-mix/wp/2014/04/01/dating-website-okcupid-is-breaking-up-with-firefox/.

Surkyn, Johan, and Ron Lesthaeghe. "Value Orientations and the Second Demographic Transition (SDT) in Northern, Western and Southern Europe: An Update." *Demographic Research*, Special Collection 3 (2004).

Swanson, Ana. "How the Rainbow Became the Symbol of Gay Pride." Wonkblog, *Washington Post*, June 29, 2015, https://www.washingtonpost.com/news/wonk/wp/2015/06/29/how-the-rainbow-became-the-symbol-of-gay-pride/?utm_term=.57687274b090.

Swartz, David L. *Culture and Power: The Sociology of Pierre Bourdieu*. Chicago: University of Chicago Press, 1997.

———. "Pierre Bourdieu and North American Political Sociology: Why He Doesn't Fit In but Should." *French Politics* 4 (2006): 84–99.

———. *Symbolic Power, Politics, and Intellectuals: The Political Sociology of Pierre Bourdieu*. Berkeley: University of California Press, 2013.

"Target's Same-Sex Registry Ad Praised by LGBT Advocacy Bloggers." *Huffington Post*, July 26, 2012, http://www.huffingtonpost.com/2012/07/26/target -same-sex-registry-ad-gay-marriage_n_1706599.html.

Téllez, Cecilia, et al. "Attitudes of Physicians in New Mexico toward Gay Men and Lesbians." *Journal of the Gay and Lesbian Medical Association* 3, no. 3 (1999): 83–89.

Therborn, Göran. *Between Sex and Power: Family in the World, 1900–2000*. New York: Routledge, 2004.

Thyer, Bruce A., and Laura L. Myers. "Religious Discrimination in Social Work Academic Programs: Whither Social Justice?" *Journal of Religion and Spirituality in Social Work: Social Thought* 28 (2009): 144–60.

Tobin, Gary A., and Aryeh K. Weinberg. *Profiles of the American University, Volume II: Religious Beliefs and Behavior of College Faculty*. San Francisco: Institute for Jewish and Community Research, 2007.

Todd, Sarah, and Diana Coholic. "Christian Fundamentalism and Anti-Oppressive Social Work Pedagogy." *Journal of Teaching in Social Work* 27, nos. 3/4 (2007): 5–25.

Tomassen, Lisa. "Lucky Charms Asks What Makes You Lucky?" *Taste of General Mills* (blog), June 3, 2014, http://www.blog.generalmills.com/2014/06/luckytobe/.

Tosh, John. "New Men? The Bourgeois Cult of Home." *History Today*, December 1996, 9–15.

"Transcript: Robin Roberts ABC News Interview with President Obama." *ABC News*, May 9, 2012, http://abcnews.go.com/Politics/transcript -robin-roberts-abc-news-interview-president-obama/story?id=16316043.

Tsai, Wan-Hsiu Sunny. "Assimilating the Queers: Representations of Lesbians, Gay Men, Bisexual, and Transgender People in Mainstream Advertising." *Advertising & Society Review* 11, no. 1 (2010).

Turner, Bryan S. *Medical Power and Social Knowledge*. London: SAGE, 1987.

———. *The Body and Society: Explorations in Social Theory*. 3rd ed. Los Angeles: SAGE, 2008.

Turner, Greg. "Mayor Menino on Chick-fil-A: Stuff It." *Boston Herald*, July 20, 2012.

Tygart, C. E. "Genetic Causation Attribution and Public Support of Gay Rights." *International Journal of Public Opinion Research* 12 (2000): 259–75.

University of California, Berkeley School of Law. Statewide Database. http://statewidedatabase.org/.

Upadhyay, Ushma D., et al. "Women's Empowerment and Fertility: A Review of the Literature." *Social Science and Medicine* 115 (2014): 111–20.

Valutis, Stephanie, and Deborah Rubin. "Value Conflicts in Social Work: Categories and Correlates." *Journal of Social Work Values and Ethics* 13 (2016): 11–24.

Vergara, Tacie L. "Meeting the Needs of Sexual Minority Youth: One Program's Response." In *Homosexuality and Social Work*, edited by Robert Schoenberg, Richard S. Goldberg, and David A. Shore, 19–38. New York: Haworth Press, 1984.

Ward, Brian W., et al. "Sexual Orientation and Health among U.S. Adults: National Health Interview Survey, 2013." *National Health Statistics Reports* 77 (July 15, 2014).

Warner, Michael. *The Trouble with Normal*. Cambridge, Mass.: Harvard University Press, 2000.

Whitley, Bernard E., Jr., and Sarah E. Lee. "The Relationship of Authoritarianism and Related Constructs to Attitudes toward Homosexuality." *Journal of Applied Social Psychology* 30, no. 1 (2000): 144–70.

Wilcox, W. Bradford. *Soft Patriarchs, New Men: How Christianity Shapes Fathers and Husbands*. Chicago: University of Chicago Press, 2004.

Wilcox, W. Bradford, and Jon McEwan. "Marriage, Single Parenthood, and the 2016 Vote." Family Studies, last modified December 7, 2016, https://family-studies.org/marriage-single-parenthood-and-the-2016-vote/.

Wilkinson, W. W. "Religiosity, Authoritarianism, and Homophobia: A Multidimensional Approach." *International Journal for the Psychology of Religion* 14 (2004): 55–67.

Wong, Curtis M. "Tylenol's 'For What Matters Most' Re-Imagines Norman Rockwell Painting with Lesbian Moms." *Huffington Post*, February 2, 2016, http://www.huffingtonpost.com/2014/12/22/tylenol-lesbian-commercial-_n_6367800.html.

Wright, James D. "Introductory Remarks." *Social Science Review* 41 (2012): 1339–45.

Yancey, George. "Who Has Religious Prejudice? Differing Sources of Anti-Religious Animosity in the United States." *Review of Religious Research* 52 (2010): 159–71.

———. *Compromising Scholarship: Religious and Political Bias in American Higher Education*. Waco, Tex.: Baylor University Press, 2011.

Yancey, George, and David A. Williamson. *So Many Christians, So Few Lions: Is There Christianophobia in the United States?* Lanham, Md.: Rowman & Littlefield, 2015.

Yenor, Scott. *Family Politics: The Idea of Marriage in Modern Political Thought*. Waco, Tex.: Baylor University Press, 2011.

Zoeller, Gregory F. "Duty to Defend and the Rule of Law." *Indiana Law Journal* 90, no. 2 (2015): 513–57.

INDEX

abortion, 97–98, 108, 141–42
American Bar Association: *see* legal
   profession
American Medical Association: *see*
   physicians
American National Election Studies, 78–
   80, 143–44, 175–76
American Psychiatric Association: *see*
   psychiatry
American Psychological Association: *see*
   psychology

Biden, Joe, 43–45
Bourdieu, Pierre, 139, 159–63, 171,
   212n34, 217n1, 217n2, 217n3
Bryant, Anita, 89–90
business, 3, 11, 27–33, 37–41, 52, 118,
   120–23, 125–29, 135–37, 153–55

Catholics, 140–42, 152, 157, 186n30
Chauncey, George, 77
Chick-fil-A, 15–16
class: *see* social class
Clinton, Bill, 2, 95, 135
Clinton, Hillary, 95, 158
contraception, 81, 97–98, 140–42
conversion therapy, 24–25, 145–46

Corporate America: *see* business
counseling: *see* social work

Defense of Marriage Act, 2–3, 35–39, 147
Democratic Party, 3, 16, 62, 76,
   138, 149, 154
diversity, 30, 34, 39, 40–41, 117–32, 134,
   146, 156, 203n10, 204n18

Eich, Brendan, 13–14
elites: authority, 155–58; definition, 16–
   21, 46–49, 159–70; location, 53–54,
   60–61, 63–65; and homosexuality,
   21–41, 45–46, 51–53, 54–60, 68–79,
   86, 105, 131–32, 145–50; and diversity,
   117–23, 128–32; and religion, 27–29,
   79–80, 139–42, 145–48; and same-sex
   marriage, 60–66
equality, 7–9, 13–14, 21, 69–70, 87, 90–
   91, 117–18, 127

family, 4–7, 33–41, 81–85, 89–113
feminism, 79, 94–96, 106–13, 135,
   156, 216n14
fertility, 81–85, 96–98, 102–13,
   142, 178–79, 196n43, 200–1n40,
   201n42, 202n48

www.ingramcontent.com/pod-product-compliance
Lightning Source LLC
Chambersburg PA
CBHW021813270326
41932CB00007B/165